Non-State Actors in Education in the Global South

Fuelled by social equity concerns, there have been vigorous debates on the appropriateness of certain non-state actors, particularly those with commercial and entrepreneurial motives, to meet universal education goals. There are further questions on the relative effectiveness of government and private schooling in delivering good learning outcomes for all.

Within this debate, several empirical questions abound. Do students from poorer backgrounds achieve as well in private schools as their advantaged peers? What are the relative out-of-pocket costs of accessing private schooling compared to government schooling? Is fee-paying non-state provision 'affordable' to the poorest households? What is the nature of the education market at different levels? What are the relationships between different non-state actors and the state, and how should they conduct themselves? The chapters in this volume present new empirical evidence and conduct critical analysis on some of these questions.

This book was originally published as a special issue of the *Oxford Review of Education*.

Prachi Srivastava is Associate Professor in Education and International Development at the University of Western Ontario, Canada, Adjunct Professor, School of International Development, University of Ottawa, Canada, and Senior Visiting Fellow at the University of Sussex, UK. She has been conducting research on non-state private actors in education in the Global South for more than 15 years, and is credited as coining the term, 'low-fee private schools'. She has published widely on global education policy, low-fee private schooling, and privatisation and the right to education.

Geoffrey Walford is Emeritus Professor of Education Policy at the University of Oxford, UK. He has authored or edited more than 30 books on education policy, private education and ethnography, and published many articles and book chapters. He has been Editor of the *British Journal of Educational Studies* and the *Oxford Review of Education*, and remains Deputy Editor of *Ethnography and Education*.

Non-State Actors in Education in the Global South

Edited by
Prachi Srivastava and Geoffrey Walford

Routledge
Taylor & Francis Group

LONDON AND NEW YORK

First published 2018
by Routledge
2 Park Square, Milton Park, Abingdon, Oxon, OX14 4RN, UK

and by Routledge
711 Third Avenue, New York, NY 10017, USA

Routledge is an imprint of the Taylor & Francis Group, an informa business

British Library Cataloguing in Publication Data
A catalogue record for this book is available from the British Library

ISBN 13: 978-1-138-57067-2

Typeset in Myriad Pro
by RefineCatch Limited, Bungay, Suffolk

Publisher's Note
The publisher accepts responsibility for any inconsistencies that may have
arisen during the conversion of this book from journal articles to book chapters,
namely the possible inclusion of journal terminology.

Disclaimer
Every effort has been made to contact copyright holders for their permission
to reprint material in this book. The publishers would be grateful to hear
from any copyright holder who is not here acknowledged and will undertake to
rectify any errors or omissions in future editions of this book.

Contents

Citation Information

The chapters in this book were originally published in the *Oxford Review of Education*, volume 42, issue 5 (October 2016). When citing this material, please use the original page numbering for each article, as follows:

Introduction
Non-state actors in education in the Global South
Prachi Srivastava and Geoffrey Walford
Oxford Review of Education, volume 42, issue 5 (October 2016), pp. 491–494

Chapter 1
Does private schooling narrow wealth inequalities in learning outcomes? Evidence from East Africa
Benjamin Alcott and Pauline Rose
Oxford Review of Education, volume 42, issue 5 (October 2016), pp. 495–510

Chapter 2
Is there a private schooling market in poor neighbourhoods in Maputo, Mozambique? Exploring the role of the non-state education sector
Joanna Härmä
Oxford Review of Education, volume 42, issue 5 (October 2016), pp. 511–527

Chapter 3
'Affordable' private schools in South Africa. Affordable for whom?
Sonia Languille
Oxford Review of Education, volume 42, issue 5 (October 2016), pp. 528–542

Chapter 4
How are private school enrolment patterns changing across Indian districts with a growth in private school availability?
Amita Chudgar and Benjamin Creed
Oxford Review of Education, volume 42, issue 5 (October 2016), pp. 543–560

Chapter 5
The myth of free and barrier-free access: India's Right to Education Act—private schooling costs and household experiences
Prachi Srivastava and Claire Noronha
Oxford Review of Education, volume 42, issue 5 (October 2016), pp. 561–578

Chapter 6

Extending access to low-cost private schools through vouchers: an alternative interpretation of a two-stage 'School Choice' experiment in India
James Tooley
Oxford Review of Education, volume 42, issue 5 (October 2016), pp. 579–593

Chapter 7

Non-state actors, and the advance of frontier higher education markets in the global south
Susan L. Robertson and Janja Komljenovic
Oxford Review of Education, volume 42, issue 5 (October 2016), pp. 594–611

Chapter 8

Towards a human rights framework to advance the debate on the role of private actors in education
Sylvain Aubry and Delphine Dorsi
Oxford Review of Education, volume 42, issue 5 (October 2016), pp. 612–628

For any permission-related enquiries please visit:
http://www.tandfonline.com/page/help/permissions

Notes on Contributors

Benjamin Alcott is a University Lecturer at the Research for Equitable Access and Learning (REAL) Centre at the University of Cambridge, UK. His current research focuses on access to schooling, the quality of state and non-state educational provision, and inequalities in learning outcomes.

Sylvain Aubry is currently working as Research and Legal Advisor with the Global Initiative for Economic, Social and Cultural Rights (GI-ESCR). He has been working on the role of the State and private actors in the delivery of education since 2012, initially with the Right to Education Project, before moving to GI-ESCR in 2013.

Amita Chudgar is Associate Professor of Education Policy at Michigan State University, USA. Her work examines the influence of home, school, and community contexts on educational access and achievement of children in resource-constrained environments.

Benjamin Creed is Assistant Professor of Educational Administration at Northern Illinois University, USA. His research examines the influence of educational policies on how students of varying backgrounds access the limited resources of an educational system. His current work explores the impact of school choice policies on district administrators' decision making, the competitive effects of school choice, and how charter school leaders attract and retain both teachers and students.

Delphine Dorsi is the Executive Coordinator of the Right to Education Project. She previously worked at UNESCO for the Right to Education Programme, providing her with a comprehensive understanding and unique perspective on the right to education. She has also worked with a number of NGOs in Europe and Africa, including Amnesty International, Save the Children, and Defense for Children International.

Joanna Härmä is a Visiting Research Fellow at the School of Education and Social Work, University of Sussex, UK. She works as a researcher and consultant, specialising on low-fee private schooling for the poor in sub-Saharan Africa and India.

Janja Komljenovic is a Lecturer of Higher Education at the University of Lancaster, UK. Her main research interests are on the cultural political economy of higher education and particularly on understanding the nature of higher education markets and industry.

Sonia Languille is currently co-leading the Higher Education Support Program at the Open Society Foundations. Her contribution to this book is based on research she conducted as a Postdoctoral Research Fellow at the Faculty of Education, University of Johannesburg, South Africa.

Claire Noronha is a Senior Consultant Researcher at Collaborative Research and Dissemination (CORD), New Delhi, India. CORD has been researching the problems of marginalised groups in accessing education in India for well over a decade. She has had a long experience in researching issues related to private schooling for the poor, most recently, in the context of India's Right to Education Act.

Susan L. Robertson is Professor of Sociology of Education at the University of Cambridge, UK. She has a long standing interest in transformations of the state, education policy-making, spatial politics, and broader issues of globalisation, development, and social justice. She is founding co-Editor of the journal *Globalisation, Societies and Education*.

Pauline Rose is Professor of International Education at the University of Cambridge, UK, and Director of the Research for Equitable Access and Learning (REAL) Centre in the Faculty of Education. She is also Senior Research Fellow at the UK Department for International Development. Prior to joining Cambridge, she was Director of the UNESCO Education for All Global Monitoring Report. Her research examines issues of educational policy and practice in relation to inequality, financing and governance, and the role of international aid.

Prachi Srivastava is Associate Professor in Education and International Development at the University of Western Ontario, Canada, Adjunct Professor, School of International Development, University of Ottawa, Canada, and Senior Visiting Fellow at the University of Sussex, UK. She has been conducting research on non-state private actors in education for more than 15 years, and is credited as coining the term, 'low-fee private schools'. She has published widely on global education policy, low-fee private schooling in the Global South, and privatisation and the right to education.

James Tooley is Professor of Education Policy at Newcastle University, UK. His work on low-cost private schools in developing countries won gold prize in the first International Finance Corporation/Financial Times Private Sector Development Competition. He is co-founder and chairman of Omega Schools, Ghana, patron of the Association of Formidable Educational Development, Nigeria, and chief mentor of the National Independent Schools Alliance (India).

Geoffrey Walford is Emeritus Professor of Education Policy at the University of Oxford, UK. He has authored or edited more than 30 books on education policy, private education and ethnography, and published many articles and book chapters. He has been Editor of the *British Journal of Educational Studies* and the *Oxford Review of Education*, and remains Deputy Editor of *Ethnography and Education*.

Non-state actors in education in the Global South

Prachi Srivastava and Geoffrey Walford

Universal education for all has recently been reaffirmed in sustainable development goal 4, which states its first target as: 'By 2030, ensure that all girls and boys complete free, equitable and quality primary and secondary education leading to relevant and effective learning outcomes'. However, scholars have noted the growth of private schooling and the increased engagement of non-state actors in education in the Global South, including for-profit and corporate entities, since the periods following the previous high-level commitments to universal education of the 1990 World Conference on Education in Jomtien and the 2000 World Education Forum in Dakar.

A vigorous debate has emerged on the appropriateness of certain non-state actors, particularly those with commercial and entrepreneurial motives, to meet universal education goals, as well as on the relative effectiveness of private schooling and its ability to mitigate against social inequities. A number of empirical questions abound, such as relative student achievement and learning outcomes; relative costs; impacts on households accessing fee-paying sectors; the nature of the market at various education levels; relationships between different types of non-state actors and between them and the state; and regulatory compulsions. There is also a need to sharpen conceptualisations on the types of non-state actors operating in the Global South, and the nature of their engagement.

This Special Issue is concerned with the growth of non-government schooling in the Global South where a great variety of non-state private providers have become increasingly active. Some of these schools are religiously-based, others are run by NGOs, civil society, community, or philanthropic organisations, but a number are entrepreneurial schools that are run either as single operations or chains and may often be profit-making. Some of these schools may charge lower fees than traditionally elite private schools, and target less well-off families who do not wish or are unable to send their children to local government schools. A number of families may feel themselves being forced into the private sector because they see the government schools as unacceptable or there is insufficient local provision.

Thus, in many countries of the Global South, the principle that the government should offer schooling to all children seems to have been superseded by the reality of a dual system where those who are able to pay opt out of government schooling into the private sector, at least for some time if not permanently, and where a variety of non-state actors with different motives operate. Such a situation raises many questions linked to equity, social mobility, and social justice. This Special Issue provides new research and ideas about some of these issues.

The first paper, by Benjamin Alcott and Pauline Rose, is concerned with the relationships between attendance at private schooling and wealth inequalities in learning outcomes. It uses data from household surveys in Kenya, Tanzania, and Uganda. The surveys themselves are high quality studies conducted in 2013, and the paper presents new and important findings derived from those surveys. The findings show that private schooling generally leads to a greater chance of children learning the basics, but does not help close the learning gap for the most disadvantaged. There are some important findings on in-country differences and other background variables. The authors argue that supporting private schooling is unlikely to narrow learning gaps, and that reforms need to reduce inequalities in the external, home, and community environments.

The second paper, by Joanna Härmä, focuses on Mozambique and the role that non-state actors play in poor neighbourhoods in Maputo. This paper presents some of the results of a census and survey of two poor neighbourhoods, and it provides new data that indicate the nature and extent of non-state provision in pre-primary, primary, and secondary education. It shows that non-state provision is still relatively modest, and that there has not been any growth of 'low-fee' private primary schools as is understood to have occurred in other countries, such as India, Kenya, Nigeria, or Pakistan. Rather, the fees in the non-governmental primary schools available are relatively high, and there is considerable inequity in terms of access. As there is no government provision at pre-primary level, it is obviously dominated by private providers, and access is influenced by the ability to pay fees. Apart from pre-primary, the main role of the non-government sector is in the provision of secondary places where the government under-provides.

The next article, by Susan Languille, focuses on private schooling in South Africa where there has been a dramatic growth in the last few decades. Many of these new schools claim to be 'affordable' or 'low-fee' private schools which are said to serve poorer families. Yet, Languille's research reveals that much of the growth in private schooling in the post-apartheid period has been designed for a growing—mostly black—middle class. She argues that the imprecision of the 'affordable' terminology used acts as a discursive device to obscure the class interests that shape South Africa's educational system. It allows segments of the state and pro-market lobbyists to frame their project in social justice terms, while the reality is very different.

There follows three articles on private schooling in India. The first two are concerned with the possible effects of the implementation of the Right of Children to Free and Compulsory Education Act, 2009, commonly known as the Right To Education Act (RTE Act) which, amongst many other changes, makes it compulsory for all private unaided schools to provide 25% of their places as free places for children from socially and economically disadvantaged backgrounds. In the first article Amita Chudgar and Benjamin Creed use data from two district-level surveys to estimate how private enrolment patterns have changed over the period from 2005–2006 to 2011–2012, during which there was a large increase in private schools. While most states were still drafting rules and regulations at the time of the second survey, the authors identified states which had adopted clearer regulations by this time. They show that the large growth in private school enrolments had not led to greater equity in rural areas, but that there was a declining caste gap and gap between poor and non-poor students in private school enrolments in the states that had adopted clearer RTE regulations.

In the second article on India's RTE Act, Prachi Srivastava and Claire Noronha report household-level data on the schooling patterns, experiences, and perceptions in one Delhi slum about accessing schooling based on a survey of 290 households and 40 semi-structured household interviews. They found very low instances of children with private school 'freeships'. Furthermore, children in free private school seats incurred the second highest costs of accessing schooling after full-fee paying students in relatively high-fee private schools. Finally, households accessing freeships and higher-fee schools experienced considerable barriers to securing a seat and admission.

The third article on India by James Tooley gives a critique of an important recent article by Muralidharan and Sundararaman (from 2015) which has gained some influence in policy circles. The original article reported some of the results from a randomised control trial which was conducted over the period 2008–2014 and involved children in 180 villages in Andhra Pradesh, India. Tooley argues that there are some major problems in the interpretation of the data obtained. In particular, identical tests were not given to the whole of the two groups of children, meaning that it is not straightforward to interpret the results in mathematics and in languages in the way the authors of the original paper do. Tooley further argues that the authors conflate two different meanings of school choice, and that 'top-down School Choice' with the use of vouchers must be seen as different from school choice where parents are paying fees. He claims that the result of these and other difficulties is that the data presented in the paper actually give a more positive view of private schooling than that of the original authors.

The article by Susan L. Robertson and Janja Komljenovic, moves on from schooling to consider developments in higher education markets. First, it reminds us that the concept of the Global South is social, spatial, and relational. Thus, there is a need to consider not only changes within the geographic entities that are commonly designated as the Global South, but also the activities of global non-state and multilateral actors within the marginal and precarious communities within the Global North or more economically developed countries. The article then presents new data and discussion of three ways in which the wheels of market-making are lubricated: through the rise of recruiters/brokers who search for international students in the Global South on behalf of higher education institutions in the Global North; through the expansion of non-profit providers of higher education which have developed new market logics; and, finally, through the growth of new financial actors working in the higher education arena providing credit for potential students whilst, at the same time, restructuring higher education into a commodity.

This is followed by an article by Sylvain Aubry and Delphine Dorsi that puts forward a human rights framework for considering the impact of the privatisation of schooling. They examine in detail various national and international human rights laws, and argue that these laws can be seen as an internationally agreed normative legal framework that should be used to provide a third way of reflecting on the current polarised privatisation debate. They recognise, of course, that a human rights framework contains inner tensions which need to be analysed. In particular, they examine the tension between the right to mandatory and free quality education for all without discrimination, and the right for parents to be able to choose a school or establish their own, which might generate inequalities. They develop and describe a framework for the evaluation of privatisation initiatives which has five dimensions based on criteria that the operation of private schools should not infringe. Their work is ongoing, but this paper provides insights into how human rights legislation might be used to make judgements about particular initiatives.

Does private schooling narrow wealth inequalities in learning outcomes? Evidence from East Africa

Benjamin Alcott and Pauline Rose

ABSTRACT

In many low- and lower-middle-income countries, private schools are often considered to offer better quality of education than government schools. Yet, there is a lack of evidence to date on their role in reducing inequalities: namely, the extent to which private schooling improves learning among the most disadvantaged children. Our paper uses household survey data from Kenya, Tanzania, and Uganda to identify whether any observed impact of private schooling on core literacy and numeracy skills differs according to children's household wealth. We demonstrate wealth gaps in access to private schooling, and use inferential models to account for observable differences between those who do and do not enrol in private schools. In Kenya and Uganda, we find that private schooling appears to improve the chances of children learning relative to their peers in government schools, but the chances of the poorest children learning in private schools remains low and is at best equivalent to the richest learning in government schools. In Tanzania, private schooling does not seem to improve poorer children's learning, whereas it does for richer children. These findings raise a caution about the extent to which private provision can help narrow learning inequalities.

Introduction

Equitable learning outcomes are a key aspect of the education Sustainable Development Goals (SDG). The SDGs emphasise the importance of all children and young people acquiring basic numeracy and literacy skills, ensuring that the most disadvantaged are not left behind. Consequently, an important concern for policy research is how best to organise education systems to achieve this.

Among the most contentious debates within education policy is whether private provision of schools is likely to aid these goals. There is no doubt that private schooling has proliferated over recent decades. In many low- and lower-middle-income countries, students attending private schools are found to have better learning outcomes than students in government schools, on average. However, the extent to which the learning gain for those in private schools is attributable to the schools themselves is still ambiguous in most of the available research (Day Ashley et al., 2014). The principal source of this ambiguity is potential selection bias: to estimate the impact of private schooling on learning outcomes, it is necessary to account for differences between children who enrol in private schools and children who do not.

In this article, our aim is to advance research in this field in a number of ways. First, we put equity at the forefront of our analyses, meaning that we focus not only on the impact of private schooling on learning, but whether any impact differs for children from more disadvantaged backgrounds. Second, we use inferential methods to provide estimates of the impact of private schooling on learning outcomes, thus attempting to account for observed differences between children enrolled in private and government schools. Third, in contrast to the more common focus on South Asia, our data come from East Africa (namely, Kenya, Tanzania, and Uganda), a region that has heretofore received far less research attention on the topic of private schooling.

In line with previous research, our findings indicate that private schooling leads to a greater chance of children learning; on average, in Kenya, Tanzania, and Uganda among children aged 11–14, our model estimates suggest that private schools increase the likelihood of children learning basic numeracy and literacy skills by between six and eight percentage points. However, our analyses indicate that private schooling does not narrow inequalities between the rich and poor for three reasons: first, the poor are far less likely to be able to access private schooling; second, even for those who do gain access to private school, their chances of learning remain low; and, third, any gain in learning that is achieved for the poorest at best only gives them the same chance of learning as the richest in government schools. In Tanzania, private schooling increases the chances of learning among children from rich households but not among those from the poorest households. For Kenya and Uganda, children from poorer households are less likely to be learning on average so, even though attending a private school increases their chances of learning, they still only have the same chance as children from wealthier households in government schools. Our findings suggest that private schooling does not help close the learning gap for the most disadvantaged, and does not help poor children reach even average rates of learning among more advantaged children.

Prior evidence on private schools, learning and equity

A recent rigorous review of the literature on private schooling finds that most of the inferential research on the impact of private schooling on learning outcomes has focused on countries in South Asia. The rigorous review concluded that most studies on learning outcomes recognise the difficulties in effectively taking account of differences in social background such that 'it may be difficult to ascertain whether achievement advantage can be fully ascribed to private schools' (Day Ashley et al., 2014, p. 14). Available quantitative studies in Pakistan find that private schooling has a positive effect on learning in comparison to government schools on average, after taking account of characteristics of children and households (Andrabi, Bau, Das, & Khwaja, 2010; Andrabi, Das, Khwaja, & Zajonc, 2011; Arif & Saqib, 2003; Aslam, 2009; Das, Pandey, & Zajonc, 2006), although Arif and Saqib (2003) note that in some districts public schools performed better than private schools. The majority of quantitative studies focusing on India draw similar conclusions (Desai, Dubey, Vanneman, & Banerji, 2009; French & Kingdon, 2010; Goyal, 2009; Kingdon, 1996; Pal, 2010). There is, however, some countervailing evidence in India: Chudgar and Quin (2012) find that the improvement associated with private school enrolment was no longer significant after they controlled for observable differences; and Muralidharan and Sundararaman (2015) and Singh (2015) both find only modest improvements in most learning outcomes.

There is not yet a commensurate body of inferential research on Eastern Africa, and the limited evidence that is available is more mixed. In Kenya, Bold, Kimenyi, Mwabu, and Sandefur (2013) find considerable differences in performance between students at private and government primary schools, of around a fifth, and that this gap persists even after using gender, district, and year fixed effects controls to account for selection biases in which children attend private school. However, the study has been criticised on the grounds that a significant proportion of students in the country do not reach Grade 8, and those who dropout are likely to belong to the most socially disadvantaged groups (Day Ashley et al., 2014). Using multi-level modelling, Dixon, Tooley, and Schagen (2013) find private schooling to be linked to better scores in mathematics and Swahili, but not in English, among children living in the Kibera slum of Nairobi, Kenya. In contrast, Lassibille and Tan (2001) find no evidence that private schools outperform public schools in Tanzania at the secondary level, although the data used by the authors are now over 20 years old.

To the best of our knowledge, there are not yet equivalent inferential studies focusing on Uganda, although available data indicate that there is a gap in learning outcomes between children in private and government schools (Uganda National Examinations Board, 2015; Uwezo, 2014b; Uwezo Tanzania, 2013). In Uganda, 33% of Grade 3 children in private schools are able to read a story at a Grade 2 level, compared to 12% of Grade 3 children in government schools (Uwezo, 2014b), and similar gaps are visible across a range of ages and grades (Mugo, Ruto, Nakabugo, & Mgalla, 2015). Even so, in absolute terms, learning outcomes are disappointing: overall, 45% of Ugandan pupils in Grades 3–7 who were in private schools were unable to read a text designed for Grade 2 classes (Uwezo, 2014b).

The research noted thus far engages with the impact of private schools on raising learning outcomes, but there is far less evidence on the extent to which it is sufficient to improve the chances of learning amongst the poorest. African countries follow the worldwide trend of sizeable learning inequalities between children from more and less advantaged households (UNESCO, 2014). In South Africa, by Grade 3 the poorest 60% are three grade levels behind the wealthiest quintile, and this increases to four grade levels by Grade 9 (Spaull & Kotze, 2015). Among eight year-olds in Ethiopia, the richest are four times more likely than the poorest to be able to read sentences (Rolleston, James, & Aurino, 2014). Cross-sectional data in East Africa show the learning of children from less advantaged households is at least one year behind that of children of the same age from more advantaged households (Jones & Schipper, 2015).

This inequality compels policy researchers to prioritise the educational needs of the most disadvantaged. The first equity concern commonly raised about private schools is whether they are accessible to the poorest. Research has noted growth in private school attendance among poorer children in some African countries, although there are differing opinions as to whether this has more to do with a preference for private schools (Dixon et al., 2013) or with the absence of adequate government school provision (Härmä, 2013; Oketch, Mutisya, Ngware, Ezeh, & Epari, 2010; Stern & Heyneman, 2013). Nonetheless, the disparity in enrolment remains considerable, with conditions in Africa similar to those in South Asia, where the most disadvantaged children are less likely to be enrolled in a private school (Alcott & Rose, 2015b; Härmä & Rose, 2012; Muralidharan & Kremer, 2008). Among children aged 10–12 in Kenya, Tanzania, and Uganda, for example, the richest are over three times more likely than the poorest to attend a private school (Alcott & Rose, 2015b).

The second equity concern is whether private schools increase the chances of the most disadvantaged learning basic literacy and numeracy skills compared with the richest. Descriptive analysis suggests that private schooling does not overcome inequalities stemming from household disparities: across rural Pakistan, rural India, Kenya, Tanzania, and Uganda, even though those in private schools are more likely to be learning than those in government schools, disadvantaged children who attend private schools are less likely to learn the basics than more advantaged children attending government schools (Alcott & Rose, 2015a, 2015b). It appears unlikely then that private schools can act as a panacea to inequalities in learning. Still, whether they can help narrow the gap between wealthier and poorer children remains an important question.

Research question and data

Our goal is to determine whether private primary schooling can help narrow learning inequalities in East African countries. Consequently, we seek to respond to this in two stages:

1. In Kenya, Tanzania, and Uganda, do private primary schools increase the likelihood that children have learned basic literacy and numeracy skills?
2. Can the provision of private schools help reduce gaps in learning outcomes between more and less disadvantaged groups?

We use data from the Uwezo ('capability' in Swahili) household surveys conducted in Kenya, Tanzania, and Uganda in 2013. Conducted by Twaweza, Uwezo surveys follow the model established in India by the Pratham organisation's Annual Status of Education Report: for each district in the country, surveyors visit 30 enumeration areas (broadly equivalent to villages), and 20 households within each enumeration area. Uwezo's sampling frame is designed in collaboration with each country's government statistical department to provide data that are representative at both the district and national levels (Uwezo, 2014a). Uwezo surveys collect information on parental background, indicators of household wealth, children's enrolment status, and an independent assessment of learning for all children of school

Table 1. Descriptive statistics for sample.

	Able to do basics (%)	Enrolled in private school (%)	Enrolled in government school (%)	Out of school (%)	Mother attended school (%)	Receive private tuition (%)	N
Kenya							
All	74	11	84	5	72	35	46,509
Poorest	58	3	84	13	47	22	12,333
Wealthiest	81	17	78	4	78	42	11,735
Tanzania							
All	49	2	86	12	67	21	37,007
Poorest	38	1	83	17	57	9	10,063
Wealthiest	63	6	87	7	76	37	9535
Uganda							
All	38	26	70	4	66	22	22,050
Poorest	26	11	80	9	52	14	5653
Wealthiest	46	29	68	3	72	25	5482

Source: Uwezo Kenya 2013, Uwezo Tanzania 2013, Uwezo Uganda 2013.

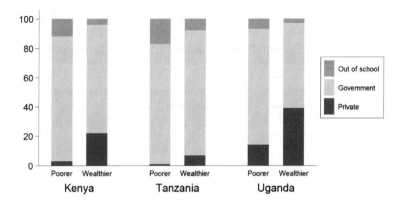

Figure 1. In Kenya, Uganda, and Tanzania, poorer children are more likely to be out of school and wealthier children are more likely to be enrolled in private schools. Source: Uwezo Kenya 2013, Uwezo Tanzania 2013, Uwezo Uganda 2013.

age. We delimit our sample to those aged 11–14, on the basis that these children should, in theory, have progressed to the end of primary school and learned the basics. This leaves sample sizes of 46,509, 37,007, and 22,050 for Kenya, Tanzania, and Uganda, respectively.

As an indicator of household wealth, for each country we group children into quartiles on the basis of a wealth index similar to that used by Saeed and Zia (2014). Our wealth index comprises housing materials and the assets used by Jones and Schipper (2015) in defining household wealth: indoor lighting, running water, a television, a radio, a computer, and a phone. In each of the three countries, children from poorer households are less likely to receive private tuition or to have a mother who attended school (Table 1).

In the Uwezo survey, families report whether each child in the household attends a government school, a private school, or is out of school. Within each country, poorer children are about three times more likely than wealthier children to be out of school, and poorer children are far less likely than wealthier children to be enrolled in a private school (Figure 1).

Private school enrolment rates also vary greatly across the three countries, from 2% on average in Tanzania to 11% in Kenya and 26% in Uganda; as such, a poor child in Uganda is more likely than a wealthy child in Tanzania to be enrolled in a private school. There is also great heterogeneity in the distribution of private schools within each country. In Kenya, for example, just 5% of children in the Western and North Eastern provinces are enrolled in private schools, compared to 15% in the Coast province and 36% in the capital, Nairobi.

The vast majority of non-state schooling in the three countries is for-profit. While systematic information is not available of the types of provision in the countries, 2012 Uwezo data from Kenya show that less than 2% of those enrolled in non-state education in the sample are in NGO-run or religious schools, while the vast majority are in private schools.[1]

For learning outcomes, children are assessed individually in literacy (both in Swahili and English in Kenya and Tanzania; only in English in Uganda) and numeracy, at up to four levels of competency in literacy and six in numeracy, all of which should have been acquired within two years of schooling (Jones & Schipper, 2015). Children are tested at each level sequentially until they reach a level they cannot complete; e.g. if they can recognise numbers but cannot perform subtraction, they are not then tested for the ability to perform multiplication (for further details, see Jones, Schipper, Ruto, & Rajani, 2014). From these learning assessments

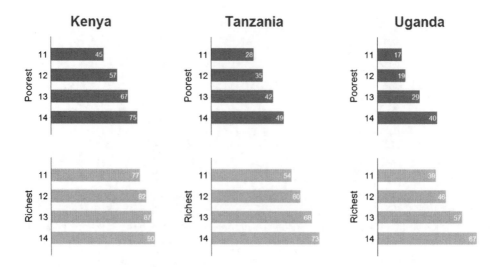

Figure 2. By age 14, the poorest children's chances of learning are three years behind those of the richest. Source: Uwezo Kenya 2013, Uwezo Tanzania 2013, Uwezo Uganda 2013.

we derive our key learning outcome for whether children have achieved the basics: whether a child is both able to read a short paragraph and to perform multiplication.

A far higher proportion of children in Kenya (74%) are able to do the basics than in Tanzania (49%) or Uganda (38%) (Table 1). Even so, a common trend across the countries is that wealth inequalities in learning are considerable (Figure 2). By age 11, the percentage-point gap between wealthier and poorer children in learning the basics runs between 22 points in Uganda and 32 points in Kenya. This gap is maintained in each country, such that by age 14 the proportion learning the basics among poorer children is only just approaching the proportion among wealthier 11-year-olds; in other words, the poorest children are three years behind the wealthiest. The size of these learning disparities compels us to focus not only on aggregate improvements among the full population, but also on conditions among the most disadvantaged.

Methodology

It is possible to use a bivariate regression to estimate the impact of private schooling (P) on a learning outcome (L), which would produce a linear probability model as represented by:

$$L = \beta_0 + \beta_1 P + \upsilon \tag{1}$$

where the estimated parameter β_0 represents the proportion of children not in private schools who have learned the basics, the estimated parameter β_1 represents the average difference from this proportion among those in private schools, and υ represents an error term that is normally distributed with a mean of zero. However, the estimate β_1 is only plausible if there is little concern of omitted variable bias. In other words, we would need to be confident that there are no substantive differences between children who do and do not enrol in private schools that would also be linked to learning.

This is highly unlikely, of course: in most countries, children from more advantaged households enrol in private schools at disproportionately high rates (e.g. Akyeampong & Rolleston,
2013; James & Woodhead, 2014; Srivastava, 2013), and this is the case in Kenya, Tanzania,
and Uganda (Table 1). As Singh (2014) has shown, in Andhra Pradesh, India, there is already
a learning gap between children attending private and government schools at the point of
enrolment. Hence, in the absence of a randomised, or as good as randomised, allocation of
students to different school types, it is important to control for indicators of bias between
those who do and do not enrol in private schools.

We use multivariate, ordinary least-squares (OLS) regression to estimate the inferential
models presented in this paper.[2] Our dependent variable of interest—whether a child has
learned the basics—is dichotomous, and, in recent years, the convention in many social-
science fields has been to estimate logistic regression models for outcomes of this nature
(Hellevik, 2009; Mood, 2010). However, we prefer to use OLS regression for this study for two
main reasons: OLS estimates are highly comparable to more complex procedures (e.g.
Abadie, 2003; Hellevik, 2009), and they provide marginal effects directly without the need
for supplementary computations (Angrist & Pischke, 2009).[3]

OLS regression estimates the average impact of an independent variable on an outcome
whilst holding constant the impact of the other independent variables included in the model.
As such, our regression models enable us to establish whether the predictive power of each
factor still holds once controlling for a range of other variables. Letting L denote whether a
child has learned the basics, we first estimate the following model for each country:

$$L = \gamma_0 + \gamma_1 P + \gamma_2 W2 + \gamma_3 W3 + \gamma_4 W4 + \gamma_5 X + \omega \tag{2}$$

in which P represents whether a child enrols in a private school, $W2$–$W4$ represents a child's
household wealth quartile, X represents a matrix of control variables, γ_0–γ_5 represent estimated parameters, and ω represents an error term. Then, in order to assess whether private
schooling can help reduce learning inequalities, we re-estimate Equation (2) separately for
the poorest and wealthiest quartiles in each country. If estimates of γ_1 differ significantly
between models for the poorer and richer subgroups in a given country, this would indicate
that private schooling has a differential impact on the chances of learning between these
groups.[4]

In the matrix of control variables (X), we account for a range of variables that past research
has identified as important to children's learning: whether a child is out of school (Alcott &
Rose, 2015a; Lewin & Sabates, 2012), their gender (Aslam, 2009; Jones & Schipper, 2015),
their age (Hungi, Ngware, & Abuya, 2014), whether their mother attended school (Abuya,
Mutisya, & Ngware, 2013; French & Kingdon, 2010), and whether the child receives private
tuition (Alcott & Rose, 2015a; Aslam & Atherton, 2012). In addition, as with prior quantitative
studies on developing countries (e.g. Jones & Schipper, 2015; Pal & Kingdon, 2010), we use
district fixed effects, via dummy variables, to minimise bias stemming from unobserved
heterogeneity within each country.[5] This is likely to be important because none of the countries are internally homogenous: within each, children in different regions grow up with
different conditions that will affect their educational opportunities. In Uganda for example,
wealth, infrastructure, and population density vary considerably by district (Lincove, 2012;
Uganda Bureau of Statistics, 2014); across countries, children in rural regions are likely to live
further from any type of school, and there are large learning inequalities between children
in rural and urban areas (Rose & Alcott, 2015).

Table 2. Model estimates for full sample.

	Kenya		Tanzania		Uganda	
	(1)	(2)	(3)	(4)	(5)	(6)
	Naïve	Controls	Naïve	Controls	Naïve	Controls
Enrolled in private school	12.7***	6.1**	23.0***	7.7***	17.1***	7.5***
95% confidence interval	(11.0, 14.3)	(4.3, 7.9)	(18.4, 27.6)	(3.5–11.9)	(14.4, 19.8)	(5.0, 10.0)
Wealth quartiles						
2nd	–	0.7	–	2.5*	–	3.0*
3rd	–	4.7***	–	5.5***	–	8.6***
4th (wealthiest)	–	9.2***	–	11.0***	–	16.6***
Out of school	−25.9***	−21.7***	−22.3***	−21.3***	−17.9***	−20.4***
Private tuition	–	6.3***	–	10.0***	–	10.2***
Female	–	4.6***	–	03.2***	–	3.5***
Mother attended school	–	4.9***	–	5.0***	–	7.4***
Age						
12	–	09.6***	–	7.6***	–	7.4***
13	–	16.5***	–	16.3***	–	18.3***
14	–	21.9***	–	24.3***	–	29.0***
District fixed effects	No	Yes	No	Yes	No	Yes
N	46,509	46,509	37,007	37,007	22,050	22,050
Adjusted R^2	0.028	0.142	0.027	0.147	0.032	0.181

Notes: To account for the sampling design of Uwezo, in all models we use population weights and cluster standard errors at the village level.
$^*p < 0.05$; $^{**}p < 0.01$; $^{***}p < 0.001$.
Source: Uwezo Kenya 2013, Uwezo Tanzania 2013, Uwezo Uganda 2013.

We recognise that there are limitations to our analysis. The cross-sectional nature of the Uwezo data means that we cannot be certain about the temporal precedence of our explanatory and control variables. For example, in order to assess the impact of private schooling on learning, it is important also to account for the influence of private tuition; however, we cannot be certain about how parents' decision to pay for private tuition interacts with their decision to pay for private schooling, e.g. whether one tends to follow the other, or vice versa. Also, household wealth influences a family's ability to pay for private tuition, but expenditure on private tuition also reduces the ability of households to afford the items from which we derive our wealth index. In addition, as the Uwezo dataset is household-based, it does not include some variables that are likely to be relevant for explaining learning outcomes. Notably, school factors are almost certainly important, such as teacher qualifications, teacher experience and class size. This means that our estimates remain prone to some forms of omitted variable bias, as is typical of OLS estimates based on survey data.

Findings

For each country, we first estimate a simple model controlling only for schooling status (Table 2: Models 1, 3, and 5 for Kenya, Tanzania, and Uganda, respectively), which we refer to as 'naïve' models because they do not control for any potential confounding variables. In all three countries, private schooling has a positive and significant association with learning the basics. We then add control variables in Models 2, 4, and 6. Comparing these to the naïve models, the apparent impact of private schooling on learning the basics remains significant and positive in each country, although it reduces by at least a half in each case. For example, in Kenya the estimated impact of private schooling versus government schooling on the likelihood a child will have learned the basics reduces from 13 to 6 percentage points when adding our model controls. In Tanzania and Uganda, the estimates change from 23 to 8 and from 17 to 8 percentage points, respectively.

This change between the sets of models implies that many of our control variables are correlated with private school enrolment and so account in part for the raw difference in learning outcomes between children in private schools and children in government schools. To help explore the association with different control variables, we estimate a series of blocked regressions for each country (presented in the Appendix 1). These regression models indicate that among our control variables, those reducing the gap most are district fixed effects, household wealth, and private tuition. Simply adding district fixed effects reduces the estimated impact of private schooling by 38% in Kenya, 42% in Uganda and 47% in Tanzania. This suggests that much of the overall difference in learning between children in private and government schools can be explained by disparities in learning between regions within each country. Even after controlling for district, gender, age, and mother's schooling, adding wealth controls further reduces the estimated impact of private schooling. The extent of this reduction runs between 14% in Uganda, 18% in Kenya, and 25% in Tanzania, suggesting that, within districts, inequalities in household wealth account for much of the apparent boost provided by private schooling. Even with all other model controls, controlling for private tuition reduces the estimated impact of private schooling by a further 21% in Kenya, 8% in Tanzania, and 18% in Uganda.

After accounting for many key control variables, private schooling still has a positive association with overall learning rates among the school-aged population; the average increase in the chances of learning the basics that is associated with private schooling compared to government schooling is between six and eight percentage points across the countries. However, as demonstrated by Figure 2, it is important not only to analyse aggregated patterns for the full population but also specifically among the most disadvantaged. Thus, we also estimate separate models for the poorest and richest quartiles in each country (Table 3).

Table 3. Model estimates of differential effects for poorer and wealthier children.

	Kenya		Tanzania		Uganda	
	(1)	(2)	(3)	(4)	(5)	(6)
	Poorest	Wealthiest	Poorest	Wealthiest	Poorest	Wealthiest
Enrolled in private school	9.4**	5.8***	−5.9	11.7***	7.4**	7.3***
	(3.5–15.3)	(3.6–8.0)	(−18.5–6.8)	(6.7–16.6)	(2.2–12.6)	(3.2–11.5)
Out of school	−35.4***	−7.9*	−26.1***	−14.5***	−22.0***	−22.5***
	(−39.8 – −31.0)	(−14.1 – −1.7)	(−29.1 – −23.2)	(−20.1 – −8.8)	(−27.0 – −16.9)	(−31.7 – −13.2)
Private tuition	8.1***	3.8***	9.6***	11.0***	12.2***	11.2***
	(5.1–11.0)	(1.8–5.9)	(4.3–14.9)	(7.6–14.5)	(7.7–16.7)	(6.7–15.7)
Female	4.4***	3.0**	2.0	3.2***	1.0	3.3
	(2.5–6.2)	(1.4–4.6)	(−0.4–4.3)	(1.0–5.4)	(−1.6–3.5)	(−0.3–6.9)
Mother attended school	4.4**	3.9**	3.8**	4.4	4.9***	7.8***
	(1.6–7.3)	(1.3–6.5)	(1.0–6.5)	(−0.0–8.9)	(2.0–7.7)	(3.5–12.2)
Age						
12	12.4***	5.8***	6.0***	7.6***	5.9***	10.1***
	(9.3–15.4)	(3.0–8.5)	(2.9–9.1)	(4.0–11.3)	(2.5–9.2)	(5.1–15.1)
13	20.9***	10.3***	13.5***	16.0***	15.1***	20.1***
	(17.8–24.0)	(7.4–13.1)	(10.2–16.9)	(12.2–19.9)	(11.2–19.0)	(14.7–25.5)
14	29.7***	14.1***	22.4***	20.9***	27.1***	31.0***
	(26.8–32.7)	(11.4–16.8)	(18.9–25.9)	(17.2–24.5)	(22.9–31.2)	(25.4–36.6)
District fixed effects	Yes	Yes	Yes	Yes	Yes	Yes
N	12,333	11,735	10,063	9535	5653	5482
Adjusted R^2	0.186	0.092	0.144	0.119	0.143	0.200

Notes: Lower and upper bounds of 95% confidence intervals are shown in parentheses.
$^*p < 0.05$; $^{**}p < 0.01$; $^{***}p < 0.001$.
To account for the sampling design of Uwezo, in all models we use population weights and cluster standard errors at the village level.
Source: Uwezo Kenya 2013, Uwezo Tanzania 2013, Uwezo Uganda 2013.

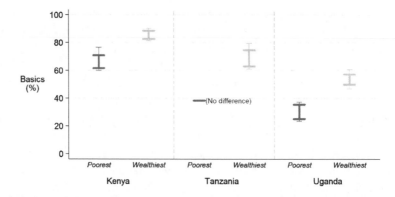

Figure 3. Model estimates of the average marginal improvement in test scores attributable to private schooling.
Note: Thicker lines show model estimates of the average improvement; thinner lines shows model estimates of the largest plausible improvement at the 95% confidence level.

The extent to which private schooling affects learning for the poorest differs between the countries. For the poorest in Tanzania (Model 3), the coefficient for private schooling is not significantly different from zero, whereas for the wealthiest (Model 4) the coefficient for private schooling is significant and positive, at 11.7 percentage points. This indicates that private schooling in Tanzania has no discernible impact on learning among children from poorer households, but it does have a positive impact on learning among children from wealthier households. For both Kenya (Model 1) and Uganda (Model 5), the coefficient for private schooling for the poorest is significant and positive, but neither is significantly different from the coefficient for private schooling among wealthier children (Models 2 and 6). This indicates that private schooling in these countries is positively related to learning for children from both poorer and wealthier households, but that this association does not vary between the groups.

To help visualise these patterns, from the models in Table 3 we plot the estimated marginal impact of private schooling against government schooling on learning the basics for the poorest and wealthiest in each country (Figure 3). The thicker lines show model estimates of the average improvements; the thinner lines show model estimates of the largest plausible improvement at the 95% confidence level. Since we did not observe any significant association among the poorest children in Tanzania in Model 3, we do not plot any apparent change in the chances of learning for this group.

This visualisation helps frame the impact of private schooling in relation to policy considerations: learning gaps between the rich and poor, and the absolute chances of learning for the most disadvantaged. First, a focus on the impact of private schooling should not mask the fact that inequities stemming from household background are sizable: while private schooling seems to improve learning among poorer children in Kenya and Uganda, it does not close the gap between poorer children enrolled in private schools and wealthier children enrolled in government schools. In Uganda, for example, private schooling increases the average poor child's chances of learning to 33%, but this compares to 50% for the richest in government schools. Second, by showing total chances of learning (rather than just changes in the chances of learning), we hope to refocus attention on the continuing challenge facing these countries, especially in Tanzania and Uganda. Even for those poorer children enrolled in private schools in these countries, fewer than 40% are learning the basics. In addition, the chances of learning are not great even among the most advantaged: in Tanzania around a quarter of wealthier children in private schools are still not learning the basics, and in Uganda this is over 40%.

Conclusion

As the focus of global education goals has shifted attention towards equitable learning outcomes, questions arise about how best to achieve this. One option that is increasingly considered in policy circles is to increase support for private schools. Our study makes a number of contributions to research on this topic. First, we help broaden the debate by presenting inferential analyses on a region, East Africa, that has thus far received limited research attention in comparison to South Asia. Second, while we control for varying conditions right down to the district level, our analysis provides countrywide patterns. Third, with household background information, we are able to examine whether the apparent impact of private schooling is equitable.

Our findings indicate that, on average, private schooling improves a child's chances of learning the basics in reading and writing. This is consistent with prior literature from a range of low- and lower-middle-income countries. However, we do not find evidence that private schools will help to close the gap in learning inequalities in the three East African countries included in the analysis. In Tanzania it appears that benefits accrue disproportionately among children from wealthier households, and in Kenya and Uganda benefits are similar across wealth groups. This implies that private schooling is unlikely to help close the wide gaps that remain between rich and poor in each country.

It should also be recalled that the poorest are much less likely to be enrolled in private school in each of the three countries. Our evidence would suggest that initiatives aimed at expanding access to private schooling to these children (for example via voucher programmes) are unlikely to be the solution to narrowing learning gaps. Expanding private schooling in Tanzania would potentially exacerbate learning inequalities; in Kenya and Uganda it would maintain the current gaps between rich and poor, at best helping the proportion of the poor learning the basics to approach current chances among wealthier children in the government school sector.

The shortcomings of private schooling for poorer children may be attributable to constraints in access among more disadvantaged households, differences in the quality of private schools available to wealthier and to poorer households, or to the inability of private schools to mitigate other drivers of disadvantage. Our data preclude us from making definitive assertions on this, although there are some clues. Preliminary analysis on government schools in the Uwezo data and on private schools in the related ASER data from Pakistan suggest that poorer and wealthier children are attending different schools from one another, with very different resource levels, within each sector (Alcott & Rose, 2015b; Jamil, Mohammad, & Saeed, 2015). In addition, besides being able to spend more on school fees to attend better resourced schools, we find that wealthier households also tend to be located in more densely populated districts, where they tend to have the opportunity of multiple schooling options close by. It is, therefore, plausible that learning inequalities reflect to some extent disparities in access and choice available to the rich and poor living in different parts of each of the countries. Even taking these issues into account, it would seem likely that factors beyond schooling have a strong impact on the different chances of children learning from poor and rich households. As such, any policy reforms need to address both the sources of inequalities within the school environment itself, and those that children bring to the school from their home and community background.

Moreover, even if policies could eliminate all barriers to private schools for poorer families, and guarantee they would be of a quality commensurate to those accessed by the more advantaged, the evidence suggests that private schools would be unlikely to offer a panacea. A significant proportion of wealthier children enrolled in private schools have not learned the basics even within a very conservative time frame. This suggests that all three countries' current private school systems, as with their government school systems, are flawed. For policymakers, transformation is more important than replication: simply expanding private school provision is unlikely to solve the global learning crisis.

Notes

1. Equivalent data from Uwezo are not available for Tanzania or Uganda, nor for Kenya beyond 2012.
2. In addition, we undertook preliminary analysis with instrumental variable methods but, as with past literature (e.g. French & Kingdon, 2010; Jones, 2013) found it difficult to identify an appropriate instrument. As such, the analysis was not considered sufficiently robust, especially when exploring heterogeneous effects for poorer and wealthier children. Further research would benefit from the consideration of identifying potential instruments at the time of collecting data.
3. We also ran all models both as logistic and probit regressions. The significance levels and relative magnitude of the predictors remain the same.
4. We compare whether γ_1 differs between the models by seeing whether there is any overlap between their 95% confidence intervals. If there is not, we deem them to be significantly different. We also corroborated the findings from these separate models by estimating models on the full sample for each country with the addition of an interaction effect between private schooling and wealth quartile. Substantive findings were the same for both approaches.
5. For Kenya, Tanzania, and Uganda, the number of districts in the 2013 Uwezo data are 156, 131, and 80, respectively.

Disclosure statement

No potential conflict of interest was reported by the authors.

References

Abadie, A. (2003). Semiparametric instrumental variable estimation of treatment response models. *Journal of Econometrics, 113*, 231–263.

Abuya, B. A., Mutisya, M., & Ngware, M. (2013). Association between mothers' education and grade six children numeracy and literacy in Kenya. *Education 3-13, 43*, 653–665.

Akyeampong, K., & Rolleston, C. (2013). Low-fee private schooling in Ghana: Is growing demand improving equitable and affordable access for the poor? In P. Srivastava (Ed.), *Low-fee private schooling: Aggravating equity or mitigating disadvantage?* (pp. 83–104). Oxford: Symposium Books.

Alcott, B., & Rose, P. (2015a). Schools and learning in rural India and Pakistan: Who goes where, and how much are they learning? *Prospects, 45*, 345–363.

Alcott, B., & Rose, P. (2015b, September 15–17). *Who learns in government schools, and why? Evidence from East Africa.* Paper presented at 13th UKFIET International Conference on Education and Development, Oxford.

Andrabi, T., Bau, N., Das, J., & Khwaja, A. I. (2010). Are bad public schools public 'bads'? Test scores and civic values in public and private schools. Retrieved from http://www.hks.harvard.edu/fs/akhwaja/papers/badpublicschools.pdf

Andrabi, T., Das, J., Khwaja, A. I., & Zajonc, T. (2011). Do value-added estimates add value? Accounting for learning dynamics. *American Economic Journal: Applied Economics, 3*(3), 29–54.

Angrist, J. D., & Pischke, J. S. (2009). *Mostly harmless econometrics: An empiricist's companion.* Princeton, NJ: Princeton University Press.

Arif, G. M., & Saqib, N. (2003). Production of cognitive life skills in public, private, and NGO schools in Pakistan. *Pakistan Development Review, 42*, 1–28.

Aslam, M. (2009). The relative effectiveness of government and private schools in Pakistan: Are girls worse off? *Education Economics, 17*, 329–354.

Aslam, M., & Atherton, P. (2012). *The 'shadow' education sector in India and Pakistan: The determinants, benefits and equity effects of private tutoring* (Education Support Programme Working Paper Series, 38). London: Institute of Education.

Bold, T., Kimenyi, M., Mwabu, G., & Sandefur, J. (2013). *The high return to low-cost private schooling in a developing country* (IGC Working Paper). Retrieved from http://r4d.dfid.gov.uk/Output/192407/

Chudgar, A., & Quin, E. (2012). Relationship between private schooling and achievement: Results from rural and urban India. *Economics of Education Review, 31*, 376–390.

Das, J., Pandey, P., & Zajonc, T. (2006). *Learning levels and gaps in Pakistan* (World Bank Policy Research Working Paper No. 4067). Washington, DC: World Bank.

Day Ashley, L., Mcloughlin, C., Aslam, M., Engel, J., Wales, J., Rawal, S., … Rose, P. (2014). *The role and impact of private schools in developing countries.* London: Department for International Development.

Desai, S., Dubey, A., Vanneman, R., & Banerji, R. (2009). Private schooling in India: A new educational landscape. *India Policy Forum, 5*, 1–58.

Dixon, P., Tooley, J., & Schagen, I. (2013). The relative quality of private and public schools for low-income families living in slums of Nairobi, Kenya. In P. Srivastava (Ed.), *Low-fee private schooling: Aggravating equity or mitigating disadvantage?* (pp. 83–104). Oxford: Symposium Books.

French, R., & Kingdon, G. (2010). *The relative effectiveness of private and government schools in rural India: Evidence from ASER data.* London: Institute of Education.

Goyal, S. (2009). Inside the house of learning: The relative performance of public and private schools in Orissa. *Education Economics, 17*, 315–327.

Härmä, J. (2013). Access or quality? Why do families living in slums choose low-cost private schools in Lagos, Nigeria? *Oxford Review of Education, 39*, 548–566.

Härmä, J., & Rose, P. (2012). Is low-fee private primary schooling affordable for the poor? Evidence from rural India. In S. L. Robertson, K. Mundy, A. Verger, & F. Menashy (Eds.), *Public private partnerships in education: New actors and modes of governance in a globalizing world* (pp. 243–258). Cheltenham: Edward Elgar.

Hellevik, O. (2009). Linear versus logistic regression when the dependent variable is a dichotomy. *Quality & Quantity, 43*, 59–74.

Hungi, N., Ngware, M., & Abuya, B. (2014). Examining the impact of age on literacy achievement among Grade 6 primary school pupils in Kenya. *International Journal of Educational Development, 39*, 237–249.

James, Z., & Woodhead, M. (2014). Choosing and changing schools in India's private and government sectors: Young lives evidence from Andhra Pradesh. *Oxford Review of Education, 40*, 73–90.

Jamil, B. R., Mohammad, U., & Saeed, S. (2015, September 15–17). *How does access and learning vary within the private sector in Pakistan?* Paper presented at 13th UKFIET International Conference on Education and Development, Oxford.

Jones, S. (2013). *Class size versus class composition: What matters for learning in East Africa?* (WIDER Working Paper No. 2013/065). Retrieved from https://www.wider.unu.edu/sites/default/files/WP2013-065.pdf

Jones, S., & Schipper, Y. (2015). Does family background matter for learning in East Africa? *Africa Education Review, 12*, 7–27.

Jones, S., Schipper, Y., Ruto, S., & Rajani, R. (2014). Can your child read and count? Measuring learning outcomes in East Africa. *Journal of African Economies, 23*, 643–672.

Kingdon, G. (1996). The quality and efficiency of private and public education: A case-study of urban India. *Oxford Bulletin of Economics and Statistics, 58*, 57–82.

Lassibille, G., & Tan, J. P. (2001). Are private schools more efficient than public schools? Evidence from Tanzania. *Education Economics, 9*, 145–172.

Lewin, K. M., & Sabates, R. (2012). Who gets what? Is improved access to basic education pro-poor in sub-Saharan Africa? *International Journal of Educational Development, 32*, 517–528.

Lincove, J. A. (2012). The influence of price on school enrollment under Uganda's policy of free primary education. *Economics of Education Review, 31*, 799–811.

Mood, C. (2010). Logistic regression: Why we cannot do what we think we can do, and what we can do about it. *European Sociological Review, 26*, 67–82.

Mugo, J. K., Ruto, S. J., Nakabugo, M. G., & Mgalla, Z. (2015). A call to learning focus in East Africa: Uwezo's measurement of learning in Kenya, Tanzania and Uganda. *Africa Education Review, 12*, 48–66.

Muralidharan, K. & Kremer, M. (2008). Public and private schools in rural India. In R. Chakrabarti & P. Petersen (Eds.), *School choice international: Exploiting public-private partnerships.* Cambridge, MA: MIT Press.

Muralidharan, K., & Sundararaman, V. (2015). The aggregate effect of school choice: Evidence from a two-stage experiment in India. *The Quarterly Journal of Economics, 130*, 1011–1066.

Oketch, M., Mutisya, M., Ngware, M., Ezeh, A. C., & Epari, C. (2010). Free primary education policy and pupil school mobility in urban Kenya. *International Journal of Educational Research, 49*, 173–183.

Pal, S. (2010). Public infrastructure, location of private schools and primary school attainment in an emerging economy. *Economics of Education Review, 29*, 783–794.

Pal, S., & Kingdon, G. G. (2010). *Can private school growth foster universal literacy? Panel evidence from Indian districts* (IZA Discussion Paper No. 5274).

Rolleston, C., James, Z., and Aurino, E. (2014). *Exploring the effect of educational opportunity and inequality on learning outcomes in Ethiopia, Peru, India, and Vietnam* (Background Paper for the UNESCO Education for All Global Monitoring Report 2013/4).

Rose, P., & Alcott, B. (2015). *How can education systems become equitable by 2030? DFID think pieces— Learning and equity (Report prepared for UK Department for International Development).* Oxford: Health & Education Advice and Resource Team.

Saeed, S., & Zia, H. (2014). Measuring gender and educational inequality: Addressing the marginalized. In *Annual status of education report: ASER Pakistan 2013.* Lahore: SAFED.

Singh, A. (2014). Test score gaps between private and government sector students at school entry age in India. *Oxford Review of Education, 40*, 30–49.

Singh, A. (2015). Private school effects in urban and rural India: Panel estimates at primary and secondary school ages. *Journal of Development Economics, 113*, 16–32.

Spaull, N., & Kotze, J. (2015). Starting behind and staying behind in South Africa: The case of insurmountable learning deficits in mathematics. *International Journal of Educational Development, 41*, 13–24.

Srivastava, P. (2013). Low-fee private schooling: Issues and evidence. In P. Srivastava (Ed.), *Low-fee private schooling: Aggravating equity or mitigating disadvantage?* (pp. 7–36). Oxford: Symposium Books.

Stern, J. M. B., & Heyneman, S. P. (2013). Low-fee private schooling: The case of Kenya. In P. Srivastava (Ed.), *Low-fee private schooling: Aggravating equity or mitigating disadvantage?* (pp. 105–128). Oxford: Symposium Books.

Uganda Bureau of Statistics. (2014). *National population and housing census: Provisional results*. Kampala: Uganda Bureau of Statistics.

Uganda National Examinations Board. (2015). *2014 PLE performance overview*. Retrieved from http://ww.uneb.ac.ug/index.php?link=Performance&&Key=PLE

UNESCO (2014). *Global monitoring report 2013/4: Teaching and learning: Achieving quality for all*. Paris: UNESCO.

Uwezo. (2014a). *Annual plan*. Retrieved from http://www.uwezo.net/wp-content/uploads/2012/08/Uwezo-Annual-Plan-2014.pdf

Uwezo. (2014b). *Are our children learning? Annual learning assessment report*. Kampala: Twaweza East Africa.

Uwezo Tanzania. (2013). *Are our children learning? Annual learning assessment report*. Dar es Salaam: Uwezo Tanzania.

Appendix 1.Block OLS model results for each country

Table A1. Kenya

Kenya	(1) Naïve	(2) + District FE	(3) + Base controls	(4) + Wealth controls	(5) + Tuition
Private schooling	12.7***	7.9***	9.4***	7.7***	6.1***
	(11.0–14.3)	(6.1–9.7)	(7.6–11.2)	(5.9–9.5)	(4.3–7.9)
Out of school	−25.9***	−21.4***	−22.1***	−21.7***	−21.0***
	(−31.5 – −20.4)	(−25.6 – −17.2)	(−26.2 – −17.9)	(−25.9 – −17.6)	(−25.2 – −16.9)
Female			4.6***	4.6***	4.6***
			(3.7–5.5)	(3.7–5.5)	(3.7–5.5)
Age 12			9.8***	9.8***	9.6***
			(8.2–11.3)	(8.3–11.4)	(8.0–11.1)
Age 13			17.0***	17.0***	16.5***
			(15.4–18.7)	(15.3–18.6)	(14.9–18.2)
Age 14			22.4***	22.5***	21.9***
			(20.8–24.0)	(20.9–24.1)	(20.3–23.5)
Mother attended school			5.8***	5.0***	4.9***
			(4.3–7.3)	(3.5–6.5)	(3.4–6.4)
2nd wealth quartile				0.8	0.7
				(−0.9–2.5)	(−1.0–2.5)
3rd wealth quartile				5.0***	4.7***
				(3.2–6.7)	(2.9–6.5)
4th (top) wealth quartile				10.0***	9.2***
				(8.1–11.8)	(7.4–11.0)
Private tuition					6.3***
					(5.0–7.7)
N	46,509	46,509	46,509	46,509	46,509
Adjusted R^2	0.03	0.10	0.14	0.14	0.14
District fixed effects	No	Yes	Yes	Yes	Yes

Notes: Parentheses show 95% confidence intervals. Estimates use population weights and errors clustered at the village level.
$^{**}p < 0.01$; $^{*}p < 0.05$.

Table A2. Tanzania.

Tanzania	(1) Naïve	(2) + District FE	(3) + Base controls	(4) + Wealth controls	(5) + Tuition
Private schooling	23.0***	12.2***	10.9***	8.4***	7.7***
	(18.4–27.6)	(7.9–16.5)	(6.7–15.0)	(4.3–12.5)	(3.5–11.9)
Out of school	−22.3***	−19.9***	−23.3***	−22.6***	−21.3***
	(−24.7 – −19.9)	(−22.1 – −17.6)	(−25.5 – −21.1)	(−24.8 – −20.4)	(−23.5 – −19.1)
Female			3.3***	3.4***	3.2***
			(2.2–4.4)	(2.2–4.5)	(2.1–4.3)
Age 12			7.7***	7.7***	7.6***
			(6.0–9.4)	(6.0–9.4)	(6.0–9.3)
Age 13			16.4***	16.3***	16.3***
			(14.6–18.2)	(14.5–18.1)	(14.6–18.1)
Age 14			24.4***	24.3***	24.3***
			(22.6–26.3)	(22.5–26.2)	(22.5–26.2)
Mother attended school			6.0***	5.1***	5.0***
			(4.2–7.8)	(3.3–6.9)	(3.2–6.8)
2nd wealth quartile				2.7**	2.5*
				(0.8–4.7)	(0.6–4.5)
3rd wealth quartile				6.0***	5.5***
				(3.8–8.3)	(3.2–7.7)
4th (top) wealth quartile				12.8***	11.0***
				(10.4–15.2)	(8.6–13.5)
Private tuition					10.0***
					(7.8–12.3)
N	37,007	37,007	37,007	37,007	37,007
Adjusted R^2	0.03	0.10	0.13	0.14	0.15
District fixed effects	No	Yes	Yes	Yes	Yes

Notes: Parentheses show 95% confidence intervals. Estimates use population weights and errors clustered at the village level.
**$p < 0.01$; *$p < 0.05$.

Table A3. Uganda.

Uganda	(1) Naïve	(2) + District FE	(3) + Base controls	(4) + Wealth controls	(5) + Tuition
Private schooling	17.1***	10.0***	10.6***	9.1***	7.5***
	(14.4–19.8)	(7.4–12.6)	(8.0–13.1)	(6.7–11.6)	(5.0–10.0)
Out of school	−17.9***	−21.3***	−22.4***	−21.6***	−20.4***
	(−22.0 – −13.9)	(−25.0 – −17.5)	(−26.0 – −18.8)	(−25.2 – −18.0)	(−24.0 – −16.8)
Female			3.9***	3.7***	3.5***
			(2.2–5.5)	(2.1–5.4)	(1.9–5.2)
Age 12			7.6***	7.5***	7.4***
			(5.4–9.9)	(5.2–9.7)	(5.2–9.6)
Age 13			18.7***	18.6***	18.3***
			(16.4–21.1)	(16.3–21.0)	(16.0–20.7)
Age 14			29.7***	29.4***	29.0***
			(27.3–32.2)	(27.0–31.8)	(26.6–31.5)
Mother attended school			9.0***	7.9***	7.4***
			(7.2–10.9)	(6.0–9.7)	(5.5–9.2)
2nd wealth quartile				3.0*	3.0*
				(0.7–5.2)	(0.7–5.2)
3rd wealth quartile				9.0***	8.6***
				(6.6–11.4)	(6.1–11.0)
4th (top) wealth quartile				17.2***	16.6***
				(14.4–20.0)	(13.8–19.4)
Private tuition					10.2***
					(7.8–12.7)
N	22,050	22,050	22,050	22,050	22,050
Adjusted R^2	0.03	0.10	0.16	0.17	0.18
District fixed effects	No	Yes	Yes	Yes	Yes

Notes: Parentheses show 95% confidence intervals. Estimates use population weights and errors clustered at the village level
**$p < 0.01$, *$p < 0.05$.

Is there a private schooling market in poor neighbourhoods in Maputo, Mozambique? Exploring the role of the non-state education sector

Joanna Härmä

ABSTRACT
In some low-income countries, low-fee private schools targeting relatively poor communities have sprung up in considerable numbers meeting growing demand. This is often the case where government is not providing enough school places, but also where parents could access government schools for their children but choose not to, due to perceived low quality of provision. This research study sought to find out if non-state schooling has developed to any considerable extent in the Mozambican context, where government education is of poor quality and learning outcomes are low. This paper reports that non-state provision is playing some role in providing places at the secondary level where government under-provides, and it is providing differentiated demand for some primary pupils. The study finds that the only level at which a true market appears to be developing is at the pre-primary level where government does not provide at all, which has resulted in complete inequity in access to early learning opportunities. At this most crucial level most schools are established, owned and run like typical low-fee private schools, i.e. as small businesses with individual owners. Overall non-government schools are few and far between and are playing a small role, with the only indications of recent growth evident at the pre-primary level.

Introduction

Can education markets function, and even play a positive role in poor countries? And are all poor countries with over-burdened or failing government school systems in the global south experiencing a boom (to a greater or lesser extent) in low-fee private schools? These questions are investigated in the context of Maputo, the capital and economic heart of Mozambique, as part of a study to understand how much non-state provision has developed in the city. The questions informing the research focus on what kind of provision, serving what levels of education, has appeared in low-income areas of a city which has hitherto not been written about in connection with this issue.

Mozambique is one of the poorest countries in the world (World Bank, 2015b), with some of the worst education indicators on record; it is ranked 178th out of 187 countries on the

UNDP's Human Development Index (UNDP, Undated). The education challenge is immense: learning assessments provide evidence that both pupils and teachers alike struggle with—and fail—tests of primary grade 4 level material (World Bank, 2015a). Not only poor learning but also under-provision of school places may have spurred some growth in non-state schooling in Maputo. An area of particular interest is the pre-primary level, as it was known at the outset that there is no government provision at this level. Private fee-paying options are found to be the only recourse for parents, and there is evidence that a market is developing at this level.

This paper addresses general questions regarding the non-state sector as a whole: is there a non-state school sector that serves poor inhabitants of Maputo, and if there is, is it growing? If such schools are found, what are their key characteristics, and to what extent are the different schooling levels served? The paper addresses these research questions, first introducing the context for the study, then moving on to how the study was carried out. The paper then reports the types of schools that were found, followed by the main study findings. A discussion section and conclusions bring the paper to a close.

The Mozambican context

The Mozambican context is characterised by considerable poverty, with 82% of the population living below the international $2 per day poverty line. The country's population is relatively small, at approximately 25.8 million people, 69% of whom live in rural locations; nationally the average length of time spent in school is just 3.3 years (UNDP, 2014). Only 32% of children reach primary grade 7, the final year of the cycle. The gross intake rate in this last year of primary is just 49%, down from the gross intake into primary 1 of 158% (UIS, 2014).

A recent World Bank study provides evidence of the extremely low quality of education in Mozambique. The study tested teachers and pupils in primary class 4, and found that the average teacher score across tests of Portuguese, mathematics and pedagogy was just 29%. Pupils fared even worse, scoring on average 24% across Portuguese, mathematics and non-verbal reasoning tests (World Bank, 2015a, p. 1), echoing earlier SACMEQ results.

Low learning is the result of poor teacher knowledge and also rampant absenteeism: 45% of teachers and 56% of pupils were found to be absent during unannounced visits (World Bank, 2015a, p. 1). In addition, 16% of teachers were at school but not teaching. A minority of 39% of teachers were actually found in class and teaching (World Bank, 2015a, p. 2).

Poverty proves a major obstacle, with many children not eating breakfast before school (Paulo, Rosario, & Tvedten, 2011; World Bank, 2015a); these children were found to score 10 percentage points lower than children who had eaten (World Bank, 2015a, p. 1). Poverty is also an obstacle to children being prepared to enter school at primary grade 1 as there is currently no fee-free provision of pre-primary education.

There are little data on the extent of access to early learning opportunities, and the National Institute for Statistics does not even mention pre-primary education (INE, 2013a, 2013b, 2013c); older survey evidence shows that in 2008 in Maputo city 16% of children aged between three and four years were in some early learning programme; nationally 2% of the poorest and 13% of the richest children received such opportunities (UNICEF, 2008). The need for pre-primary education and forms of child care for very young children is considerable; in the most recent MICS survey, 33% of children were left without adequate supervision and care (UNICEF, 2008).

Secondary education consists of three years, grades 8–10 (serving children aged 14–16), and families must pay enrolment, tuition and boarding (where relevant) fees, though poor families are meant to benefit from reduced fee levels (UNESCO IBE, 2010). Nationally there are too few secondary schools, meaning excessively large catchment areas. Insufficient places, combined with the fees involved mean low levels of participation: of the one-third of pupils who reach grade 7 (the end of the primary cycle), only 61% make the transition to secondary school. The NER in 2013 was 18%, and in 2011 only 11% of youths aged 15–24 years had completed their secondary education (Demographic and Health Survey, 2011).

The Maputo context

The national picture of poverty and educational outcomes is bleak, while that of Maputo is somewhat better. The city has historically been divided between the *cidade de cimento* and the *cidade de canico*, or the formal, well-developed city and the unplanned peripheral *bairros*, or neighbourhoods. The poorest living conditions are found in the latter, though there is considerable variation between *bairros* (Bertelsen, Tvedten, & Roque, 2014). Urban poverty exists in tense, sometimes dangerous, and densely populated areas with slum characteristics such as unregulated growth, lack of common infrastructure for water, electricity, roads, and more, and homes made precariously of unsuitable and impermanent materials (Bertelsen et al., 2014; Paulo et al., 2011).

There have been some indications of general improvement—though things may have worsened again with the global economic crisis (there is no more up-to-date information available). In Maputo, the National Household Survey of 2008/09 had shown a drop in the poverty rate from 54% in 2002/03, to 37% (INE, 2010; MPD, 2010 cited in Paulo et al., 2011, p. 15). This was reflected through increasing ownership of consumer durables and increased access to health, education, and water (MPD, 2010 cited in Paulo et al., 2011). In Maputo the net enrolment rate at the primary level has reached 96% with very little in the way of gender gap, while the national NER is 86%. The primary completion rate is 93% as compared with 77% nationally (MPD, 2010 cited in Paulo et al., 2011, p. 17).

Access to secondary schooling has been expanding somewhat with private schools being established, while expansion of government provision has failed to keep pace. However private schools, generally regarded as being of good quality, are unaffordable to the poor, commonly costing between 3100 and 4400 Meticais per month, compared with 300 at public schools (Paulo et al., 2011, p. 38). Some private schools have very many more girls than boys, and this gender imbalance is reflected in wider tensions in society. Many young men who have completed their secondary education find themselves in the same position of unemployment and dependence as their peers who did not invest the time and money in education. Therefore disillusionment regarding the benefits of secondary schooling may be leading more young men to drop out in search of economic opportunities (Paulo et al., 2011).

While certain indicators of socioeconomic well-being have been improving, there remain serious tensions in society with great sensitivity to prices for basic commodities. There have been violent popular uprisings in 2008 and 2010 due to changes in prices for petrol, public transportation, food, water, and energy, with government subsidies resulting from the agitation (Paulo et al., 2011). Those in poverty have extremely small disposable incomes: Table 1 shows that the poorest 20% have only 8.8% of their income to dedicate to health, education, and any other family needs. This has clear implications for the poor's ability to access early childhood care and learning opportunities for their young children, and secondary education for older children.

Table 1. Percentage of household expenditure per item and expenditure per capita by wealth, in Maputo.

Ownership	Food	Housing	Transport	Furniture	Other	Expenditure per capita
Maputo City average	23.4	36.6	7.4	11.2	21.3	2,175 Meticais*
Richest quintile	17.8	37.6	8.3	12.6	23.6	4,396 Meticais
Poorest quintile	47.9	32.1	4.7	6.4	8.8	417 Meticais

*There were 50 Meticais to the US dollar in March 2016.
Source: MPD (2010) cited in Paulo et al. (2011, p. 16).

There is limited up-to-date information on earnings in Maputo to contextualise the school costs and teacher salaries as outlined in the report below. However Table 1 reports information on per capita expenditure in Maputo for 2009. More current and perhaps more relevant for looking at non-state provision in low-income areas characterised by high levels of informality, one qualitative study provides data on the earnings of women in the informal market trading sector in Maputo in relation to earnings in the formal sector. It is stated that while low, 3000 Meticais per month is a common salary for a low-income employed person, and 6000 Meticais would be considered 'respectable' for a maid or a guard. Using the detailed accounts of incomings and outgoings of a very small sample of market traders, the authors find that very conservatively a trader selling only bread and peanuts could earn 4000–4500 Meticais per month. However, traders selling a variety of about five common products could earn between 7000 and 10,000 Meticais, which is comparable to a low though respectable salary for a full-time employee in the formal sector (Pedersen & Havemann, 2013). It should be noted that since these limited existing data were published between 2009 and 2013, major economic upheavals in Mozambique mean that this information may already be dated, including the more recent data on market traders' earnings by Pedersen and Havemann (2013).

In terms of what is known about the extent of private schooling to date, the National Institute of Statistics states that 2% of the country's primary schools are private, while at secondary level it is 28% (INE, 2013c, pp. 19–20). As government does not provide at the pre-primary level, by far the largest share of private provision is at this level with 100% of schools being non-state. A recent market study on the non-state sector for Opportunity International (Reichel & Chiulele, 2013) finds a relatively thriving market for private pre-primary schools, highlighting that there appears to be growing demand. It found similar types of secondary schools to those found in this study, but does not mention any private primary schools.

How the study was carried out

Private schools and how they are reported in this study

The aim of this research was to find all schools that exist in the chosen geographical areas, and (except for government schools) to document their key characteristics in some detail, meaning that the study takes the form of a census plus a survey of two case study areas. All non-government school proprietors or managers/principals (except for two who refused to participate) were interviewed using a structured questionnaire. It was anticipated that this would be possible due to the expectation that a relatively small number of schools would be found.

All schools not owned and managed by the government, and that teach the formal, standard curriculum at any level and for any combination of levels, between pre-primary and *preuniversitario* (grade 12) were covered in the census-survey. All schools were included, irrespective of socioeconomic level, size, infrastructure and facilities, registration status, or staffing (numbers and qualifications). This also meant that private schools with government-provided teachers were also included despite this important difference between them and fee-dependent private schools. Child care centres providing crèche (day care) services only, were not included. However, where schools with pre-primary upwards also had a crèche, information was also gathered regarding this level. Private (supplemental) tutoring centres and 'cramming' centres were not included, nor were purely Qur'anic or Bible schools teaching only religion.

Selection of case study areas

The United Kingdom's Department for International Development (DFID), which commissioned the study, specified an interest in low-income areas characterised by poor (and often privately provided) infrastructure, informality, and a dearth of public services. The aim was to discover whether low-income families are turning to the non-state sector or not. The two study areas selected were the districts Nhlamankulu, covering 8 square kilometres and KaMaxakeni, with 12 square kilometres. Table 2 provides a picture of the level of development of these districts, and the percentages of households possessing certain assets. The districts have poorer socioeconomic indicators than the average for the province, and Nhlamankulu tends to have somewhat poorer indicators than KaMaxakeni. Despite this latter fact, there is relatively little in the available data to clearly distinguish one area from another in terms of poverty status. Therefore, the extensive local knowledge of the fieldwork supervisor was relied upon in conjunction with discussion with the fieldwork team leader, to confirm the choice of these two areas.

Table 2. Selected indicators of standard of living and socioeconomic status in study districts—percent of households possessing each characteristic/asset.

	Nhlamankulu	KaMaxakeni
Walls—cement block	67	84
Walls—zinc	19	5
Walls—bamboo, etc	8	7
Roof—concrete	12	2
Roof—zinc	83	93
Floor—cement	84	92
Toilet—flush	29	19
Toilet—latrine	70	80
Toilet—none	1	1
Electricity	54	67
Water—piped from mains	15	4
Radio	67	69
TV	59	63
Car	10	8
Motorbike	1	1
Bicycle	5	5

Source: INE (2013a, 2013b).

The methodology

In October 2015, a team of experienced researchers was assembled and given defined geo-graphical areas for each to cover for the school mapping and survey. The researchers combed the entirety of their assigned areas to find what schools existed, and were instructed in how to do this; they walked the streets asking repeatedly from local people where schools existed, to find them all, even if hidden from view. It was anticipated that only a relatively small number of non-state schools would be found, so all school proprietors were asked to take part in the survey; school mapping and interviewing took place concurrently. In several cases an appointment had to be made to come back to speak with the relevant person. All of the necessary local government authorities (pertaining to education and more generally) were approached for their approval for the research, including the neighbourhood secre-taries. Stamped letters were shown at every school and the purpose of the research was explained and informed consent obtained.

Analysis of the data from this study is simple, using only descriptive methods due to the very small number of observations: 53 schools are included in the dataset serving all levels and coming from all ownership types/categories, meaning insufficient numbers of obser-vations for more complex, multivariate analysis.

What non-state schools were found in this study

This study set out to document all non-government schools in the selected study areas of Maputo. The types of schools found included: government schools, fully independent com-munity schools, community schools with some government support, and private schools. Firstly, government schools are those owned, run, staffed and maintained by the govern-ment, though fees are charged at the secondary and upper secondary levels. No fees are charged at the primary level, and these schools remain the default option for most Mozambican children, with many schools (at all levels) running multiple shifts of relatively short school days in order to meet the high demand. Actual enrolments at the government schools in the study areas are not reported here as the survey was of non-state schools only (however all existing schools were listed), and no reliable EMIS data were available for this purpose. The government is not involved in provision of pre-primary education at all, and the primary school cycle enrols children aged six into primary grade 1.

Several different types of non-state schools are found in the study areas, including those operated not-for-profit for community self-help purposes. The latter schools were referred to as 'community schools' because they had initially been established by the community, or community members had urged their church leaders to establish a school. Yet not all so-called community schools are the same: some are funded mostly or fully through user fees but on a not-for-profit basis, while others are supported by the government. These latter schools received all or some of their teachers from the government, meaning that civil service teachers are deployed to work in these schools and their salaries are paid by the government. Other running costs at these schools were covered through registration fees. While this means a material difference within the group, in practice, whether staffed by civil service teachers or not they were all referred to, and referred to themselves, as 'community schools'. Even where teachers were civil service teachers, the community reportedly viewed these schools, very often run by a church mission, as having greater control over teachers. This distinguishes the schools from government schools, and as a result they were reported as having long waiting lists of prospective pupils.

What Kingdon refers to as 'genuinely private schools' (2007, p. 183) are those independently established, owned and managed, and fully dependent on fee income, a similar definition to that used by Day Ashely et al. (2014). They can be profit-orientated or not-for-profit, but are more usually for-profit. Private schools can be owned by a broad range of people or organisations, including religious organisations, corporations, individuals, or groups of individuals (but are most usually owned by individuals). Purely private schools in their varying forms can target the less well-off, the middle classes, and the wealthy. Private schools for the wealthy are not new and provide perhaps the most commonly held image of what 'private education' means. What is relatively new and still quite rare in the selected areas of Maputo is the phenomenon of *low-fee private schools*. Such schools have been found in other contexts to often be unknown to and unregistered with the government, however this too proved to be uncommon in the sampled areas. This study found schools serving from pre-primary through senior secondary levels, falling under these four types of provision: government, private, community schools with government funding, and independent community schools.

The survey findings

Schools and their basic characteristics and facilities

This section outlines some basic characteristics of the non-state schools found, however firstly it is noted that identical numbers of government and non-state schools were found: 55 of each. The 55 government schools found serve primary through senior secondary levels in the study area. These schools have extremely large enrolments, as they cater for up to three shifts per day, meaning that the size of each government school dwarfs the typical non-government school. Of the latter, 55 were found but only 53 surveyed. Fifty-one of the participating 53 non-state schools serve 13,119 pupils, across which the average enrolment is 257 pupils, of which 53% are female (Table 3; two surveyed schools were unable or unwilling to provide enrolment information). Of note, there are more girls than boys at every level except for primary level, and in some secondary schools there were found to be very many more girls than boys enrolled. Part of this imbalance is explained by the population being 51.3% female (INE, 2013a, 2013b, p. 11); an extreme gender imbalance in favour of girls in private secondary schools was also found by Paulo et al. (2011).

No evidence was found of any 'mushrooming' of small, unregistered private schools, which is one hallmark of an expanding and unregulated private school market. No unregistered schools were found that are not (reportedly) in the process of applying for registration; in the case of primary and upwards, registration is with the Provincial Directorate of Education, while for pre-primary schools it is the Provincial Directorate of Women and Social Affairs. It was found that even in fairly poorly developed neighbourhoods, very few schools reported not having been inspected in 2015 (a few had been inspected in 2014 or 2013), and in the case of pre-primary schools, two out of six schools currently applying for registration have already been inspected this year. Only one (pre-primary) school out of 53 reported never having been inspected.

Table 3 shows that while secondary schools are few, they serve the largest share of pupils. As compared to other contexts in which non-state schooling has been researched, the primary level has negligible coverage with relatively few parents opting out of the fee-free government system. The total enrolment at this level is spread over seven school years, as opposed to two or three years for other levels. While the numbers of pre-primary pupils are much fewer than at the secondary level, pre-primary schools have the largest number of separate schools, most likely due to parents' desire to keep small children closer to home, meaning that demand is more localised at this level. They also represent 100% of provision.

Nearly 40% of surveyed non-state schools are owned by individuals, however 19 of the 21 schools concerned are concentrated at the pre-primary level, where the lack of government provision provides a clear market opportunity. Over half (53%) of all schools are owned by religious organisations (nine schools, mostly at the pre-primary and primary levels), and the community (19 schools, 10 of which serve pre-primary, with the rest spread across levels). Removing pre-primary schools from the equation, nearly 77% of schools (serving primary, secondary or *preuniversitario*) are owned by religious or community groups, and only two are owned by private individuals.

In terms of school financing, 87% are reliant on user-fees, 2% on community contributions, and the balance receive the bulk of their recurrent costs from the government through having civil service teachers deployed to the schools. One school receives funding from the mission on top of their user fees, and one school with a majority of user-fee funded teachers also received five government-provided teachers.

One of several factors distinguishing pre-primary schools from the other schools found is that there has been much more recent growth than at other levels, as illustrated in the last row of Table 3. While the mean year of establishment is nearly the same across levels (except for primary), 10 out of 38 pre-primary schools have opened after 2010, five of these in 2015 alone, the only discernible uptick in NSP supply. Non-state primary schools have a much longer history and slower growth than at the secondary levels (which only appeared from the mid-1990s), with the first non-state primary school opened in 1975, and the rest established relatively evenly across the years. The last two primary schools were established in 2012, meaning no evidence of sharply increasing supply (or presumably demand either) at this level. Several respondents during the survey expressed the view that 'everyone uses the government primary schools because they are free'.

Table 4 presents ownership information not by distinct schools (many of the 53 schools serve a combination of levels) but by the numbers of schools serving an individual level.

Table 3. Selected characteristics of surveyed non-state schools, by level served.

Characteristic	Pre-primary	Primary	Secondary	Preuniversitario
Schools serving this level	38	11	9	7
Lowest enrolment	9	25	162	16
Highest enrolment	150	1616	1782	180
Average enrolment	61	402	747	229
Average per year group	n/a*	57	249	115
% female enrolment	50.3	48.6	58.4	53.1
Total children enrolled	2263	4023	5231	1602
Number schools registered	32	11	8	6
Applying for registration	6	0	1	1
Unregistered, not applying	0	0	0	0
Inspected in 2015	34	10	8	5
Never inspected	1	0	0	0
Mean year of establishment	2001	1995	2001	2004
No. established after 2010	10	2	1	1

*Year group separations are not as clear at this level as for other levels.

Table 4. School ownership types, by level.

Ownership	Pre-primary	Primary	Secondary	*Preuniversitario*
Individual	20	1	1	1
Community	10	7	6	1
Religious organisation	5	2	2	4
Private company	0	0	0	1
Other	3	1	0	0
Total	38	11	9	7

This table shows that at the pre-primary level individual school ownership is the most common, while at all other levels community schools are predominant, followed by religious groups.

The extent of physical facilities varies greatly; nine pre-primary schools have just one or two rooms and a further 11 have three rooms; most (82%) report having sufficient suitable furniture. Of the 38 pre-primary schools, 74% were in owned premises, while seven were in rented accommodation and two were in space granted for free (such as from a religious mission/church). Researchers judged that while 84% of schools had safe, suitable premises, 8% were in totally unsuitable premises, with two schools' locations deemed dangerous to children. Six schools hold classes outside due to insufficient all-weather rooms. It is clear the infrastructure varies greatly at this level, however all schools were deemed to be making efforts to keep the premises as clean and hygienic as possible.

With regard to primary level and above, no school was found operating in an unsuitable building, which is consistent with the lack of an unregistered private school sub-sector, marking it as extremely different from other cities where unregistered schools are booming. Nearly all were in purpose-built buildings roughly meeting standards, while the rest were in converted buildings which were suitable for school use. All were well-maintained or semi well-maintained and kept clean except in the case of one secondary school which was deemed to be in an unacceptably dirty and unhygienic condition.

In terms of basic facilities all schools from primary to upper secondary had a water source, usually mains-piped water, and toilets, including ones specifically for girls. All schools had sufficient classroom furniture to accommodate students. However secondary schools were severely lacking in some necessary facilities for quality teaching and learning at this level: five out of seven upper-secondary schools have no laboratory, four had no library, and six had no computers. At the secondary level, two out of seven schools with data have laboratories, three had libraries, and one had computers.

Teachers and teaching at non-government schools

Teaching in the study schools that do not receive government support is not lucrative employment. Yet as far as proprietors or principals could tell, only a handful of teachers have other forms of employment outside of the school, and 47 proprietors out of 53 stated that teachers are not allowed to charge their students for extra lessons/tuition outside of regular school hours. However teachers may still supplement their earnings through providing private tuition to other children. The mean salary for a private sector teacher of 'average' experience is 3812 Meticais or US$76 per month (Table 5), which compares unfavourably with a

Table 5. Teacher salaries per month by level and by teacher sector.

Monthly salary	Private sector teachers*	Civil service teachers
Lowest	1403	6000
Highest	14,025	24,600
Inexperienced teacher (mean)	3241	6500
Average teacher (mean)	3812	11,166
Experienced teacher (mean)	5681	20,300

*Numbers of observations: crèche: 24; pre-primary: 37; inexperienced teachers: 35; average teachers: 36; experienced teachers: 38. Private sector teachers indicates that these are teachers who are paid out of fee income paid by parents.

Notes: Proprietors reported the monthly salary and the number of months per year that this is paid. The yearly salary was then calculated and divided by 12 to arrive at the monthly salary reported here. The average number of months that private sector teachers are paid for is 11.22 months per year.

market trader selling only bread and peanuts, as documented by Pedersen and Havemann (2013).

Table 5 separates out the salaries of private sector teachers, which is taken to mean those teachers who are paid out of school fee income, from the salaries of the civil service teachers who work at some of the sample schools. The table shows that the salaries of private sector teachers are extremely low in comparison with civil service pay levels. Six schools have government (civil service) teachers, five of these having only government teachers. Two of the five schools serve primary only, two serve secondary only, and one serves primary and secondary. The sixth school has five teachers that are government-provided but 30 that are paid by the school. Across the five schools with only civil service teachers, the mean salary for a teacher of average experience is 11,166 Meticais, or nearly three times that of a private sector teacher.

The levels of pedagogical and subject content knowledge that teachers have attained are extremely important to their ability to provide good quality education. Yet while the on-paper qualifications attained by teachers often do not accurately reflect these levels of actual attainment, in this study teachers' highest academic qualifications and teaching qualifications provide the only available proxy measure of teachers' competence. Teachers should have a good general education, and it is also required (by regulation) that teachers gain a recognised teaching qualification. Table 6 provides the numbers of teachers teaching each

Table 6. Distribution of teachers by general education level and schooling level taught.

General education level	Pre-primary	Primary	Secondary	Preuniversitario
Up to Primary 7	30 (20%)	2 (2%)	0	0
Up to Secondary 10	64 (43%)	3 (3%)	3 (2%)	0
Up to Preuniversitario 12	54 (37%)	44 (43%)	23 (15%)	5 (5%)
Studying for Bachelors		22 (21%)	13 (9%)	11 (10%)
Degree completed		11 (11%)	56 (37%)	62 (59%)
Masters or higher degree completed		0	2 (1%)	0
Basic Education Certificate Certificado de Ensino (básico)*		11 (11%)	2 (1%)	0
Higher certificate in teaching (Curso de Ensino Superior, UP/ UCM)*		10 (10%)	48 (31%)	22 (21%)
Other			6 (4%)	5 (5%)
Total	148	103	153	105

*These teachers have teaching qualifications as their highest education level attained.

Table 7. Numbers of teachers by teaching qualification and schooling level taught.

Teaching qualification	Pre-primary	Primary	Secondary	Preuniversitario
None	52 (35%)	7 (7%)	11 (7%)	5 (5%)
Magisterio Primaria	15 (10%)	4 (4%)	1 (1%)	0
UEM/CFP 10"/11ª	0	0	1 (1%)	4 (4%)
CFPP 6ª/7ª + 3 anos	0	2 (2%)	0	0
Instituto do Magistério Primário (IMP)	0	0	9 (6%)	0
10th grade + 1 year training	12 (8%)	15 (15%)	0	1 (1%)
12th grade + 1 year training	7 (5%)	21 (20%)	14 (9%)	5 (4%)
Educatora Infantil	6 (4%)	0	0	0
Instituto do Magisterio Primario	4 (3%)	26 (25%)	0	0
Bacharelato / Licenciatura (UP/UCM)	1 (1%)	27 (26%)	104 (68%)	65 (62%)
No response	51 (34%)	0	0	0
Other	0	1 (1%)	12 (8%)	25 (24%)
Total	148	103	153	105

level, with their general education qualifications, while Table 7 presents teachers' teaching qualifications. Most teachers handle only one level, though some teachers/care-givers were responsible for both crèche and pre-primary, and a few teachers teach both secondary and *preuniversitario* levels.

It is clear that most pre-primary teachers are vastly under-educated and unqualified for the important and demanding work that they do, with a fifth having just primary education and another 43% just up to grade 10, and over a third have no teaching qualification at all. Based on researchers' observations, in 89% of pre-primary schools the teachers were found to be working with their classes, with 8% having the majority of teachers found in-class, while only one school (3%) had very little teaching activity going on when researchers entered the school.

In keeping with the relatively well-regulated non-state sector in Maputo, there are few untrained teachers teaching at higher levels: 5% at the *preuniversitario* level and 7% at primary and secondary levels respectively (Table 7). As expected, education and qualification levels tend to increase with the level taught, with *preuniversitario* teachers the most highly qualified. In only one poorly managed and maintained secondary school, few teachers were observed to be present and in their classrooms working; however in all other schools all or the majority of teachers were working.

Irrespective of qualifications already gained, teachers benefit from further professional development in the form of in-service training. Proprietors were asked whether they provide any training for their teachers, and if so, what type (Table 8). The most common is for the proprietor or an experienced member of staff to instruct teachers in the basics; of note, at the pre-primary level proprietors report sending their staff on external training courses and also hiring in consultants/trainers to come and provide training. It should be noted that the survey collected no evidence as to the effectiveness or usefulness of this training, however this training may go some way to make up for the lack of prior education and qualifications. Yet with seven pre-primary schools providing no training at all, it is likely that quality of provision in the sector at that level varies enormously.

With regard to how classes and classrooms are arranged, the two schools in the sample that serve both primary and pre-primary levels use multi-grade teaching in grouping together primary 1 with the pre-primary class. And with regard to all of the 38 schools serving the pre-primary level, 29 schools provide dedicated teachers for each pre-primary class at all times, but nine schools stated that this is not the case. In addition, 13 schools stated that

Table 8. Numbers of proprietors reporting providing different types of training, by level.

Type of in-service training	Pre-primary	Primary	Secondary	Preuniversitario
Basic instruction from proprietor or other member of staff	16	3	3	4
Seminars for all teachers as a group, from a proprietor or other member of staff	2	3	3	2
Training seminars by external trainer/ consultant	7	2	2	1
Teachers sent on external training course	8	0	0	0
No training is provided at the school	7	3	2	1

there is no separate, age-appropriate curriculum for pre-primary levels that is distinct from primary school material, most likely due to a lack of government leadership on this issue. In terms of pupil–teacher ratios, these differ drastically by level. At the pre-primary level it is the lowest at just 12 children per teacher/carer, and it is highest at the primary level with 39 pupils per teacher. At secondary level there is a relatively high 34 pupils per teacher, but only 15 at the *preuniversitario* level.

Competition, the clientele, and the costs of private schooling

Competition in this 'market' is much less than in other contexts with larger numbers of schools. Only half of all proprietors feel that they need to compete with other schools to attract clients; several of the community schools have long waiting lists of pupils. Many of the proprietors reasoned that there was no competition because there were no other schools close by; schools were indeed found to be fairly far apart, while the majority of pupils travel by foot, from 1.5 to 3 kilometres away.

The costs of attending a private school are high, even for those with stable employment, and the clientele of the schools was assessed as being mostly middle class, with few really poor families. The term 'middle class' should be viewed in the context of societies where there is an enormous divide between the truly wealthy (or elites) and the bulk of the population. In the study areas as in other African contexts, what is viewed as 'middle class' in a particular location will often include better-off residents of informal settlements. The majority of proprietors stated that the parents of their pupils include civil servants and highly qualified private employees (81%); skilled workers or labourers (21%); domestic workers (43%); and small business owners (25%). Only 13% of proprietors reported that they cater to the children of manual labourers or petty traders (6%) or employees in small or informal businesses (11%). Only 21% of proprietors believe that their clientele includes poor families, while 55% cited the lower-middle classes and 64% cited the established middle classes as being amongst their clientele. Thirteen percent of proprietors believe the bulk of their clientele to be poor, while the remainder believe the majority of their clients are middle class (51%) or at least lower-middle class (36%).

There are indications that parents do not find the costs easy to manage, making budgeting and piecemeal payments necessary. Only a quarter of proprietors reported that parents are regular and reliable at paying school fees, and while these reports come only from proprietors, the responses tally with research from all other contexts where the author has studied low-fee private schooling, including from the household perspective (Härmä, 2011a, 2011b). Yet a considerable 38% of proprietors stated that parents are for the most part regular and only sometimes late with paying. Twenty-one percent stated that parents are frequently irregular and need to be chased in order to get full payment; and 9% reported them to be extremely difficult to extract payment from. In some cases parents will remove their child from the school when it becomes clear that they will not be able to pay the fees, so the school loses out, however this was not cited as a very common occurrence; half of proprietors reported that this happens only from time to time. In order to retain clients, proprietors allow all schedules and instalments of payments in the hope of eventually receiving full payment. They also accept lower fees in some limited circumstances. Parents are irregular with paying fees often due to their own employment and incomes being irregular, sometimes in the informal sector.

The complete costs of attending non-state schools

Non-state schools in the selected areas of Maputo are expensive for those on low incomes. Table 9 provides the full costs of attending the surveyed non-state schools, and it should be borne in mind that these are the costs of educating one child at the relevant level. Taking all costs combined, the schools become more expensive as the levels progress, as expected. Yet the data can be treated as representing the lower bound of school costs, as other studies find that proprietors tend to under-estimate the costs as compared to parents' spending reports (as in Härmä, 2011b). Another caveat to make is regarding the very small numbers of observations for all levels except for the pre-primary level. In addition, transportation makes up a large proportion of costs at the post-primary levels. This is explained by older children being more likely to be sent longer distances to schools, particularly considering the general dearth of secondary schools. However it is difficult to account for the differences in actual school fees across the educational levels, while intuitively, textbooks cost much more for older children. The final row of the table provides the yearly sum divided by 10 months; however many of these costs (such as registration, uniforms, and books) must be

Table 9. All costs (per annum) of attending fully private surveyed schools.

Fee type	Pre-primary	Primary	Secondary	Preuniversitario
School fee	12,618	11,800	5362	9721
Registration fee*	1119	487	967	967
Exams	0	363	370	370
Uniform	275	429	387	387
Books	166	1503	2122	2122
Materials	0	583	620	620
Transport	0	0	10,457	10,457
Total per annum	14,178	15,165	20,285	24,644
Total divided by 10 months	1418	1517	2029	2464

Notes: The numbers of observations for fee levels are low (except for the pre-primary level where there are 38 observations): six at the primary level; four at the secondary level; seven at the upper secondary level.
*Roughly half of all 53 schools charged registration fees only upon first enrolling at the school; where this was the case, it was on average 1004 Meticais at the pre-primary level; 1338 at the primary level; 699 at the secondary and *preuniversitario* levels.

paid at the start of the year, meaning an extra challenge for less well-off households. Schools with government funding do not charge fees, but do charge registration fees and some charge for examinations.

Bearing in mind from the information on earnings provided above that 10,000 Meticais per month would be quite a 'reasonable' salary, then to have a child in pre-primary, a child in primary, and a third in secondary school, would consume well over 50% of the household's total income. This can easily be considered unsustainable, and it should be taken as no surprise that most children attend government primary schools, and that most of the clientele of the surveyed schools are reported as being of lower-middle to upper-middle classes. In addition to these costs, it is likely that many children also take extra tuition, adding even more to household expenditure.

Discussion

A key aspect of the non-state sector in Maputo is its diversity: there are different models of ownership and outlook; the community or church-owned schools are established and run from a different impetus than a for-profit private school, and five of the schools are staffed entirely with government-provided teachers. These schools are not in the control of a single private individual; there appears to be great community support behind them. One such school's head teacher reported that such schools are established as a result of concerted efforts and requests on the part of the community for a well-run school for their children. It is likely that such schools will continue to endure and have long waiting lists, and particularly so at the government-supported schools where no fees are charged at any level.

It appears that there is little scope for private primary schooling; as one proprietor of a more up-market pre-primary and primary school stated, the market for the primary level is extremely small. She owned two pre-primary schools that were full, but she said that people only spend where they have to, and that most families in Maputo have no chance of affording private pre-primary schooling, and that they will for sure use government primary schools. The anecdotal evidence suggests that household poverty may be the barrier to demand for even low-fee private schooling.

The market can therefore be assessed as being quite stable, with no boom in provision taking place. It appears likely that more government-subsided community schools would find an eager audience, but the market for user fee-reliant schools appears to be limited, illustrating that even in some densely-populated urban contexts, there is little to no market for private primary schooling. Future research that would explore the issue from the demand (household) side, is needed to fully understand the dynamics of demand, and whether or not poverty means that even at the lowest possible unit costs (made up mostly of teacher salaries), a market for low-fee private schooling is not feasible.

Non-state activity serving the pre-primary level stands out: five of the existing 38 schools were found to have opened in 2015, indicating that there is growing demand at this level, and it is likely that as awareness of the importance of this level of education grows, that the market may also expand. Pre-primary is also the level at which the largest number of schools are owned by private individuals running the schools for their livelihood, more similarly to the model of low-fee private schools in contexts such as India and Nigeria.

The non-state pre-primary sector in the study areas most closely resembles a market of private providers, with no competition from the government. This development may have serious consequences for what is already an extremely unequal city. For the most part children have been entering government primary schools from a position of equality at least in respect to prior formal learning experiences. But as the market for fully private pre-primary education expands to absorb those who can afford to pay fees, a considerable proportion of poor families, likely to comprise approximately the lower two quintiles of wealth, will remain excluded from this opportunity. Poorer, more disadvantaged children will therefore enter government primary schools at a further disadvantage, while evidence suggests that the poorest, and more specifically the poor in poorer countries, gain the most from effective early childhood programming (Gertler et al., 2014; Grantham-McGregor, Fernald, Kagawa, & Walker, 2014).

At the other end of the spectrum, the demand for the community and church-owned secondary schools indicates strong demand for good-quality education, that is clearly not being met by the government sector. It is important that as more and more pupils approach completion of the primary cycle, that they are not put off by a dearth of opportunities for further learning.

Lack of access on either end of the primary schooling cycle is of concern for social equity, however as the lower end of schooling caters the most to all segments of society, getting the foundations right from the early years is arguably of greater urgency than expanding access to secondary schooling. It is recognised that the Mozambican government faces financial constraints in extending government provision, yet focusing too much on primary schooling is an approach that has not worked well for other countries.

Harnessing the potential of the private sector at the pre-primary level to quickly expand provision could be a sensible partnership option for the government and its international development partners to consider, although only where parents' purchasing power would be supported. In addition, while lower unit costs are often an attraction of the low-fee private sector, if these costs are low due to hiring staff with extremely low educational attainment and no qualifications, then it will likely prove a false economy. Any partnership for expansion must be accompanied by required minimum standards.

Conclusions

The non-state sector in the sampled areas of Maputo is diverse despite being small, and growing at a very slow pace. It is not characterised by fierce competition between a range of privately and individually-owned schools existing close together, as in Lagos, Nairobi, Accra, Lahore and Delhi. The likely explanation for why there does not appear to be a thriving private sector is its unaffordability for most people, even with teacher salaries (the key determinant of how low the fees charged can feasibly be) as low as were found in this study. Irrespective of the sector, there is clear excess demand for good quality provision with strong moral values and management at the secondary level, as well as for pre-primary schooling. Both areas of demand are due to a lack of, or insufficient, government provision.

If pre-primary education continues to be left solely to the market, and all those who can pay start to take up private school places, then this runs the risk of making an unequal society even more unequal. If the market broadly is not providing widely in areas of urban Maputo, then it will surely not provide for the vast rural areas of the country. In the interests of universality and equity, it would be preferable to invest more in the government system used so widely at the primary level, and which will be the only provider in many rural and remote areas of the country. Secondary school provision should be expanded and management strengthened. And as a matter of urgency, provision should be extended downwards to the pre-primary level. Ensuring early childhood learning opportunities of good quality to all children in Mozambique, and not just in Maputo, is crucial to success in later grades, for children, families, and the country.

Disclosure statement

No potential conflict of interest was reported by the author.

References

Bertelsen, B., Tvedten, I., & Roque, S. (2014). Engaging, transcending and subverting dichotomies: Discursive dynamics of Maputo's urban space. *Urban Studies, 51*, 2752–2769.

Day Ashley, L., Mcloughlin, C., Aslam, M., Engel, J., Wales, J., Rawal, S., & Rose, P. (2014). *The role and impact of private schools in developing countries*. London: Department for International Development.

Demographic and Health Survey. (2011). Mozambique: 2011. Retrieved from http://dhsprogram.com/publications/publication-fr266-dhs-final-reports.cfm

Gertler, P., Heckman, J., Pinto, R., Zanolini, A., Vermeersch, C., Walker, S., & Grantham-McGregor, S. (2014). Labor market returns to an early childhood stimulation intervention in Jamaica. *Science, 344*, 998–1001.

Grantham-McGregor, S., Fernald, L., Kagawa, R., & Walker, S. (2014). Effects of integrated child development and nutrition interventions on child development and nutritional status. *Annals of the New York Academy of Sciences, 1308*, 11–32.

Härmä, J. (2011a). Low-cost private schooling in India: Is it pro poor and equitable? *International Journal of Educational Development, 31*, 350–356.

Härmä, J. (2011b). *Study of private schools in Kwara State* (DfID-ESSPIN Report KW326).

INE (2010). *Inquerito sobre Orcamento Familiar 2008/09*. Maputo: Instituto Nacional de Estatistica.

INE (2013a). *Estatisticas do Distrito KaMaxakeni, November 2013*. Mozambique: National Institute for Statistics.

INE (2013b). *Estatisticas do Distrito Nhlamankulu, November 2013*. Mozambique: National Institute for Statistics.

INE (2013c). *Estatisticas E Indicadores Sociais 2012–2013*. Maputo: Instituto Nacional de Estatistica.

Kingdon, G. G. (2007). The progress of school education in India. *Oxford Review of Economic Policy, 23*, 168–195.

Paulo, M., Rosario, C., & Tvedten, I. (2011). *'Xiculungo' revisited: Assessing the implications of PARPA II in Maputo 2007–2010* (CMI Report R2011:1).

Pedersen, K. K., & Havemann, T. (2013). The surprising tale of Maputo sales ladies. Retrieved from http://www.clarmondial.com/the-surprising-tale-of-maputos-sales-ladies/

Reichel, B., & Chiulele, M. E. (2013). *Identification of educational institutions eligible for 'school improvement loans'*. Maputo: Opportunity International.

UIS. (2014). Mozambique country profile. UNESCO Institute for Statistics. Retrieved from http://www.uis.unesco.org/DataCentre/Pages/country-profile.aspx?code=MOZ&regioncode=40540

UNDP. (2014). Human development report 2014. Country profile Mozambique. United Nations Development Program. Retrieved from http://hdr.undp.org/en/countries/profiles/MOZ

UNDP. Undated. Human development index and its components. Retrieved from http://hdr.undp.org/en/content/table-1-human-development-index-and-its-components

UNESCO IBE. (2010). World data on education Mozambique. UNESCO IBE, 7th edn. Retrieved from http://www.ibe.unesco.org/fileadmin/user_upload/Publications/WDE/2010/pdf-versions/Mozambique.pdf

UNICEF. (2008). Multiple indicator cluster survey 3 report. Retrieved from http://www.childinfo.org/files/MICS3_Mozambique_FinalReport_2008.pdf

World Bank. (2015a, March). *Mozambique service delivery indicators* (Report no. 95999). Washington, DC: World Bank.

World Bank. (2015b). Poverty and equity Mozambique. Retrieved from http://povertydata.worldbank.org/poverty/country/MOZ

'Affordable' private schools in South Africa. Affordable for whom?

Sonia Languille

ABSTRACT

The paper sets out to challenge the notions of 'affordable' private schools in the context of South Africa. It is guided by one main question: 'affordable private schools for whom?' It argues that, contrary to claims by its public and private proponents, affordable private schools in South Africa do not cater for poor children. Their rise has coincided with the emergence, in the post-apartheid period, of a—mostly black—middle class. However, despite its imprecision, the 'affordable' terminology can also be interpreted as a discursive device that obscures the class interests and distributional choices that actually shape South Africa's education system. It allows the social forces in favour of the expansion of private education—segments of the state and pro-market lobbyists—to frame their project in social justice terms. The paper concludes that the state's ambiguous position towards the so-called 'affordable' or 'low-fee' private schools reflects national leaders' delicate balancing act between contradictory objectives, which is overly determined by their embrace of an orthodox macro-economic model that constrains the fiscal space for public education.

Introduction

Over the last three decades, worldwide, the education field has been increasingly invested by business-oriented actors. The global trend of education privatisation has varied in intensity and taken diverse forms according to countries' specific contexts (Ball, 2009; Robertson & Dale, 2013). The present paper examines the conditions of internalisation of the neoliberal education agenda in South Africa by focusing on one of its ingredients: the rise of so-called 'affordable'—also referred to as 'low-fee' or 'low-cost'—private schools that purportedly target the poor (Tooley & Dixon, 2005). While access to basic education has greatly improved in South Africa since the end of apartheid, educational performances have remained low. Additionally, access to quality education is unequally distributed, along social class, racial, and spatial lines (Chisholm, 2005). Proponents of private education claim that a thriving private schooling market would help the state fulfil the constitutional right to basic education and to 'fix' the 'learning crisis' in public education.

Private basic education in South Africa remains, in comparison with other low- and middle-income countries, relatively small. In 2015, only about 4.4% of students in basic education were enrolled in 'independent schools'—the country's official terminology (DBE, 2015). In comparison, in 2013, in Brazil, private education enrolment represented 16.2% of total enrolment at primary level and 12.9% at secondary level. In India, the figures were, respectively, 17% and 41.9% in 2003 (UNESCO Institute of Statistics, last year available). However, in recent years, privatisation initiatives have mushroomed in South Africa—in the realms of discourse and practice—that call for more research. The present paper does not provide a comprehensive study of affordable private schooling in South Africa. It sets out to challenge the notions of 'affordability' and 'low-fee' in the South African context. It is guided by one main question: 'affordable private schools for whom?' It aims at challenging a narrative, under consolidation within South African policy-making circles and in the media, which posits 'low-fee' or 'affordable' private schools as a credible alternative to free quality public education for all.

The definition of an 'affordable' or 'low-fee' private school is contentious. James Tooley and Pauline Dixon, the researchers who have been instrumental in promoting the concept of 'private schools for the poor' in developing countries, have never properly operationalised the notion. Tooley proposed the following definition: '"low-cost" private schools are those affordable by a family on or below the poverty line, if total fees for all children in school amount to between 10% and 11% of total family income' (Tooley, 2013 cited in Mcloughlin, 2013, p. 15). However, this threshold remains arbitrary and its characterisation as 'low' highly debatable. Similarly, as noted by Srivastava (2016), Pearson Corporation, the world leading publishing and media multinational company that is actively involved in the promotion of 'affordable learning' in developing countries (Junemann & Ball, 2015), has never precisely defined the notion.

The present paper argues that, contrary to claims by its public and private proponents, 'affordable' or 'low-fee' private schools in South Africa do not cater mainly for poor children. Their rise has been intricately linked to the emergence, in the post-apartheid period, of a—mostly black—middle class, whose educational interests are not fulfilled by the government education sector. The latter has indeed become increasingly segmented between a small elite sector, which charges high tuition fees and delivers high-quality education, and a large under-resourced sector, where learning conditions have deteriorated.

The paper is based on extensive press reading, the examination of the grey literature and official speeches, an analysis of budget data and education statistics. As in other developing countries, South Africa's private education sector is characterised by a lack of robust information on its coverage, especially for the unregistered, so-called 'fly-by-night', private schools (Lewin & Sayed, 2005). The present analysis focuses on registered, for-profit and non-profit, private schools. In addition, semi-structured interviews were conducted in 2015 with the owners of two school chains (Spark Schools and Pioneer Academies), three private investors involved in the sector, the executive director of a private schools association, as well as seven parents and five teachers from the four Spark schools in Johannesburg.

The paper is organised as follows. The first section centres on what the literature says about the social background of children attending 'low-fee' private schools in developing countries. The second section describes South Africa's affordable private education landscape, an exercise hindered by the contentious definition of 'affordable learning'. The third section shows how the rise of so-called 'low-fee' private schooling in South Africa has coincided with the emergence of new middle classes since the end of apartheid. Finally, the last section argues that, despite its imprecision, the 'affordable' and 'low-fee' terminology can be interpreted as a discursive device that obscures the class interests and distributional choices that actually shape South Africa's education system. It allows the social forces in favour of the expansion of private education—segments of the state and pro-market lobbyists—to frame their project in social justice terms. Here, the state is not considered a homogeneous entity. It is important to differentiate, using Southall's (2004a, p. 532) terminology, between state 'senior managers', members of the ruling class, and the 'civil petty bourgeoisie', whose specific interests may diverge. The paper concludes that the state's ambiguous position towards the so-called 'low-fee' or 'affordable' private schools reflects national leaders' delicate balancing act between contradictory objectives, which is overly determined by their embrace of an orthodox macro-economic model that constrains the fiscal space for public education.

Affordable private schooling for whom? A review of the literature

In sub-Saharan Africa, private schools are not a recent phenomenon. During colonial times, formal schooling was introduced by missionary institutions. Today, in most African countries, the education system is organised around public, non-profit private, and for-profit private sectors, according to configurations specific to each country, moulded by history and by singular and evolving relations between the state and the private sector (Kitaev, 2007). In recent years, a paradigm shift has occurred: while for decades, private education was chiefly reserved for a small wealthy elite, so-called 'low-fee', 'low-cost', or 'affordable' private schools have emerged that purportedly serve the educational needs of the poor. Junemann and Ball (2015) or Srivastava (2013) have underlined the heterogeneity of the category. According to Srivastava (2016), two main moments can be identified in the 'low-fee' private school movement. The 'first wave' has been characterised by the creation of small, individual schools, following a family business-type model. More recently, corporate-backed branded chains of 'low-cost' private schools have emerged: this is the 'second wave'.

The rising—material and discursive—role played by private education in Africa has coincided with the growing interest of private investors, international aid agencies, and the academia for the African middle class(es) (ADB, 2012; Ravaillon, 2009). This social category reveals itself to be extremely malleable and its contours vague (Melber, 2013). However, it also reflects social dynamics currently at play in African countries, including social mobility trajectories (Darbon, 2012). Advocates of the 'low-cost' for-profit schools have explicitly mobilised the notion of the wealth of the 'bottom of the pyramid' (Prahalad, 2006) to legitimise these educational business endeavours (Stanfield, 2015).

The existing literature on affordable private education in the global South has mainly focused on the first wave of 'low-fee' private schools. A growing share of this literature has contested one core claim of their proponents, i.e. private education would be affordable to the poor. A recent literature review on the topic (Ashley et al., 2014) stresses the absence of conclusive evidence on whether 'low-fee' private schools geographically reach the poor. While private schools are mainly located in urban areas, they are increasingly present in rural areas. However, this does not mean that they are increasingly accessible to the poor. Moreover, several authors have exposed 'the structural exclusion of the very poor, girls and marginalised groups' (Macpherson, 2014, p. 295) from the 'low-fee' private schools sector. Indeed, despite claims about private schooling enhancing poor parents' educational choices, patterns of private education enrolment are, in practice, shaped by wealth and social status (see Härmä & Rose, 2012, on India; and Bhatta & Budathoki, 2013, on Nepal). Lewin (2007, p. 60) points out that, in sub-Saharan Africa, without significant state subsidies, the so-called 'low-fee schools for the poor' cannot cater for the children from the lowest two quintiles.

The literature also sheds light on two potential important effects of the rise of so-called affordable private schooling. At the household level, the payment of school fees, even relatively modest, leads a significant number of families to cut back on other essential expenditure (see Härmä, 2009, on India) and feeds households' indebtedness (see Akaguri, 2014, on Ghana). At the national level, the expansion of private education can deepen the stratification of the country's education system (Härmä & Rose, 2012) and negatively impact the quality of education delivered in government schools (see Di John, 2007, on Latin America).

The bulk of the literature on 'low-fee' private schooling in developing countries consists of econometric analyses that compare education performances in public and private schools. Despite the existing insights mentioned above, the question of 'affordability' of 'low-fee' private schools remains insufficiently investigated. Besides, as pointed out in Ashley et al. (2014, p. 28), the existing literature does not rely on a consistent definition of who the 'poor', 'poorest', 'lower income', and 'disadvantaged' are.

In South Africa, the production of knowledge about 'low-fee' private schooling has been monopolised by the Centre for the Development of Enterprise (CDE), a think tank that promotes the alleged virtues of choice and competition as the most efficient route towards quality education for all. The country's major corporations are among CDE's core funders. The centre is also linked to global actors—individuals and corporations—dedicated to the world spread of market ideology in education, such as Pauline Dixon and the Pearson Corporation.

The centre explicitly intends to influence education policy, its regulatory framework, and funding. Since their first report on 'low-fee' private schools (CDE, 2010), they have consistently claimed that 'low-fee' private schools in South Africa would increasingly serve poor communities, especially in townships. Besides, given their alleged intrinsic efficiency, these schools should benefit from higher public subsidies, in the name of the right of the poor to access quality education. Despite the hybrid nature of its reports—policy advocacy documents underpinned by research that has never been peer-reviewed—the CDE has asserted itself as the most authoritative voice on the subject in the country. Not only are their arguments regularly presented as scientific evidence in South African media, their reports are also regularly cited by prominent international scholars in their studies on private schooling or educational marketisation (Ashley et al., 2014; Junemann & Ball, 2015), accrediting the scientific credibility of CDE's claims. One may contend that South Africa is currently experiencing what Goldie, Matthew, Huriya, and Lubienski (2014, p. 1) call, in their analysis of the rise of charter schools in the United States, an 'echo chamber' phenomenon 'where a small, or unrepresentative, sample of studies is repeatedly cited to create momentum around a policy proposal'. The remainder of the article aims to contribute to challenging this dominant narrative about affordable private schooling in South Africa.

Affordable schooling in South Africa: a contentious delineation

Private education has long been an integral component of South Africa's education landscape. Today's oldest schools were opened up by religious institutions in the second half of the 19th century. Until the mid-20th century, state-subsidised church-run schooling remained the only source of formal education for black children. With the *Bantu Education Act* (1950), the apartheid regime asserted the state control over Blacks' education, which led to the closure of most missionary schools. Despite the anti-private education stance of the apartheid regime, about 100 private schools were set up between 1948 and 1990. Some of these schools—both prestigious institutions and commercial 'street academies' (Muller, 1992)— were established as a direct response to apartheid, to cater for black learners. However, in the early 1990s 'most of the learners [in the independent sector] were white and found in traditional, high-fee, religious schools' (Hofmeyr & Lee, 2004, p. 143).

The specific public–private mix that characterises South Africa's education system today hinges on the historical choice, at the time of the democratic transition, to discard the option of free compulsory basic education. The 1996 *South Africa School Act* granted public schools the autonomy to charge tuition fees and to set their amount annually, through their governing bodies. The 1998 *Norms and Standards for School Funding* organised a public funding of schools based on a quintiles system, classifying schools according to the poverty of their surrounding community. In 2007, schools in quintiles 1 and 2 were classified as 'no-fee' schools, a status extended to quintile 3 schools in 2009. Elite public schools may actually charge relatively high fees. For instance, in 2015, Parktown Boys' High School in Johannesburg, one of the oldest and best performing schools in the country, charged R36,700 a year (€2,620). This 'partial privatisation of public school funding' (Motala & Dieltiens, 2008, p. 125), which was explicitly introduced to prevent white middle classes from exiting the public education system (Fiske & Ladd, 2004), has contributed to the relatively small size of South Africa's private education sector (Fleisch & Woolman, 2004). But in a context of inadequate and declining government resources for basic education (Chisholm, 2016; Nordstrum, 2012), this funding system has also deepened the social segmentation of the public education system, between affluent schools and no-fee, under-resourced schools. As recognised by the Minister of Education, 'inequalities in terms of resources available at public schools remain due to the disparity in households' ability to supplement the funding of public schools' (Motshekga, 2015). These dynamics within the public education system are key to understand the middle class exit out of a resource-starved government sector.

Whilst South Africa's independent education sector remains today relatively small, it has, over the last decade, expanded significantly. Between 2006 and 2015, the number of institutions increased by 58% and the number of enrolled students by 60% (from a very low base), while the total enrolment in basic education only grew by 4.2%. The geographical distribution of independent schools has been skewed in favour of the two wealthiest provinces, especially Gauteng (11.6% of learners enrolled in independent schools) and, to a lesser extent, the Western Cape (4.6% of learners enrolled in independent schools). However, the Eastern Cape Province, one of the poorest provinces, which has experienced a quasi-collapse of its education system in recent years, has recorded a marked increase in the size of its independent sector: between 2006 and 2013, the number of learners enrolled in independent schools increased by 95%, the second fastest growth in the country.[1]

As in most countries, South Africa's independent education sector is characterised by its heterogeneity (Motala & Dieltiens, 2008). As an illustration, fees charged by schools that are members of the Independent Schools Association of Southern Africa range from R0 to R250,000 per year (i.e. about €20,000 for a boarding school). Low-fee private schools can be sub-divided in two broad categories: non-profit and for-profit schools. The former are certainly the most numerous. According to the law, they are eligible to state subsidies below a certain fee level, following a progressive scale. In addition to single low-fee schools that fit Srivastava's 'first wave' model, South Africa hosts several non-profit low-fee private school chains (inc. Vuleka, BASA Educational Institute Trust schools, the LEAP schools, 2 Oceans Education Foundation, African School for Excellence), which run schools in townships following a traditional philanthropic or charity model, funded by individual and corporate donations.

The number of formally for-profit low-cost schools has certainly grown in recent years, especially with the setting up of branded chains. Three self-proclaimed 'affordable' or 'low-cost' corporate-backed chains have recently emerged. The oldest, Curro Meridian Schools (seven schools; 6,000 learners in 2015, from age five to grade 12) are part of Curro Holding (42 privately-managed educational institutions, 36,000 pupils), which is listed on the Johannesburg Stock Exchange. Curro's first school was established in 1998. Spark Schools, a chain of pre-primary and primary schools, was set up in 2012 (four schools in 2015; about 1000 pupils from grade R to grade 4). In 2014, Pearson invested R28 million (€2M) in the chain, through its Pearson Affordable Learning Fund. Pioneer Academies are the most recent addition to the market; the first school opened in January 2015. The three chains operate on a strictly for-profit basis.

Assessing the scope of the private sector segment that targets the lower end of the market is hampered by the absence of a formal definition of what a 'low-fee' or 'affordable' private school is. In 2009, an IFC study defined them as those charging less than R635 per month over 10 months (cited in CDE, 2010) but the criteria to determine the figure remain unknown. In 2013 a CDE report considered fees of less than R7,500 a year (CDE, 2013), a level implicitly endorsed by the government (National Treasury, 2015a, p. 37). In 2015, the CDE chose a higher threshold: 'low-fee schools' would be those charging fees below R12,000 and those charging fees below R6,000 would serve 'poor communities' (CDE, 2015, p. 13).

In 2015, the three 'affordable' corporate-backed private school chains charged fees ranging from R15,360 a year (Curro Meridian) to R15,750 a year (Spark Schools) and R32,350 a year (Pioneer Academies), excluding registration and stationary fees or uniform cost. The School Investment Fund, a public–private partnership that invests in 'low-cost' educational institutions, claims to address the educational needs of 'low income households' (PIC, 2012, p. 2) and targets private schools that cater for households earning below R400,000 a year and charge annual fees ranging from R8,000 to R22,000.

The three chains make the alleged 'low cost' of their schools a core marketing argument. According to Stacey Brewer, from Sparks Schools: 'We're providing an education model that's affordable to the country'.[2] Meridian Schools are explicitly branded by Curro as 'highly affordable' (Curro, 2014, p. 10). However, even according to the company's own financial documentation, the notion of affordability appears very relative: 'The Meridian and Curro Academy models have school fees that are affordable in independent schooling and comparative to that of the state school fee paying schools'. However, according to the law, fee-paying public schools are actually located in communities belonging to wealth quintiles 4 and 5.

How do these fee levels compare with South Africa's actual income levels and distribution? In 2012, about 62% of South Africans were considered poor, poverty being closely tied to race: about 71% of Africans were poor against 4% of Whites. The wage distribution is also characterised by a high degree of inequality: in 2015, whilst the average wage was about

R8700 a month, the median earning amounted to R3,640 a month, bearing in mind that the number of dependents per wage earner is higher in poor households than in non-poor households (Finn, 2015). In 2014, about 78% of the adult population earned an average personal monthly income of less than R2,000 per month (FinMark Trust, 2014). A R12,000 school fee—the CDE threshold—would represent 50% of the yearly income of a poor house-hold made up of two adults and two school-going children. Based on the most recent study on poverty (Budlender, Leibbrandt, & Woolard, 2015), the household per capita poverty line was R1319 per month in 2015. If one uses this poverty benchmark, a low fee according to Tooley's definition (see Introduction) would be around R130 a month. Even though this threshold remains arbitrary and highly debatable, we are obviously extremely far from the CDE's R12,000 or R6,000 thresholds and the government view on low-fees. The various so-called 'affordable' or 'low-fee' fee levels stand in sharp contrast with the actual income conditions of the vast majority of South Africans.

Affordable for whom? Private schooling for the emerging middle classes

The rise of so-called 'affordable' private schools in South Africa has actually coincided with the emergence of—mainly black—middle classes since the democratic transition. Interestingly enough, in their study of middle-class identity in Soweto, Phadi and Ceruti (2011, p. 99) identified 'affordability' among the six broad themes used by their Sowetan informants to describe the middle class. These authors also highlighted that South African townships have, over the last decades, undergone a process of social stratification. This social transformation of township undermines the CDE's claims based on the discursive conflation between 'township' and 'the poor': the increasing number of 'low-fee' schools located in townships—even if a reality—does not imply that these schools increasingly cater for the poor.

There are various ways of defining the middle class: in reference to the 'middle share of the national income distribution', to an 'absolute level of affluence and life style' (Visagie & Posel, 2013) or to professional occupations (Rivero, Du Toit, & Kotze, 2003). Scoping the middle class can also rely on self-identification as 'middle', a strategy that allows us to unravel the extreme diversity of this social category (Phadi & Ceruti, 2011). Even though they use various definitions and income thresholds, the existing studies have all documented a sig-nificant growth in the African middle class since 1994 (Rivero et al., 2003; Stats SA, 2009; Udjo, 2008; Visagie & Posel, 2013). This dynamic has mainly been driven by affirmative action within public institutions, the restructuring of the health and education professions and a steady increase in the number of Africans employed by the private sector in white-collar positions. Only a tiny, but visible, 'black corporate bourgeoisie' has been propelled up by the Black Economic Empowerment programmes (Southall, 2004a, 2004b).

Historically, across the developed and developing world, education has been a critical ingredient of middle class formation, both in subjective terms, as an identity marker for its members, and in objective terms, as the key instrument for upward social mobility (Lentz, 2015). During apartheid, the aspiring black petty bourgeoisie was impeded from accessing a decent education, with the Bantu education 'explicitly premised on the intention of training new generations of menial workers and setting a ceiling on their upward mobility' (Posel, 2010, p. 169). In post-apartheid South Africa, education has become central to the preoccu-pations and consumption patterns of the emerging middle classes. As argued by James

(2014, p. 32), when deciding upon their spending and borrowing, members of the new black middle class 'recognise the kinds of things that bring returns in the longer term, with education primary among these'. A mother of a learner at Spark Schools, a single parent with several dependents, an employee in the corporate sector, forcefully illustrates this investment in education:

> When it comes to education, I will never, never compromise. That comes first. That is the only thing you will ever give a child … It's tough financially. At the same time … I would rather cut on certain things that I feel I need.[3]

The seven parents of learners at Spark Schools, who were interviewed for this research, do not constitute a representative sample but they provide a telling snapshot of this emerging middle class, its sociological diversity, and the reasons behind their choice of 'low-cost' private schooling. Four are self-employed, one father running a survival-type business, others, more established SMEs; three occupy low to mid-level management positions in the corporate or parastatal sector. The vast majority of learners at Spark Schools are black. Some parents do not struggle to pay the annual contributions; yet, for others, especially single parents, the payment of fees entails sacrifice. But even for those who can pay upfront, the affordability of the fees had been a determining factor in choosing Spark Schools and the annual rise in fees is a matter of major concern.

The second factor that has led parents to opt for 'affordable' private schools relates to the educational conditions in government schools. Their view on public schools is shaped more by hearsay than by robust information about the actual educational realities in those schools. This rejection of public schools is consistent across all parents who were interviewed. Like their counterparts in Lima (Balarin, 2015), these South African parents are not ideologically motivated. Their choice of a private school is driven by pragmatic reasons, not a commitment to the 'market'. Some Spark School parents actually recognise the direct and vicious relationship between the rise of private schools and the deterioration of learning conditions in public schools and acknowledge that they participate in the deepening of education inequalities in the country. But even those who are politically committed to quality public education for all as a public good and a key promise of the historical struggle against apartheid do consider private schools as their unique solution to guarantee a bright future to their children.

Spark Schools parents' views on the 'public vs. private' debate reveal however the double dimension of the relation between education and middle class formation: an objective component—an exit of the public system driven by a real deterioration of education in the government sector—and a subjective component: attending a private school provides the members of this—heterogeneous—group with 'distinction' from lower social categories. Attending a private school has become a central ingredient of a middle class social status. These views also illustrate the historical shift in the black petty bourgeoisie's perception of their class position, as highlighted by James (2014, p. 20), from a 'downward identification to its working class counterparts' during apartheid to an 'upward identification toward those better off than they are', since the democratic transition. These 'affordable' private schools may actually instil fairness within the education system. They would enable emerging black middle classes to break the circle of social reproduction that select public and private schools perpetuate through enrolment priority for alumni's children and fee levels that remain out of the reach of lower middle classes. Under South Africa's current schooling conditions, these 'affordable' private schools may indeed constitute an engine of social mobility and offer a unique opportunity for these emerging classes to consolidate their fragile social position.

'Affordable private schooling' as a discursive device to legitimate the expansion of private education

This last section argues that, precisely due to its built-in imprecision and relative character, the 'affordable' terminology works as a discursive legitimising device for the various social forces that promote the advancement of private sector interests in South Africa's education. The absence of clarity about 'to whom?' these schools are affordable allows one to frame a privatisation expansion project in social justice terms. This is true for both the state, as 'commodifying agent' (Jessop, 2002, cited in Ball, 2009, p. 97), and for the CDE, as the most prominent actor in a local policy network advocating for private education 'for the poor'.

The second section demonstrated that the R12,000 threshold chosen by the CDE to assess the number of 'low-fee' schools in South Africa was set at a level incommensurate with a notion of affordability defined from the perspective of the majority of the population. Had the CDE chosen to apply the criteria defined by James Tooley, their main source of inspiration, they would have reached a dramatically lower number of (registered) 'low-fee' schools. However, this CDE threshold has the immediate consequence of inflating the number of so-called 'low-fee' schools and accrediting the view that private schools increasingly cater for the poor. 'To convey a sense of inevitability and magnitude' (Junemann & Ball, 2015, p. 51) certainly serves a major objective of the CDE's advocacy in favour of increased state subsidies for private schools. Yet, if private providers need a massive injection of public funding to reach out to the 'real' poor, it remains to be demonstrated that this would be more effective than expanding the fiscal space for public education.[4]

The ambiguity of the 'affordable' terminology is equally instrumental for the state. According to many private sector proponents, the state would be unequivocally anti-private schools. On the other hand, state officials are quick to portray themselves as the defenders of the people against unscrupulous entrepreneurs who set up low-quality educational businesses and abuse gullible parents. State funding practice towards 'low-fee' private education demonstrates that the reality is much more complex than this simple state–private sector dichotomy.

Ideologically, the *Freedom Charter* officially remains the political reference of the ruling alliance, made up of the ANC, South Africa's communist party, and COSATU, the trade unions' federation. The document, which was adopted in 1955 as the political platform of the anti-apartheid struggle, solemnly declared that 'Education shall be free, compulsory, universal and equal for all children'. This conception of education as a public good remains deeply entrenched in large segments of the education bureaucracy. It explains the 'antipathy'[5] or 'hostility'[6] of technocrats towards private schools. Moreover, for pragmatic or ideological reasons, cash-strapped provinces have used the subsidies to private schools as a financial adjustment variable. In the face of general budget cuts, they have regularly decreased or postponed their disbursements to independent schools.

On the other hand, discourses in state power circles strikingly converge with the CDE rhetoric. Public subsidies to private schools are legitimised on two, somehow contradictory, grounds: independent schools would increasingly cater for the poor and, at the same time, would allow the state to concentrate public funding on public schools where poor children are enrolled. According to the National Treasury, the most powerful government administration, 'numerous low-fee independent schools now cater to poorer families (...) Fees at these schools are below R7500 per annum' (2015a, p. 37). At the same time, 'the independent school sector plays a key role in the delivery of education in that it frees up state resources for use on poorer schools' (2015a, p. 22). These views are relayed by some provincial governments, especially in the two wealthiest provinces, Western Cape and Gauteng, where the independent education sector has a significant size. According to Debbie Schaffer, Western Cape's Member of the Executive Council (MEC) for Education, the province intends 'to encourage the expansion of independent schools that provide quality education to poor learners. It will increase access to schooling and the competition between private and public schools'.[7] This ambition reflects a cross-partisan embrace of the virtues of the private sector in education: the Western Cape is ruled by the Democratic Alliance, the main opposition party. A 2013 judgement by the Constitutional Court confirmed the valence of these views across the highest levels of the state apparatus. According to the Court, 'independent schools constitute a saving on the public purse' and contribute to fulfilling the constitutional right to basic education (CC, 2013, p. 18). Public subsidies to independent schools were granted a constitutional value.

This accounting approach of the relation between the constitutional right to basic education and public subsidies to private schools is conveniently consistent with the National Treasury's prevailing macro-economic orthodoxy and fiscal consolidation priority, which actually condition the design and funding of all sector policies (Pons-Vignon & Segatti, 2013). The ideological imperative of cost-cutting assigned to all government departments is ingeniously framed as a way towards a more equitable education system whereas it constitutes the root cause of the under-funding of no-fee public schools. The claim that 'low-fee' private schools are a source of savings for the state mis-frames the question raised by the fiscal challenges faced by South Africa's basic education. It substitutes an accounting perspective to political-economy considerations about the country's economic development model, its tax system, and mechanisms of social redistribution. The political nature of the state budget, as a site of power struggles that determine the society's redistributive choices, is being obscured. 'Low-fee' private schools actually organise a transfer of the cost of education from the state to households from low to medium middle class groups. Ultimately, the incidence of the supposed savings falls on individual and corporate tax payers; the most affluent segments of the society are implicitly cleared of their responsibility for financially supporting quality public education for all.

Given the relative small size of South Africa's independent sector, state direct funding to non-profit providers has remained relatively marginal. Since 2000, the spending share for independent schools in total provincial education expenditures has been stable at around 0.5%. However, the state financial support towards the independent sector has increased in volume, and more rapidly than total education expenditures: actual subsidies transferred to these schools increased by 80% between 2001/02 and 2012/13 (in constant terms).[8] This increase directly reflects the growth in enrolment, not an increased financial effort of the state. On the other hand, the state also mobilises equity considerations to legitimise its policy of subsidies to independent schools. As noted earlier, these subsidies are only granted to non-profit private schools and are based on their fee level. However, as the government itself recognises, independent schools that charged fees between R18,000 and R30,000 in 2013 are 'middle and upper middle class schools with good facilities' (DE, 2006, p. 50). Yet, these schools are granted subsidies.

Moreover, in recent years, the emergence of 'low-cost' for-profit private schools chains has given rise to a new mode of public funding of private schooling, also legitimised on equity grounds. To date, Spark Schools and Pioneer Academy have not benefited from public funding. However, domestic and international public entities have financially supported the development of Curro Meridian schools. In 2010, the International Finance Corporation directly participated to Curro's strategic expansion through a 10-year concessional loan of US$9.4 million. In 2011, the Public Investment Corporation (PIC), the largest investment manager in Africa, wholly owned by the South African government, partnered with Old Mutual, the largest financial service provider in Southern Africa, to set up the Schools and Education Investment Impact Fund of South Africa. The PIC invested R1 billion in this School Fund, which provided Curro with R440 million (€30 million), on concessional terms, to develop 11 new Meridian schools (Curro, 2013). This amount is equivalent to 20% of the Department of Basic Education 2015 development budget to address the current public schools backlog and the infrastructure maintenance needs of the 24,000 existing public schools.[9] The PIC's status—public or private—is a contentious issue. Yet, it is an institutional investor under the government's direct control and its clients include South Africa's largest pension fund, the Government Employees Pension Fund. Its massive support to a for-profit educational venture, listed on the stock exchange, whose CEO received emoluments of about R8 million in 2014 (about €570.000) (Curro, 2015), is being portrayed as a social-ly-minded project. The 'less privileged South Africans' are claimed to be the main beneficiaries of the scheme; 'quality [would] no longer be a preserve of the elite' (PIC, 2012). Nevertheless, as shown earlier, the fee charged by Curro Meridian schools can hardly be considered afforda-ble to most South Africans.

Conclusion

Despite the claims made by various actors—the National Treasury, the PIC, edu-preneurs, and their ideological outlet (the CDE)—South Africa's 'affordable', 'low-fee', or 'low-cost' private schools do not target the 'bottom of the pyramid'. Ball (1998, p. 128) pointed out the coin-cidence between the development of educational markets and the 'widespread middle-class concerns about maintaining social advantage in the face of national and international labour market congestion'. In South Africa indeed, far from a 'miracle' solution[10] to address the low quality of public education provided to poor children, the rise of 'affordable' schools needs to be understood in conjunction with the emergence of black middle classes since the democratic transition, their aspiration to social mobility, and their consumption patterns. As in other developing or emerging countries (Härmä & Rose, 2012), affordable private schools in South Africa fill a gap. Under-funded government public schools do not provide the emerging middle classes with learning conditions conducive to the consolidation of their upward social mobility. At the same time, sending one's children to a private school has become a central ingredient of a middle class social status. It cannot be considered only a choice 'by default' (Balarin, 2015). Yet, as pointed out in the existing literature (Akaguri, 2014; Härmä, 2009), 'affordable' school fees fuel the vulnerability of the most fragile segments of this heterogeneous social category.

Whilst so-called 'affordable' fee levels stand in sharp contrast with the actual income of the vast majority of South Africans, the paper argued that the use of the imprecise 'affordable' terminology, associated with undefined social categories such as 'less privileged', 'lower income groups', and the 'poor', fulfils an ideological function. It enables state officials, edu-preneurs, and their lobbyists to legitimise education privatisation as a response to the predicaments of the public education system. However, the path towards a greater com-modification of education also raises tensions within the state, especially between an impor-tant segment of the education bureaucracy, rather hostile to private providers, and the state power. Paraphrasing Ball (1990, p. 43), South Africa's state policy toward 'affordable' private schooling may be considered 'an amalgam, a blending of tensions, a managing of nascent contradictions'. These tensions echo those nurtured by state macro-economic policy choices and reflect a difficult synthesis between the legacy of the anti-apartheid struggle, the Marxist component of the ruling alliance, and the conversion of the ANC dominant faction to neo-liberalism (Segatti & Pons-Vignon, 2013).

One may conclude that ANC government leaders, in devising their policy and funding toward private schooling, are attempting a delicate—if not impossible—balancing act between deeply contradictory objectives. To promote their class interests, as allied to the corporate bourgeoisie, they need to organise the ideological and material conditions of the penetration of traditionally non-economic domains like education by domestic and international capital. In the neoliberal era, this constitutes a privilege mode of the reproduction of capitalism (Ashman & Fine, 2013). They also need to secure the existence of elite schools—public and private—that are attended by their children and key instruments of their social reproduction. At the same time they have to promote the interests of their main constituency, chiefly composed of low- to medium-level civil servants (Southall, 2004a), this emerging middle class that increasingly views affordable private schooling as their unique solution to consolidate their fragile social position. Yet, as custodians of the liberation struggle legacy, their main source of political legitimacy, ANC state leaders need to constantly reaffirm their commitment to free education as a public good. They cannot, too openly, defend and financially support private sector interests in education. The conditions of access to quality education constitutes indeed an important site of social conflicts and potential destabilisation for the government. But, ultimately, the parameters of this challenging reconciling exercise are overly shaped by the ANC fundamental choice of an economic model based on macro-economic orthodoxy that structurally constrains the fiscal space for public education. In this context, the built-in ambiguity of the 'affordability' terminology provides a useful discursive tool to the advocates of the extension of the market in education. It enables them to frame their project in social justice terms and to lessen entrenched social resistances by converting state officials and the general population to the alleged virtues of the market.

Notes

1. The author's own calculations based on DBE, *Education statistics in South Africa* and *School realities*, several years.
2. Interview, Johannesburg, 8 April 2015.
3. Interview, Johannesburg, 18 November 2015.
4. The argument builds on Lewin (2007, p. 62).
5. Interview, executive director, ISASA, Johannesburg, 7 April 2015.
6. Interview, private provider, Gauteng province, 13 May 2015.
7. See http://groundup.org.za/article/manenberg-school-highlights-public-versus-private-education-debate_2724?utm_source=GroundUp+Newsletter&utm_campaign=f061bb41d0-GroundUp_Newsletter_5_February_20153_5_2015&utm_medium=email&utm_term=0_21dfeb9ddb-f061bb41d0-163114961, (25 January 2016). For Debbie Schaffer, 'Sir Barber rocks, he's great'.

8. The author's own calculations based on provincial education budget estimates, several years.
9. Budget data from National Treasury (2015b).
10. On 'policy magic' in education policy-making see Ball (1998).

Acknowledgements

The author would like to thank two anonymous reviewers and Geoffrey Walford for providing valuable feedback on earlier versions of the article. Although some of this paper is critical of affordable for-profit private school chains she is most grateful to Stacey Brewer for allowing her to conduct interviews with teachers and parents of Spark Schools.

Disclosure statement

No potential conflict of interest was reported by the author.

References

ADB. (2012). *Annual development effectiveness review 2012: Growing African economies inclusively*. Tunis: African Development Bank.

Akaguri, L. (2014). Fee-free public or low-fee private basic education in rural Ghana: How does the cost influence the choice of the poor? *Compare, 44*, 140–161.

Ashley, L. D., et al. (2014). *Education rigorous literature review. Role and impact of private schools in developing countries*. London: DFID.

Ashman, S., & Fine, B. (2013). Neo-liberalism, varieties of capitalism, and the shifting contours of South Africa's financial system. *Transformation, 81*, 144–178.

Balarin, M. (2015). *The default privatization of Peruvian education and the rise of low-fee private schools: Better or worse opportunities for the poor?* (ESP Working Paper 65). London: Privatisation in Education Research Initiative.

Ball, S. J. (1990). *Politics and policy making in education: Explorations in sociology*. London: Routledge.

Ball, S. J. (1998). Big policies/small world: An introduction to international perspectives in education policy. *Comparative Education, 34*, 119–130.

Ball, S. J. (2009). Privatising education, privatising education policy, privatising educational research: Network governance and the 'competition state'. *Journal of Education Policy, 24*, 83–99.

Bhatta, P., & Budathoki, S. B. (2013). *Understanding private educationscape(s) in Nepal* (ESP Working Paper 57). London: Privatisation in Education Research Initiative.

Budlender, J., Leibbrandt, M., & Woolard, I. (2015). *South African poverty lines: A review and two new money-metric thresholds* (Southern Africa Labour and Development Research Unit Working Paper 151). Cape Town: SALDRU, University of Cape Town.

CC. (2013). *Case CCT 60/12 [2013] ZACC 10*. Pretoria: Constitutional Court of South Africa.

CDE. (2010). *Hidden assets: South Africa's low-fee private schools*. Johannesburg: Centre for Development and Enterprise.

CDE. (2013). *Affordable private schools in South Africa*. Johannesburg: Centre for Development and Enterprise.

CDE. (2015). *Low-fee private schools: International experience and South African realities*. Johannesburg: Centre for Development and Enterprise.

Chisholm, L. (2005). Introduction. In L. Chisholm (Ed.), *Changing class: Education and social change in post-apartheid South Africa* (pp. 1–28). London & Cape Town: Z Books, HSRC Press.

Chisholm, L. (2016). University protests are important—but school fees also matter. *The Conversation.* Retrieved from https://theconversation.com/profiles/linda-chisholm-220916/articles

Curro. (2013). *Integrated annual report 2012.* Durbanville: Curro.

Curro. (2014). *Rights issue 2014: Circular to shareholders.* Durbanville: Curro.

Curro. (2015). *Integrated annual report 2014.* Durbanville: Curro.

Darbon, D. (2012). Classe(s) moyenne(s): Une revue de la littérature: Un concept utile pour suivre les dynamiques de l'Afrique. *Afrique contemporaine, 244*(4), 33–51.

DBE. (2015). *Education statistics in South Africa.* Pretoria: Department of Basic Education.

DE. (2006). *Amended national norms and standards for school funding.* Pretoria: Department of Education.

Di John, J. (2007). Albert Hirschman's exit-voice framework and its relevance to problems of public education performance in Latin America. *Oxford Development Studies, 35*, 295–327.

FinMark Trust. (2014). *FinScope consumer South Africa 2014.* Johannesburg: FinMark Trust.

Finn, A. (2015). *A national minimum wage in the context of the South African labour market* (SALDRU Working Paper No. 153). Cape Town: SALDRU.

Fiske, E., & Ladd, H. (2004). Balancing public and private resources for basic education: School fees in post-apartheid South Africa. In L. Chisholm (Ed.), *Changing class: Education and social change in post-apartheid South Africa* (pp. 57–88). London & Cape Town: Z Books, HSRC Press.

Fleisch, B., & Woolman, S. (2004). On the constitutionality of school fees: A reply to Roithmayr. *Perspectives in Education, 22*, 111–123.

Goldie, D., Matthew, L., Huriya, J., & Lubienski, C. (2014). Using bibliometric and social media analyses to explore the 'echo chamber' hypothesis. *Educational Policy, 28*, 281–305.

Härmä, J. (2009). Can choice promote Education for All? Evidence from growth in private primary schooling in India. *Compare, 39*, 151–165.

Härmä, J., & Rose, P. (2012). Is low-fee private primary schooling affordable for the poor? Evidence from rural India. In S. Robertson, K. Mundy, A. Verger, & F. Menashy (Eds.), *Public private partnerships in education: New actors and modes of governance in a globalizing world* (pp. 243–258). Cheltenham: Edward Elgar Publishing.

Hofmeyr, J., & Lee, S. (2004). The new face of private schooling. In L. Chisholm (Ed.), *Changing class: Education and social change in post-apartheid South Africa* (pp. 143–174). London & Cape Town: Z Books, HSRC Press.

James, D. (2014). *Money from nothing: Indebtedness and aspiration in South Africa.* Stanford, CA: Stanford University Press.

Jessop, B. (2002). *The future of the capitalist state.* Cambridge: Polity.

Junemann, C., & Ball, S. J. (2015). *Pearson and PALF: The mutating giant.* Brussels: Education International.

Kitaev, I. (2007). Education for All and private education in developing and transitional countries. In P. Srivastava & G. Walford (Eds.), *Private schooling in less economically developed countries: Asian and African perspectives* (pp. 89–110). Oxford: Symposium Books.

Lentz, C. (2015). *Elites or middle classes? Lessons from transnational research for the study of social stratification in Africa* (Working Paper of the Department of Anthropology and African Studies No. 161). Mainz: Johannes Gutenberg-Universität.

Lewin, K. M. (2007). The limits to growth of non-government private schooling in sub-Saharan Africa. In P. Srivastava & G. Walford (Eds.), *Private schooling in less economically developed countries: Asian and African perspectives* (pp. 41–66). Oxford: Symposium Books.

Lewin, K. M., & Sayed, Y. (2005). *Non-government providers of secondary education: Exploring the evidence in South Africa and Malawi.* London: DFID.

Macpherson, I. (2014). Interrogating the private-school 'promise' of low-fee private schools. In I. Macpherson, S. Robertson, & G. Walford (Eds.), *Education, privatisation and social justice case studies from Africa, South Asia and South East Asia* (pp. 279–302). Oxford: Symposium Books.

Mcloughlin, C. (2013). *Low-cost private schools: Evidence, approaches and emerging issues.* London: EPS-PEAKS (DFID).

Melber, H. (2013). Africa and the middle class(es). *Africa Spectrum, 48*(3), 111–120.

Motala, S., & Dieltiens, V. (2008). Caught in ideological crossfire: Private schooling in South Africa. *Perspectives in Education, 14*(3), 122–136.

Motshekga, A. (2015). A critical review of the pace of educational change in South Africa over the past 20 years delivered at the World Social Science Forum held in Durban, 14 September 2015. Retrieved from http://www.education.gov.za/Newsroom/Speeches/tabid/298/ctl/Details/mid/1749/ItemID/3458/Default.aspx

Muller, J. (1992). Private and alternative schools—Are they part of the solution? In R. McGregor & A. McGregor (Eds.), *Mcgregor's education alternatives* (pp. 76–93). Cape Town: Juta Academic.

National Treasury. (2015a). *Provincial budgets and expenditure review: 2010/11–2016/17*. Pretoria: National Treasury.

National Treasury. (2015b). *Estimates of national expenditure. Vote 14. Basic education*. Pretoria: National Treasury.

Nordstrum, L. E. (2012). Incentives to exclude: The political economy constraining school fee abolition in South Africa. *Journal of Education Policy, 27*, 67–88.

Phadi, M., & Ceruti, C. (2011). Multiple meanings of the middle class in Soweto, South Africa. *African Sociological Review, 15*, 88–108.

PIC—Public Investment Corporation. (2012). Statement on PIC's investment in independent schools. Retrieved from http://196.33.27.195/wp-content/uploads/2012/04/Statement-On-PIC-Investments-In-Independent-Schools.pdf

Pons-Vignon, N., & Segatti, A. (2013). The art of neoliberalism: Accumulation, institutional change and social order since the end of apartheid. *Review of African Political Economy, 40*, 507–518.

Posel, D. (2010). Races to consume: Revisiting South Africa's history of race, consumption and the struggle for freedom. *Ethnic and Racial Studies, 33*, 157–175.

Prahalad, C. K. (2006). *The fortune at the bottom of the pyramid: Eradicating poverty through profits*. Upper Saddle River, NJ: Wharton School Publishing.

Ravaillon, M. (2009). *The developing world's bulging (but vulnerable) 'middle class'* (Policy Research Working Paper 4816). Washington, DC: The World Bank.

Rivero, C., Du Toit, P., & Kotze, H. (2003). Tracking the development of the middle class in democratic South Africa. *Politeia, 22*(3), 6–29.

Robertson, S., & Dale, R. (2013). The social justice implications of privatisation in education governance frameworks: A relational account. *Oxford Review of Education, 39*, 426–445.

Segatti, A., & Pons-Vignon, N. (2013). Stuck in stabilisation? South Africa's post-apartheid macro-economic policy between ideological conversion and technocratic capture. *Review of African Political Economy, 40*, 537–555.

Southall, R. (2004a). Political change and the black middle class in democratic South Africa. *Canadian Journal of African Studies, 38*, 521–542.

Southall, R. (2004b). Black empowerment and corporate capital. In R. Southall (Ed.), *The state of the nation. South Africa 2004–2005* (pp. 455–478). Cape Town: HSRC Press.

Srivastava, P. (Ed.). (2013). *Low-fee private schooling: Aggravating equity or mitigating disadvantage?*. Oxford: Symposium Books.

Srivastava, P. (2016). Questioning the global scaling-up of low-fee private schooling: The nexus between business, philanthropy and PPPs. In A. Verger, C. Lubienski, & G. Steiner-Khamsi (Eds.), *The 2016 world yearbook on education: The global education industry*. New York, NY: Routledge (forthcoming).

Stanfield, J. (2015). Affordable learning: Transforming education at the bottom of the pyramid. In P. Dixon, S. Humble, & C. Counihan (Eds.), *Handbook of international development and education* (pp. 131–148). Cheltenham: Edward Elgar.

Stats SA. (2009). *Profiling South Africa middle class households, 1998–2006. Statistics South Africa report 03-03-01*. Pretoria: Statistics South Africa.

Tooley, J. (2013). *School choice in Lagos state*. London: DFID.

Tooley, J., & Dixon, P. (2005). *Private education is good for the poor: A study of private schools serving the poor in low-income countries*. Washington, DC: Cato Institute.

Udjo, E. O. (2008). *The demographics of the emerging black middle class in South Africa* (Bureau of Market Research Reports Paper No. 375). Pretoria: University of South Africa.

Visagie, J., & Posel, D. (2013). A reconsideration of what and who is middle class in South Africa. *Development Southern Africa, 30*, 149–167.

How are private school enrolment patterns changing across Indian districts with a growth in private school availability?

Amita Chudgar and Benjamin Creed

ABSTRACT

The private school sector in India has grown significantly but the equity implications of this growth are not well understood. Traditionally private schools have been patronised by more educated and better-off families. Evidence also suggests a preference for enrolling male children in private schools. With the growth in the private school sector it is unclear whether these conventional patterns of private enrolment are changing. The (uneven but ongoing) implementation of the Right to Education (RTE) Act will likely create further opportunities for private school access. If research finds that access to the private sector remains uneven across the society in spite of this growth, then it may offer a note of caution against relying on private provision, and it may also provide an indication of the potentially significant and continued importance of public provision of education. In this paper we use district-level data from 2005–2006 and 2011–2012 to estimate how private enrolment patterns have changed alongside an appreciable growth in number of private schools. While 2011–2012 is too soon to evaluate the impact of RTE (as most states were still drafting rules and regulations) we identify states that eventually adapted clearer RTE regulations to investigate if private school enrolment patterns were changing differently in these states. The data show that a large growth in the private sector has not made patterns of private school enrolment more equitable in rural areas. In urban districts the data indicate a declining caste gap in private enrolment and a decline in the private enrolment gap between poor and non-poor students in states which eventually went on to adopt clearer RTE regulations.

Introduction

The private school sector in India has grown rapidly in recent years (e.g. Mehta, 2011; Srivastava, Noronha, & Fennell, 2013). Families who exercise choice to attend private schools are systematically different from those who do not. Such families tend to be better off, more educated, and more informed (e.g. Chudgar & Quin, 2012, Woodhead, Frost, & James, 2013). There is also some evidence that private schooling may be demanded disproportionately for male children in the Indian context (e.g. Azam & Kingdon, 2013). In this paper we analyse how these economic, social, and demographic gaps in private school enrolment have changed (or not) across rural and urban districts, over time, in light of the growth in private school availability.

Our primary motivation behind asking these questions is to better understand the equity implications of growing school choice in India. This focus on equity departs from a vast majority of private school literature that attends to issues of performance (or quality) (see Chudgar and Quin [2012] for a related review of the literature). If the private sector options are seen as the solution to the country's educational woes then it is important to understand who is participating in this sector. If research finds that access to the private sector is uneven across the society, then it may offer a note of caution against relying on private provision, and it may also provide an indication of the potentially significant and continued importance of public provision of education.

This investigation is also timely in light of the 'Right of Children to Free and Compulsory Education Act, 2009' (RTE) enacted by India's Parliament in 2009. Among several important implications of this Act, Section 12(1)(c) has received particular attention due its potential to increase the private school choices available to Indian parents. While the implementation of the Act and specifically Section 12(1)(c) across the states remains uneven and problematic, it has contributed to shifting the school choice landscape in the country. The data used for this study from 2005–2006 and 2011–2012 offer an early glimpse of some of these potential changes in a post-RTE context.

Relevant background and literature

School enrolment in India has improved dramatically over recent years, moving from nearly 25 million non-enrolled children in 2003 to less than eight million in 2009 (World Bank, 2011). According to more recent official reports at the primary school level, India might have reduced these numbers even more drastically to about 1.37 million non-enrolled as of 2012 (National University of Educational Planning and Administration [NUEPA], 2014). As more students enrol, government-run school systems face greater pressure to absorb the influx. Private schools, particularly those that charge lower fees compared to regular private schools, have at the same time emerged as an alternative to the government school system. In the brief review of the literature below, we explore several related aspects of this dynamic context that are relevant to our paper.

Private schools in India

The private school sector in India is heterogeneous, incorporating a few different arrangements under the broad umbrella term (Mehta [2005, 2011], Pal and Kingdon [2010], and Srivastava et al. [2013] provide more detailed discussions of these differences). There are private schools that receive government funding, also known as 'aided' schools. There are private schools that do not receive any government support; these are the 'unaided' schools. The unaided schools may further be 'recognised' or 'unrecognised'. Schools are granted the 'recognised' status when they meet certain basic infrastructural, curricular, and teaching norms. (Sections 18 and 19 of RTE Act now require all schools to obtain recognition, but in practice unrecognised schools continue to exist.) Finally, cutting across both recognised and unrecognised unaided private schools are 'low-fee private schools' which are also growing in popularity (Tooley & Dixon, 2003). According to a recent NUEPA report nationally, around

17% of all schools were private unaided schools and 5% were private aided schools (NUEPA, 2014). The private unaided schools enrolled 28.95% and the private aided schools enrolled 5.53% of the total student population from grades 1 to 5 and these schools enrol 25.49% and 12.97% respectively at grades 6–8 (NUEPA, 2014).

A comparison of India's National Statistical Survey Organization data from 1995–1996 to 2007–2008 provides a more nuanced view of how private enrolment patterns had changed and grown in the period leading up to the legislation of the Act (Srivastava et al., 2013). In rural areas, for instance, at the primary level (grades 1–4 or 1–5 depending on the state[1]), 20% of boys were likely to be enrolled in private schools, an increase of 12 percentage points since 1995–1996. In comparison, close to 16% of rural girls were likely to be enrolled in private schools, an increase of eight percentage points over the same time period. Similarly, in urban areas, there was a 40 percentage point increase in boys' private school participation; in 2008–2009 60% of urban boys were enrolled in private schools at the primary levels. For girls, the increase is 36 percentage points and in 2008–2009 57% of urban girls were enrolled in private schools, compared to 21% in 1995–1996. These trends reveal a particularly large increase in private enrolment in the rural areas in the last few years. Also, relevant to this paper, these data indicate that in spite of a general increase in private enrolment, girls and rural children were less likely to enrol in private schools compared to boys and urban children.

Who enrols in a private school?

We next briefly discuss a general profile of the families who seek private schooling for their children and children who enrol in these schools.

Families who select private schools tend to be better off

In a recent paper utilising nationally representative data from India, Chudgar and Quin (2012) illustrated the systematic differences between families who enrol in private schools, across urban and rural India. For instance, they noted that rural families who enrolled their children in government schools had a household income of around Rs. 35,000, which was half that of families with students in private unaided schools. Similarly, the highest adult education levels (as measured in years of education) or asset levels of private school families were all almost twice as much as non-private school families. A similar pattern was noted in urban areas, indicating wide socioeconomic disparities between these two types of families. Woodhead et al. (2013) provided supporting evidence to these observations using the longitudinal *Young Lives* data, which followed two cohorts of students, born in 2001–2002 and 1994–1995, from the state of Andhra Pradesh.

In fact, the gaps between public and private school families seem to persist even when focusing on families of children who attend the relatively less expensive, 'low-fee' private schools (Singh & Bangay, 2014). In a survey of 250 households, focus group interviews in 13 villages, and visits to 26 schools in rural Uttar Pradesh, Härmä (2009) found that parents indicated a general preference for an improved government school system which functions well and is well-staffed. However, given the state of available government schools, parents who could afford to choose opted for low-fee private schools over government schools. Importantly, Härmä (2009) found that low-fee private schools remained out of reach for the poorest families and those from scheduled castes. Evidence from the same household survey and school visits indicated that enrolment in low-fee private school was related to parental occupation, parental education levels, and aspirations. Overall then, these families who are choosing private schools—despite typically preferring a better government-run school system and being price conscious—tend to be comparatively more educated and wealthier than families who send their children to government schools (Härmä, 2009, 2010, 2011). Chudgar and Quin (2012) found similar evidence in their nationally representative data. In both the rural and the urban contexts, they created a proxy for low-fee private schools based on the maximum cost of attending a government school in the district. The results confirmed that even these less expensive private schools were patronised by families who were better off than families whose children attended government schools.

Potential male bias in private school enrolment

Within families who exercise choice, data indicate a potential systematic bias in favour of the male child (e.g. Azam & Kingdon, 2013; Maitra, Pal, & Sharma, 2011; Pratham, 2012; Woodhead et al., 2013). Researchers have explored this male bias in a few different ways in the literature. Studies like the ASER report provide a descriptive national sense of private school enrolment across rural India, which indicate that girls are less likely to enrol in private schools (Pratham, 2012). Woodhead et al. (2013) also provided descriptive evidence, but because of the unique longitudinal nature of their data, they were able to offer several additional insights. They found that at younger ages, private school enrolment of urban boys and girls looks similar. But as children get older, around age 10 or as they leave primary school, gender gaps begin to appear and widen in urban areas. In rural areas, the gender gap begins and remains persistent through younger ages, but like the urban area it widens as the children get older. In fact, they noted that in the younger cohort, the gender-based differences in private school enrolment may have increased. Maitra et al. (2011) used a nationally representative dataset and found that the female disadvantage in private school enrolment continues even after accounting for differences in the home background and the school enrolment decision.

Similarly, scholars have found indirect evidence of female disadvantage in terms of differences in educational expenditure on male versus female children. Azam and Kingdon (2013) used a nationally representative dataset to study enrolment and expenditure decisions for male versus female children. They found that at primary and middle school age groups, the key difference between boys and girls appeared to be not in terms of enrolment decision, but in terms of expenditure decisions. They noted that disproportionate enrolment of boys in private school may be key in explaining these patterns. Bhatkal (2012) added further nuance to these patterns. She found not only a widening male–female private enrolment gap but also a male–female educational expenditures gap, even after a female was enrolled in a private school.

Private schools may be unevenly or non-randomly distributed

Just as 'who' chooses private school is a non-random phenomenon, there is some evidence that the choice of 'where' private schools establish may also be non-random. To put it differently, the growth in the private sector, both in terms of increased enrolment and a greater number of private schools, is non-random. For instance, Pal (2010) used data from five northern Indian states from the PROBE survey to determine if the development level of a village correlates with private school establishment. She found that villages that have better infrastructure—such as concrete roads, piped water, electricity, phone lines, and postal services—and low quality government schools are more likely to have private schools. Using ASER 2009 data from rural India, Chudgar (2012) also found that the presence of private schools is associated with higher levels of public infrastructure, greater availability of both private and government services, better roads, better access to electricity, and somewhat surprisingly a stronger government school system. Andrabi, Das, and Khwaja (2008) discussed the association between private school establishment and village characteristics using data from Pakistan. They also suggested that private schools were located in larger villages, with better infrastructure. They further noted that these are likely to be villages where previous investments were made in girls' secondary education, which in turn, provides a pool of potentially inexpensive teachers for private schools today.

Contrary to these studies that focused on villages, Rangaraju, Tooley, and Dixon (2012) argued that private schools are geographically available to all residents of the city of Patna, in Bihar, India. They conducted a street by street survey of Patna, collecting GPS data on the location of both government and private schools, and found that nearly all government schools had at least 10 private schools within a one kilometre radius. This suggests that the unevenness described in the above studies is likely more relevant in the more rural contexts of India, highlighting the importance of separate rural–urban data analysis.

The literature indicates that in general private school enrolment and even private school establishment may be uneven across different social and economic circumstances. The growth in private school sector and the implementation (albeit uneven) of RTE may help equalise some of these patterns. We next briefly discuss some relevant details of RTE before turning to our analysis.

Right to Education Act: some relevant background

The passage of the Right to Education (RTE) Act is the first national law to provide specific legislation giving children aged 6–14 the right to free and compulsory education at a neighbourhood school up to the 8th grade. Relevant to this paper, RTE includes a mandate related to school choice in Section 12 of the Act: all private schools, except for unaided minority schools,[2] must reserve at least 25% of their class I seats for disadvantaged children in their local community. The Act notes that these schools 'shall admit in class I, to the extent of at least twenty-five per cent of the strength of that class, children belonging to weaker section and disadvantaged group in the neighbourhood and provide free and compulsory education till its completion' (Ministry of Law and Justice [MoLJ], 2009, Section 12, Subsection c).

Given that private schools are not accessed equally across different social groups, in theory the idea of increasing private school supply for disadvantaged children is equity-enhancing and desirable. However the available data indicate this may not be the case in practice, at least not yet. The proportion of available seats filled under Section 12(1)(c) in the 2013–2014 school year for all of India increased to 29% but there was substantial variation across states—from an 88.24% fill rate in Madhya Pradesh to 0.21% in Andhra Pradesh (Sarin et al., 2015). Similarly, the proportion of private schools admitting at least one student under Section 12(1)(c) across India was at approximately 21.9% with wide variation across states—Rajasthan had the highest private school participation rate at nearly 65% compared to 0.1% private school participation in Andhra Pradesh in 2013–2014 (Sarin et al., 2015).

Low-levels of parental awareness along with an uneven response of private schools may in part explain these numbers. Mehendale, Mukhopadhyay, and Namala (2015) use the contexts of Karnataka and Delhi to suggest that the use of legalese, the lack of bilingual documentation of the rules and regulations associated with RTE, and the presentation of materials may hinder the participation of families from disadvantaged group. Similarly, the RTE Forum (2014) report also notes uneven awareness about the law among parents as a factor in understanding a large proportion of unused seats in many states.

It is also far from clear how private schools are responding to the new mandate. There are some not so surprising indications that the elite private schools exhibit uneven compliance with the Act and exhibit concerns about receiving timely and adequate reimbursement from the government (for instance, RTE Forum, 2014). There is indeed evidence of delay in government reimbursements in different states (e.g. Mehendale et al., 2015) and instances of litigations from private schools (e.g. Mahapatra, 2012).

Perhaps the most significant factor in the limited uptake of Section 12(1)(c) however may be the performance of states themselves in identifying rules and regulations to implement RTE. The first major deadline for RTE was 31 March 2013—the goals laid out in the Act were to have been met by this date. However, the actual implementation timeline for RTE was quite uneven across the states (for example, RTE Forum Report, 2014). According to the 62nd Central Advisory Board of Education (CABE) meeting, by October 2013, 25 states had norms for admission under Section 12(1)(c). In 2012–2013, 13 states and union territories reported admission under this section and in 2013–2014, 16 states and union territories had reported admissions under Section 12(1)(c) (Khare, 2013).

A 2015 report titled 'State of the Nation: RTE Section 12(1)(c)' (Sarin et al., 2015) provides a comprehensive assessment of how the various states have succeeded or not in clarifying rules and regulations for the implementation of this subsection of the Act. The report aims to 'assess the rules and notifications issued by different states to implement Section 12(1)(c)' (Sarin et al., 2015, p. 19), and present statistical indicators of how the state has performed in terms of available seats, and enrolment. The authors evaluate each state's performance on five major categories identified by the report. These categories include important stages in the implementation of the Act and are generated with the needs of the 'primary stakeholder' in mind (Sarin et al., 2015, p. 19). The five categories are: 'Clarity in defining eligibility and documentation required'; 'Process of information outreach/awareness'; 'Selection process'; 'Transparency in reimbursement provision and reimbursement process'; and 'Grievance mechanism and monitoring' (Sarin et al., 2015, p. 20). These five categories are used to generate a 21-criteria rubric. A state received a green, yellow, or red rating on each criterion. Green rating indicates most clarity in rules and notification and the implementation mechanism. Red indicates the worst performance where 'either we found no mention of a process or a definition, or if the rules and notifications failed to provide any clarity or understanding, thus confusing or dissuading someone from attempting to access the law' (Sarin et al., 2015, p. 21). The authors also note that the limitations of their work notwithstanding, their systematic and large-scale efforts yield a far more exhaustive understanding of a state's RTE rules and regulations than a parent or a single stakeholder may reasonably obtain. None of the states or union territories analysed for this report received a perfect score of 21 on all the criteria. The top five performers in terms of 'number of green' received were Rajasthan (16), Gujarat (16), Delhi (14), Tamil Nadu (12), and Maharashtra (11). Based on this report, these are the states we later identify in our analysis as eventually having the clearest rules and regulations around RTE implementation.

In sum, the implementation of RTE varies from state to state. In addition to this, private schools and parents are probably responding differently to the Act depending on their status (in the case of schools) and access to information and resources (in the case of parents). Even in the presence of RTE the equalising benefits of RTE may be too complex yet to actually realise for lower income and uneducated families. It is likely therefore that even post-RTE the parent population vying for private schools might not have changed drastically so far.

With this background we now turn to the data and methods we employed to understand how private school enrolment patterns have changed (or not) in light of growth in private schooling options. To the extent allowable by the data, we also conduct a separate analysis of states where eventually RTE rules and regulations were most clearly established.

Data and variables

Our primary interest in this analysis is to conduct a longitudinal assessment and observe both private school enrolment patterns and the growth in the number of private schools. We therefore utilise two different datasets from two time points. We used the India Human Development Survey I (2005–2006) and II (2011–2012) to generate district-level measures of private school enrolment, enrolment gaps, and other district background covariates. Both surveys are nationally representative covering over 40,000 households each. We also use the District Information System for Education (DISE) data from 2005 and 2011 to obtain the district-level count of number of private schools. In 2005–2006 DISE did not collect information on unrecognised schools (NUEPA, 2007, p. xviii), but by 2011–2012 such information was available (NUEPA, 2014, p. xviii). However, for the sake of consistency between the two datasets we used only the recognised private school information from both rounds. In order to analyse rural and urban data separately we generate a rural panel and an urban panel with 527 and 428 districts across the two years.

For our analysis, we decided to focus on children in lower primary and upper primary groups, as defined by the respective states. According to the National University of Educational Planning and Administration (2014), 11 states in our dataset treat grades 1–4 as lower primary and grades 5–7 as upper primary. In 22 other states, grades 1–5 are treated as lower primary and grades 6–8 are treated as upper primary. Accordingly, we generated the lower and upper primary enrolment measures from the IHDS data and obtained the commensurate lower and upper primary school count information from the DISE data.

The counts of private lower and upper primary schools from the DISE data are the main independent variables of interest. We refer to these counts henceforth as 'private school supply'.[3] As additional controls, and to describe district background factors that may also be associated with private enrolment levels, we used the IHDS household level data and generated proportion of Muslim households, Other Backward Castes (OBC) households, Dalit and Adivasi households, where OBC and Dalit Adivasi serve as indicators of caste status. We also generated district-level averages of household income, household assets, and average male and female education levels using the IHDS data. Finally, we also generate an indicator variable to identify districts in the five states which eventually implemented clear RTE rules and regulations as indicated in the Sarin et al. (2015) report discussed above.

The outcomes of interest are 'gaps' in private enrolment[4] for lower and upper primary level for rural and urban areas. We defined three gaps in private school access: gender gap (male compared to female private enrolment); poverty gap (non-poor compared to poor[5] private enrolment); and caste gap (other castes compared to OBC, Dalit, and Adivasi private enrolment). Using the IHDS data we measured the proportion of all school-going children from each subgroup that were enrolled in private school, and then subtracted the difference between the two subgroups to measure the gap. For example, in a given district if male private enrolment as a proportion of all male enrolment is 20 percentage points, and female private enrolment as a proportion of all female enrolment is 15 percentage points then the male–female gap in this district is five percentage points. Put differently, that is the proportion by which female enrolment will have to increase in private schools to be at a par with relative male private enrolment.

Methods

We first create a descriptive table to examine changes in the total number of private schools in each district. This also provides a look at changes at the district level in overall private school enrolment, district-level characteristics, and changes in the gaps of private enrolment along gender, poverty, and caste status.

Regressions

While the above allow us to look at overall changes, we want to account for other factors which may correlate with changes in the enrolment and outcome gaps. We first model the change in the district gaps at time t as a function of the private school supply and average household characteristics at the district level at time t (Equation [1]). Y_{it} represents the gap of interest for district i at time t.

$$Y_{it} = \beta_1 SS_{it} + D_{it}\gamma + \beta_2 T_t + \varepsilon_{it} \tag{1}$$

where SS is the number of private schools in district i at time t, or what we call the private school supply. Coefficient β_1 associated with this variable is the quantity of interest. D represents a vector of district-level characteristics including the proportion of Muslim, Otherwise Backward Caste, Dalit/Adivasi households, the average highest education levels for males and females in the household, and the average household income and asset for the district. Finally, T is a year dummy and ε_{it} is an idiosyncratic error term clustered at the district level. We use the Pooled Ordinary Least Squares (POLS) model to estimate the association of private school supply on the gaps of interest, controlling for district characteristics and changes across time. For this and the fixed effects analysis, we estimate each equation on four subgroups: rural-lower primary, rural-upper primary, urban-lower primary, and urban-upper primary.

If private school supply increased randomly across districts, the POLS model of the relative increase in private school supply with the gaps may suffice. However, as noted earlier private schools do not randomly appear across contexts (e.g. Andrabi et al., 2008; Chudgar, 2012; Chudgar and Creed, 2014; Pal, 2010). The growth in private schools in a district is likely related to idiosyncratic district attributes which may also influence the gaps in private enrolment. Not accounting for these attributes would bias our inferences. But many of these unique district attributes may not be observable or measurable which makes accounting for them difficult. To address this issue we employ a Fixed Effects (FE) approach to better understand the relationship between private school growth and our outcomes of interest.[6] The FE approach uses each district as its own control or compares a district to itself over time. This approach thus accounts for all of the time invariant district characteristics regardless of whether they are observed or not. We model this in Equation (2) by including a series of district dummies, *District*.

$$Y_{it} = \beta_1 SS_{it} + D_{it}\gamma + \beta_2 T_t + District_i\delta + \varepsilon_{it} \qquad (2)$$

In model 2 of particular interest once again is coefficient β_1 associated with changes in private school availability in district over time.

In addition, in model 3 we introduce to the FE model a variable identifying districts from the states which were identified as eventually having the most clear rules and regulations around RTE. The districts within these states are indicated by the variable *RTEREG*, and a term which captures the interaction of strength of RTEREG and the growth in private school availability is expressed as, $SS_{it}xRTEREG_{it}$. For this final analysis we do not use upper primary data, given Section 12(1)(c)'s focus on class I.

$$Y_{it} = \beta_1 SS_{it} + \beta_2 RTEREG_{it} + \beta_3 SS_{it}xRTEREG_{it} + D_{it}\gamma + \beta_4 T_t + District_i\delta + \varepsilon_{it} \qquad (3)$$

With this final model we can ask if growth in private school supply matters differently across districts where eventual RTE rules and regulations were clearer versus districts where this was not the case.

Results

Table 1 presents an overview of the change in private school enrolment proportions from 2005 to 2011 for all students and for different subgroups. These enrolment proportions are used to create the private enrolment gap outcome measures we use from Table 2 onward. First looking at each column separately, overall, the proportion of students of any category enrolled in private schools was larger in urban settings than in rural. Male, non-poor, non-marginalised caste students are more likely to enrol in private schools compared to female, poor, and marginalised caste students regardless of year, grade, or location. The poor, non-poor differences in private enrolment are particularly larger and noteworthy.

Next, comparing 2005 to 2011 columns for rural and urban data, the rate of change over time provides additional insights. Lower primary private school enrolment increased by 11 percentage points in rural districts and by seven percentage points in urban settings. Upper primary private enrolment grew but at a slower rate, three percentage points in rural contexts and four percentage points in urban settings. Across each subcategory (male–female, poor–non-poor, and so on) private enrolment has increased uniformly over time. The only exception is the proportion of poor students at upper primary level—in rural contexts there is no change and in urban contexts there is a decrease in the proportion enrolled in private schools. Of note, female and poor private enrolment in general grew at a slower rate than male and non-poor private enrolment despite starting at a lower level. This and further gaps are explored in Table 2 and forward.

Table 2 describes the average changes in several key variables over time across rural and urban districts including the key outcome of interest, gaps in private enrolment and key

Table 1. Private school enrolment proportions for rural and urban districts by year.

	Rural districts			Urban districts		
	2005	2011	Change (2011–2005)	2005	2011	Change (2011–2005)
Lower primary						
Private enrolment	0.22	0.33	0.11	0.60	0.67	0.07
Male private enrolment	0.24	0.36	0.12	0.62	0.69	0.07
Female private enrolment	0.19	0.30	0.10	0.59	0.66	0.08
Private enrolment for students above poverty line	0.27	0.40	0.12	0.66	0.73	0.07
Private enrolment for students below poverty line	0.10	0.15	0.05	0.41	0.42	0.02
Private enrolment for non-maginalised caste	0.33	0.45	0.12	0.65	0.75	0.09
Private enrolment for maginalised caste	0.19	0.30	0.11	0.57	0.65	0.08
Upper primary						
Private enrolment	0.21	0.24	0.03	0.53	0.56	0.04
Male private enrolment	0.22	0.26	0.04	0.57	0.59	0.03
Female private enrolment	0.19	0.21	0.02	0.49	0.52	0.04
Private enrolment for students above poverty line	0.25	0.27	0.02	0.58	0.61	0.03
Private enrolment for students below poverty line	0.12	0.12	0.00	0.38	0.30	−0.08
Private enrolment for non-maginalised caste	0.29	0.32	0.03	0.60	0.63	0.04
Private enrolment for maginalised caste	0.18	0.21	0.03	0.46	0.54	0.08

explanatory variable of interest, average number of private schools per district. While Table 1 reports the average private enrolment separately for each subcategory, by year and location across districts, Table 2 reports the average within-district gap in private enrolment for these three subcategories. So for instance in 2005 on average five percentage point more females would have to enrol in rural lower primary private schools to equalise the male–female or gender gap in private enrolment.

Again, looking at each column separately, the positive values of the gap measures reveal that regardless of the year, school level, or location of the district private school enrolment disproportionately favours male, non-poor, and non-OBC, SC/ST caste group children. The male–female gaps in private school enrolment appear to be somewhat steady and smaller. Interestingly, in rural areas male–female gaps are smaller at upper primary level and in urban areas they are smaller at lower primary levels. The caste gaps are bigger than gender gaps (in other words proportionally far more OBC/SC/ST children would have to enrol in private schools than females to even out caste differences in private enrolment patterns). Here again in rural districts at upper primary level these gaps seem to diminish. Across rural and urban data and both levels of education perhaps the most striking are the large gaps in private access between non-poor and poor children which closely reflect the patterns in Table 1.

Next comparing 2005 to 2011 columns for rural and urban data, over time, in rural areas, the gender gap has marginally increased at both lower and upper primary levels whereas in urban areas this gap has slightly declined. The average gaps in access between children from OBC and SC and ST caste groups and general caste groups have remained stable in rural areas. Gaps based on caste exhibit an interesting pattern in urban settings: increasing private enrolment gaps at the lower primary level and declining private enrolment gaps at

Table 2. Descriptives for rural and urban districts by year.

	Rural districts		Urban districts	
	2005	2011	2005	2011
Average private enrolment patterns across districts				
Gender gap, lower primary private	0.05	0.06	0.04	0.03
Gender gap, upper primary private	0.03	0.05	0.07	0.06
Poverty gap, lower primary private	0.17	0.24	0.25	0.31
Poverty gap, upper primary private	0.12	0.13	0.20	0.26
Caste gap, lower primary private	0.13	0.13	0.08	0.11
Caste gap, upper primary private	0.09	0.09	0.14	0.10
Average number of private schools per district				
Lower primary private schools	161	250	155	241
Upper primary private schools	98	163	99	159
District level control variables				
Household asset	9.64	12.51	15.88	18.34
Highest female education level in the household	3.18	4.28	6.72	7.67
Highest male education level in the household	6.08	6.84	8.99	9.52
Average household income level	40,656.76	99,340.23	69,845.34	163,458.90
Proportion Muslim households	0.08	0.08	0.17	0.16
Proportion OBC households	0.38	0.38	0.31	0.34
Proportion Dalit/Adivasi households	0.33	0.34	0.19	0.21

Note: District sample sizes are as follows; Rural 2005, $n = 219$–265; Rural 2011, $n = 221$–262; Urban 2005, $n = 157$–206; and Urban 2011, $n = 140$–222.

upper primary levels. Once again, the patterns associated with poverty gaps are most striking. Over time in urban areas at lower and upper primary levels proportionally fewer poor children are enrolling in private schools. In rural areas this is particularly true at lower primary level, and while marginal in magnitude the patterns at upper primary level also move in the same direction.

This increase in inequity between non-poor and poor private access stands in contrast with the growth in private school enrolment and private school supply in both areas. In urban areas, on average, districts had 155 lower primary private schools in 2005; this number was up to 241 schools per district in 2011. In rural areas the growth is almost the same in magnitude from 161 schools per district in 2005 to 250 schools per district by 2011. The growth at upper primary level is in fact somewhat larger, and it is especially large in relative and absolute terms in the rural areas.

In terms of the other variables, urban districts are more affluent and educated compared to the rural districts. Both sets of districts have improved in terms of economic and educational indicators during this time period. The religious and cast composition of these districts however have more or less remained stable over time on average which is not unexpected.

The pooled OLS regressions in Table 3 investigate the association between the enrolment gaps and the availability of private schools across district, holding constant various district observable attributes noted in Table 2. As the name implies, this analysis pools 2005 and 2011 observations, with a dummy variable indicating year. In urban districts, at lower primary level the growth in private school supply is associated with a decline in the private enrolment gap between the castes. In the rural area at both lower and upper primary levels the increased presence of private schools is in fact associated with an increase in the male–female gap in private access. However, the pooled OLS approach is inadequate as we discussed in the methods section. Controlling for district observables may not be enough in this case, as there may be important unobservable district attributes associated with the growth in

Table 3. Pooled OLS regression, estimating gender, poverty, and caste gaps in private enrolment in rural and urban districts.

	Rural districts						Urban districts					
	Lower primary			Upper primary			Lower primary			Upper primary		
	Gendergap	Povertygap	Castegap	Gendergap	Povertygap	Castegap	Gendergap	Povertygap	Castegap	Gendergap	Povertygap	Castegap
Lower primary private schools	**0.000*** (**0.000**)	0.000 (0.000)	-0.000 (0.000)				-0.000 (0.000)	-0.000 (0.000)	**-0.000***** (**0.000**)			
Upper primary private schools				**0.000*** (**0.000**)	0.000 (0.000)	-0.000 (0.000)				-0.000 (0.000)	-0.000 (0.000)	-0.000 (0.000)
Proportion Muslim households	-0.014 (0.046)	0.096 (0.104)	-0.350*** (0.099)	-0.003 (0.077)	0.133 (0.111)	-0.036 (0.122)	0.009 (0.088)	-0.007 (0.121)	-0.519*** (0.107)	0.253** (0.127)	0.305* (0.160)	-0.409*** (0.146)
Proportion OBC households	0.024 (0.046)	0.107 (0.078)	-0.021 (0.099)	-0.024 (0.065)	0.131 (0.094)	0.064 (0.102)	-0.063 (0.079)	-0.106 (0.119)	-0.183* (0.098)	0.153 (0.113)	0.455*** (0.170)	-0.051 (0.137)
Proportion Dalit/Adivasi households	0.014 (0.058)	0.144 (0.103)	0.117 (0.130)	0.004 (0.083)	0.100 (0.111)	0.036 (0.136)	-0.008 (0.106)	0.291** (0.136)	0.011 (0.129)	0.235*** (0.128)	0.535*** (0.194)	0.174 (0.181)
Household asset	-0.002 (0.004)	0.020*** (0.007)	0.012 (0.007)	0.008 (0.005)	0.007 (0.006)	0.011 (0.009)	-0.000 (0.005)	-0.019** (0.010)	0.002 (0.008)	0.000 (0.008)	-0.000 (0.012)	0.022* (0.011)
Highest female education level in the household	-0.007 (0.008)	-0.026** (0.012)	-0.010 (0.012)	-0.016 (0.011)	0.003 (0.011)	-0.026** (0.012)	-0.009 (0.010)	0.021 (0.013)	0.008 (0.012)	-0.022 (0.015)	-0.010 (0.020)	-0.018 (0.017)
Highest male education level in the household	0.009 (0.009)	0.025* (0.013)	0.019 (0.016)	0.008 (0.011)	0.009 (0.014)	0.006 (0.016)	-0.002 (0.013)	0.013 (0.019)	-0.019 (0.017)	0.038* (0.020)	0.014 (0.028)	-0.012 (0.022)
Average household income level	0.000 (0.000)	0.000 (0.000)	-0.000 (0.000)	-0.000 (0.000)	0.000 (0.000)	0.000** (0.000)	-0.000 (0.000)	0.000 (0.000)	-0.000 (0.000)	-0.000 (0.000)	0.000** (0.000)	-0.000 (0.000)
2011 year dummy	0.003 (0.022)	0.007 (0.024)	-0.005 (0.034)	0.013 (0.026)	-0.057** (0.029)	-0.083** (0.035)	0.019 (0.029)	-0.009 (0.059)	0.044 (0.039)	-0.024 (0.043)	-0.119 (0.076)	-0.056 (0.055)
Constant	0.009 (0.074)	-0.199* (0.117)	-0.050 (0.124)	-0.045 (0.099)	-0.145 (0.135)	-0.051 (0.147)	0.156 (0.125)	0.221 (0.170)	0.341* (0.184)	-0.254 (0.184)	-0.285 (0.272)	0.072 (0.221)
Observations	523	482	449	507	441	427	422	352	404	410	297	386
R-squared	0.015	0.101	0.073	0.026	0.059	0.059	0.022	0.078	0.117	0.025	0.063	0.074

Note: Robust standard errors in parentheses.

$^{***}p < 0.01$; $^{**}p < 0.05$; $^{*}p < 0.1$.

Table 4. Fixed effects regression, estimating gender, poverty, and caste gaps in private enrolment in rural and urban districts.

| | Rural districts | | | | | | Urban districts | | | | | |
| | Lower primary | | | Upper primary | | | Lower primary | | | Upper primary | | |
	Gendergap	Povertygap	Castegap	Gendergap	Povertygap	Castegap	Gendergap	Povertygap	Castegap	Gendergap	Povertygap	Castegap
Lower primary private schools	0.000 (0.000)	-0.000 (0.000)	-0.000 (0.000)				-0.000 (0.000)	-0.000 (0.000)	-0.000*** (0.000)			
Upper primary private schools				0.000 (0.000)	0.000 (0.000)	0.000 (0.000)				-0.000 (0.000)	-0.000 (0.000)	-0.000 (0.000)
Proportion Muslim households	-0.530 (0.532)	0.938 (0.872)	0.179 (0.995)	0.496 (0.711)	-0.227 (0.871)	-0.676 (0.890)	0.198 (0.442)	1.581* (0.854)	0.179 (0.655)	0.634 (0.597)	0.630 (1.283)	-0.118 (0.875)
Proportion OBC households	-0.033 (0.215)	-0.163 (0.218)	-0.421 (0.325)	0.154 (0.214)	-0.403* (0.225)	-0.003 (0.254)	0.088 (0.261)	-0.502 (0.317)	0.070 (0.283)	-0.142 (0.325)	1.053* (0.629)	-0.215 (0.403)
Proportion Dalit/Adivasi households	0.112 (0.402)	-0.093 (0.372)	0.857* (0.516)	-0.084 (0.324)	-0.252 (0.469)	0.878** (0.425)	0.007 (0.368)	-0.114 (0.511)	-0.262 (0.391)	0.484 (0.426)	0.132 (0.739)	0.208 (0.523)
Household asset	-0.011 (0.013)	0.007 (0.015)	-0.006 (0.027)	-0.030* (0.017)	0.008 (0.017)	-0.009 (0.027)	-0.017 (0.017)	-0.011 (0.028)	0.028 (0.027)	-0.024 (0.028)	-0.012 (0.043)	0.014 (0.029)
Highest female education level in the household	0.020 (0.030)	-0.014 (0.033)	0.004 (0.038)	-0.017 (0.038)	-0.045 (0.043)	0.000 (0.049)	-0.003 (0.030)	-0.022 (0.046)	0.023 (0.041)	0.021 (0.037)	0.012 (0.075)	-0.010 (0.059)
Highest male education level in the household	0.004 (0.026)	0.078** (0.031)	-0.051 (0.045)	0.012 (0.032)	0.039 (0.038)	-0.012 (0.043)	0.019 (0.032)	0.072 (0.048)	-0.034 (0.046)	0.045 (0.042)	0.113 (0.072)	-0.042 (0.064)
Average household income level	-0.000 (0.000)	0.000 (0.000)	-0.000 (0.000)	0.000 (0.000)	0.000 (0.000)	0.000* (0.000)	-0.000 (0.000)	0.000 (0.000)	-0.000 (0.000)	-0.000 (0.000)	-0.000 (0.000)	-0.000 (0.000)
2011 year dummy	0.034 (0.035)	0.022 (0.041)	0.105 (0.072)	0.069 (0.052)	-0.028 (0.057)	-0.042 (0.080)	0.042 (0.064)	0.060 (0.110)	0.017 (0.082)	0.026 (0.082)	0.019 (0.154)	-0.012 (0.089)
Constant	0.097 (0.239)	-0.290 (0.289)	0.389 (0.443)	0.192 (0.314)	0.177 (0.346)	-0.010 (0.438)	0.111 (0.353)	-0.148 (0.531)	-0.143 (0.557)	-0.212 (0.463)	-1.107 (0.754)	0.413 (0.590)
Observations	523	482	449	507	441	427	422	352	404	410	297	386
R-squared	0.020	0.140	0.071	0.031	0.032	0.062	0.011	0.089	0.045	0.039	0.087	0.020
Number of districts	265	254	238	264	245	237	219	202	210	216	190	207

Note: Robust standard errors in parentheses.
*** $p < 0.01$; ** $p < 0.05$; * $p < 0.1$.

Table 5. Fixed effects regression, estimating gender, poverty, and caste gaps in private enrolment in rural and urban districts with varying strengths of RtE implementation.

	Rural districts			Urban districts		
	Lower primary			Lower primary		
	Gendergap	Povertygap	Castegap	Gendergap	Povertygap	Castegap
Lower primary private	0.000	−0.000	0.000	−0.000	0.000	−0.000***
schools	(0.000)	(0.000)	(0.000)	(0.000)	(0.000)	**(0.000)**
Clear RTE Regulations	−0.028	0.061	0.098	0.080	0.134	0.026
(RTEREG)	(0.054)	(0.049)	(0.078)	(0.066)	(0.102)	(0.091)
Private supply × RTEREG	0.000	0.000	−0.000	−0.000	−0.000*	−0.000
	(0.000)	(0.000)	(0.000)	(0.000)	**(0.000)**	(0.000)
Proportion Muslim	−0.527	0.920	0.146	0.254	1.651*	0.193
households	(0.536)	(0.886)	(0.991)	(0.438)	(0.862)	(0.660)
Proportion OBC	−0.012	−0.236	−0.483	0.092	−0.485	0.070
households	(0.208)	(0.218)	(0.326)	(0.256)	(0.309)	(0.283)
Proportion Dalit/Adivasi	0.106	−0.072	0.832	0.046	−0.061	−0.249
households	(0.403)	(0.372)	(0.518)	(0.358)	(0.498)	(0.389)
Household asset	−0.010	0.002	−0.009	−0.017	−0.009	0.028
	(0.012)	(0.014)	(0.027)	(0.017)	(0.028)	(0.027)
Highest female education	0.018	−0.003	0.011	−0.005	−0.024	0.023
level in the household	(0.030)	(0.033)	(0.039)	(0.029)	(0.045)	(0.041)
Highest male education	0.005	0.073**	−0.057	0.018	0.070	−0.035
level in the household	(0.026)	(0.031)	(0.046)	(0.032)	(0.049)	(0.046)
Average household	−0.000	0.000	−0.000	−0.000	0.000	−0.000
income level	(0.000)	(0.000)	(0.000)	(0.000)	(0.000)	(0.000)
2011 year dummy	0.035	0.015	0.097	0.020	0.030	0.009
	(0.035)	(0.041)	(0.073)	(0.064)	(0.112)	(0.084)
Constant	0.076	−0.216	0.468	0.107	−0.209	−0.147
	(0.235)	(0.281)	(0.446)	(0.346)	(0.527)	(0.560)
Observations	523	482	449	422	352	404
R-squared	0.021	0.154	0.078	0.026	0.109	0.045
Number of districts	265	254	238	219	202	210

Note: Robust standard errors in parentheses.
***$p < 0.01$; **$p < 0.05$; *$p < 0.1$.

private schools. We therefore present the results of district fixed effects analysis, where we compare a district to itself and account for district observed and unobserved characteristics that are time invariant.

Taking into account several observable changes in the district over time, and accounting for district-level time invariant unobservable factors the greater presence of private school has no significant association with gender, poverty, or caste gaps in rural private enrolment as seen in Table 4. According to these data, in the rural areas, the growth in the number of private schools (Table 2), has not translated into any systematic decline in the social, economic, or demographic gaps in private school enrolment within districts. The patterns exhibited by urban data in Table 3 are different. Growth in private schools is associated with reduction in the caste gaps in private access in the urban areas at the lower primary level. In other words, all else being equal, urban districts that experienced a growth in private school supply at lower primary level also experienced more equitable private enrolment across different castes over time.

We also investigate if the patterns of private enrolments were changing differently in districts in states that were identified as having the clearest rules and regulations for Section 12(1)(c) by Sarin et al. (2015). Table 5 shows this analysis.

Of particular interest in this table is the interaction term between private school supply and RTEREG term. The coefficient associated with this variable indicates how growth in private school supply is associated with changing private enrolment gaps in districts in states where RTE rules and regulations were eventually clearly articulated. In the rural areas, no interaction terms are statistically significant. In urban areas, data for districts which eventually had clearer RTE rules and regulations and also experienced a growth in private school supply between 2005 and 2011 indicate a decline in private enrolment gap between rich and poor students.

Discussion

The private school sector in India has experienced significant growth in the last several years. The analysis of two waves of IHDS and DISE data together show both a growth in private enrolment over time and a growth in the number of private schools over time. While overall private enrolment levels are higher in urban areas in relative terms, private enrolment has grown appreciably in the rural areas. In absolute numbers, the number of private schools per rural district on average is also outstripping the average number of private schools per urban district. Our interest was to understand if and how this growth is translating into more equitable access to private schools across gender, caste and economic groups. While this analysis is not suitable for causal claims, the results reveal some important associations or the lack thereof.

The descriptive data indicate that these gaps in private school access may generally be stable or widening over time. The large and growing gaps in private enrolment between rich and poor students were particularly noteworthy. We next applied a range of more advanced analytical approaches to better understand if district-level growth in private school supply is associated with attenuating gaps in private access. In other words, as the number of private schools increased over time did proportionally more female, poor, OBC/ST/SC enrol in private schools? In the rural areas, the answer is no. The appreciable growth in private school supply in rural areas has not translated into more equitable enrolment patterns across gender, caste, and poverty levels according to these data. The large growth in rural areas both in terms of private supply and private enrolment has simply maintained the social, economic, and demographic status quo. In urban areas it appears to have bridged some of the caste gaps at lower primary levels, but overall here too there is no consistent support for more equitable private enrolment patterns.

We also attempted to understand how these enrolment patterns may differ across states which went on to define clearer rules and regulations for Section 12(1)(c). We limited this analysis to lower primary grades. In rural areas again our results yield no significant patterns. In urban areas we do find that a growth in private school supply in these states is related to declining private enrolment gaps between poor and non-poor students. This may speak to the potentially important role of state regulations in addressing poor–non-poor gaps in private access. It is worth noting that each of these five states, identified as states with clearer rules and regulations, were also states where by 2011–2012 some of these regulations were in place. Yet, it would be premature to consider our analysis an evaluation of Section 12(1)(c) of RTE given the negligible amount of time between states formulating these rules and regulations and the data collection.

It may perhaps be unrealistic to expect that private school enrolment patterns will be or should be egalitarian. Proponents of market mechanisms may argue, perhaps, the whole point of providing choice is that different families can exhibit their preferences differently and the resultant segregation is an unavoidable by-product. For those who are sceptical of the value of market-based provision, concerns about equal access to private options may seem unimportant for entirely different reasons. However, in studying equity in access our interest is not to promote one versus the other form of provision, rather it is to understand who is accessing and who is being left out of these market-based systems. Such an investigation is useful to understand both the limits of market-based solutions and the potentially crucial role of the government in education provision. If the growth in the education 'market' simply maintains the status quo between those who do and don't participate in such a market, as these data indicate to an extent, then the continuing importance of the public sector, with its many limitations, cannot be overstated. Such a comprehensive perspective may be important to embrace as private sector education in India continues to grow.

Notes

1. As each state sets grade classifications, there is some variation across states. Srivastava et al. (2013) report the enrollment of students within the grades corresponding to the state's classification: either grades 1–4 or grades 1–5 are classified as primary dependent on the state.
2. It was determined by the Indian Supreme Court in the *Society for Unaided Private Schools of Rajasthan vs Union of India* case that the 25% seat reservation was constitutional and applied to all unaided schools, excepting private unaided minority schools. See Mehendale et al. (2015) and Sarangapani, Mehendale, Mukhopadhyay, and Namala (2014) for further information related to the court case and the updated rules surrounding Section 12(1)(c).
3. To measure private school supply it would be ideal if we had not just the number of such schools, but the actual number of seats available in these schools but this information is not available in the DISE data from 2005 and 2011.
4. We include both private aided and private unaided enrolment in the private category.
5. Whether a student is non-poor or poor is operationalised based on the POOR variable in IHDS II. IHDS II provides a dichotomous variable for whether a student is poor or not based upon the household's monthly per capita consumption and the Tendulkar (2012) poverty line. The poverty line varies by state, rural/urban context, and by month of the interview. See http://www.ihds.info/sites/default/files/ihds2usersguide01.pdf, p. 25 for more information. As this study is not a direct evaluation of RTE, we focus on the overall trends in comparable measures rather than use the state definitions for 'economically weak sections'.
6. We estimate the fixed effects model instead of the random effects model because the assumption for random effects, i.e. there is zero correlation between the observed explanatory variables and unobserved district variables, or that unobserved variables are orthogonal to D_{it} (District observed), seems unrealistic.

Disclosure statement

No potential conflict of interest was reported by the authors.

Funding

The research reported here was supported by the Institute of Education Sciences, U.S. Department of Education, through Grant R305B090011 to Michigan State University. This grant supports MSU's doctoral training program in the economics of education. The opinions expressed are those of the authors and do not represent views of the Institute or the U.S. Department of Education.

References

Andrabi, T., Das, J., & Khwaja, A. I. (2008). A dime a day: The possibilities and limits of private schooling in Pakistan. *Comparative Education Review, 52*, 329–355.

Azam, M., & Kingdon, G. G. (2013). Are girls the fairer sex in India? Revisiting intra-household allocation of education expenditure. *World Development, 42*, 143–164.

Bhatkal, T. (2012). *Gender bias in the allocation of education expenditure: Evidence from Andhra Pradesh, India* (Unpublished masters thesis). University of Oxford, UK. Retrieved from http://r4d.dfid.gov.uk/PDF/Outputs/Younglives/gender-bias-in-the-allocation-of-education-expenditure.pdf

Chudgar, A. (2012). Variation in private school performance: The importance of village context. *Economic and Political Weekly, 47*(11), 52–59.

Chudgar, A. & Creed, B. (2014). *How does demand for private schooling vary across locations with different private school supply? Analysis of data from rural India.* (Occasional paper no. 222). National Center for the Study of Privatization in Education: New York, NY.

Chudgar, A., & Quin, E. (2012). Relationship between private schooling and achievement: Results from rural and urban India. *Economics of Education Review, 31*, 376–390.

Härmä, J. (2009). Can choice promote Education for All? Evidence from growth in private primary schooling in India. *Compare, 39*, 151–165.

Härmä, J. (2010). *School choice for the poor?: The limits of marketisation of primary education in rural India.* Brighton: Consortium for Research on Educational Access, Transitions and Equity.

Härmä, J. (2011). Low cost private schooling in India: Is it pro poor and equitable? *International Journal of Educational Development, 31*, 350–356.

Khare, A. (2013). Summary record of discussion of the 62nd Meeting of the Central Advisory Board of Education (CABE) held on 10th October, 2013—regarding. Retrieved from http://mhrd.gov.in/sites/upload_files/mhrd/files/document-reports/Sumrec62CABE_0.pdf

Mahapatra, D. (2012, April 12). SC upholds constitutional validity of Right to Education Act. *The Times of India.* Retrieved from http://articles.timesofindia.indiatimes.com/2012-04-12/news/31330617_1_rte-act-private-schools-seats-for-poor-children

Maitra, P., Pal, S., & Sharma, A. (2011). Reforms, growth and persistence of gender gap: Recent evidence from private school enrollment in India. Retrieved from http://papers.ssrn.com/sol3/papers.cfm?abstract_id=1965152

Mehendale, A., Mukhopadhyay, R., & Namala, A. (2015). Right to Education and inclusion in private unaided schools. *Economic & Political Weekly, 50*(7), 43.

Mehta, A. C. (2005). *Elementary education in unrecognized schools in India—A study of Punjab based on DISE 2005 data.* National Institute of Education Planning and Administration.

Mehta, A. C. (2011). *Elementary education in India: Analytical Report 2008–2009.* New Delhi: National University of Educational Planning and Administration and Department of School Education and Literacy, Ministry of Human Resource Development Government of India.

Mehta, A. C. (2014). *District report cards 2011–12 Volume 1: Elementary education in India—Where do we stand?* National Institute of Educational Planning and Administration.

Ministry of Law and Justice. (2009). *The right of children to free and compulsory education act, 2009.*

National University of Educational Planning and Administration. (2007). Elementary education in India: Progress towards UEE. Flash Statistics: DISE 2005–06. New Delhi: National Institute of Educational Planning and Administration.

National University of Educational Planning and Administration. (2014). Elementary education in India: Progress towards UEE. Flash statistics: DISE 2013–2014. New Delhi: National University of Educational Planning and Administration. Retrieved from http://www.dise.in/Downloads/Publications/Documents/Flash%20Statistics2013-14.pdf

Pal, S. (2010). Public infrastructure, location of private schools and primary school attainment in an emerging economy. *Economics of Education Review, 29,* 783–794.

Pal, S., & Kingdon, G. (2010). *Can private school growth foster universal literacy? Panel evidence from Indian districts* (IZA Discussion Paper No. 5274). Retrieved from http://ftp.iza.org/dp5274.pdf

Pratham. (2012). *ASER 2012 annual status of education report (Rural).* New Delhi: Pratham.

Rangaraju, B., Tooley, J., & Dixon, P. (2012). *The private school revolution in Bihar: Findings from a survey in Patna Urban.* New Delhi: India Institute.

RTE Forum. (2014). *Status of implementation of the Right of Children to Free and Compulsory Education Act, 2009: Year 4 (2013–2014).*

Sarangapani, P. M., Mehendale, A., Mukhopadhyay, R., & Namala, A. (2014). Inclusion of marginalized children in private unaided schools: The RTE Act, 2009. Retrieved from http://policy-practice.oxfam.org.uk/publications/inclusion-of-marginalized-children-in-private-unaided-schoolsthe-rte-act-2009-346615

Sarin, A., Kuhn, S., Singh, B. D., Khangta, P., Dongre, A., Joshi, E. . . . Rahman, F. (2015). *State of the nation: RTE Section 12(1)(c).* Indian Institute of Management-Ahmedabad.

Singh, R., & Bangay, C. (2014). Low-fee private schooling in India: More questions than answers? Observations from the young lives longitudinal research in Andhra Pradesh. *International Journal of Educational Development,* early online version published August 30, 2014, doi: 10.1016/j.ijedudev.2014.08.004.

Srivastava, P., Noronha, C., & Fennell, S. (2013). Private sector study: Sarva Shiksha Abhiyan. Report submitted to DFID India. Retrieved from http://www.prachisrivastava.com/dfid-sarva-shiksha-abhiyan-private-sector-study.html

Tendulkar, S. D. (2012). Expert group on methodology for estimating poverty. Government of India: Planning Commission.

Tooley, J., & Dixon, P. (2003). *Private schools in India: A case study from India.* UK: CfBT Research and Development.

Woodhead, M., Frost, M., & James, Z. (2013). Does growth in private schooling contribute to Education for All? Evidence from a longitudinal, two cohort study in Andhra Pradesh, India. *International Journal of Educational Development, 33,* 65–73.

World Bank. (2011). India Country overview—September 2011. Retrieved from http://www.worldbank.org/en/country/india

The myth of free and barrier-free access: India's Right to Education Act—private schooling costs and household experiences

Prachi Srivastava and Claire Noronha

ABSTRACT
We examine relative household costs and experiences of accessing private and government schooling under India's *Right of Children to Free and Compulsory Education Act, 2009* in the early implementation phase. The Act deems that no child should incur any fee, charges, or expenses in accessing schooling. Private schools are mandated to allocate 25% of their seats for free via 'freeships' for socially and economically disadvantaged children. Furthermore, the Act has a number of provisions attempting to ease barriers to admission and entry to all schools, including private schools. This paper reports household-level data on the schooling patterns, experiences, and perceptions in one Delhi slum accessing schooling based on a survey of 290 households and 40 semi-structured household interviews. We found very low instances of children with private school freeships. Furthermore, children in 'free' private school seats incurred the second highest costs of accessing schooling after full-fee-paying students in relatively high-fee private schools. Finally, households accessing freeships and higher-fee schools experienced considerable barriers to securing a seat and admission.

Introduction

Attempts to provide free and compulsory education in India predate independence, and have been contentious. Legislating the *Right of Children to Free and Compulsory Education Act, 2009* (RTE Act) was no different, which took nearly a decade and a number of draft bills (see Srivastava & Noronha, 2014b, tracing its history). Among the most contentious aspects of the Act is the mandatory allocation of 25% of seats in private unaided schools in Class 1 (or pre-primary as appropriate) for free to 'economically weaker sections' (EWS) and 'disadvantaged groups' until the completion of elementary education (Class 8) (Section 12[1][c], Government of India, 2009).

Private schools are to be subsidised by the states at per pupil state expenditure or the tuition fee charged by the school, whichever is less (Section 12[2], Government of India,

71

2009). Students meeting eligibility criteria for EWS and disadvantaged groups are meant to be granted access through a 'freeship'. Thus, children in free private school seats are subject to the Act's wider compulsions that: 'no child shall be liable to pay *any kind of fees or charges or expenses* which may prevent him or her from pursuing and completing' elementary education (Section 3[2], Government of India, 2009, emphasis added).

In principle, free elementary education in India existed in the government sector prior to the RTE Act, and was meant to be guaranteed by the constitution and in national education policies (Tilak, 1996a). Additionally, in certain states, such compulsion may have also existed for specific kinds of private schools. For example, in Delhi—the location for this study—private unaided schools allotted land at concessional rates by the Delhi Development Authority were meant to be providing free seats to 25% of their students much before the institution of the RTE Act. In 2004, a Supreme Court judgment instructed the Director of Education to examine whether conditions were being met, and to take action against schools found not to comply (see Juneja, 2005; Srivastava & Noronha, 2014a, 2014b, for elaboration on the pre-RTE context in Delhi). Thus, in principle, one would hope to find Delhi administration and schools relatively adept at instituting the provision given the previous compulsion.

What is new in the post-RTE context is the universalising aspect of the Act in Delhi and elsewhere in India—i.e. *all private unaided schools in every state* are meant to provide free education to a proportion of their students, in addition to existing compulsions on government schools for all students. A more stringent reading of Section 3(2) above extends the implication of 'free' education beyond 'fee-free', more commonly understood as tuition fees, *to include all costs incurred as a result of any charges or expenses.*

In its idealised form, the RTE Act, thus, envisions the inclusion of all children into elementary education regardless of their socio-economic background. As such, the RTE Act also mandates the removal of other barriers to accessing schooling. For example, government and private schools are meant to: be non-discriminatory; institute policies for continuous enrolment throughout the year; have age-appropriate enrolment, prohibit screening or admission testing; have transparent admissions procedures; and institute 'child-centric' pedagogic practices.

Given the commitment to free and barrier-free schooling for all children, including a proportion of those accessing otherwise fee-paying private schools, we sought to shed light on: (1) whether and to what extent out-of-pocket household costs were incurred when accessing government, private unaided (full-fee), and private unaided (freeship) provision; and (2) enrolment patterns and household perceptions and experiences of accessing schooling under the RTE Act. This paper reports data from one Delhi slum (Karampur),[1] and is part of a larger study conducted in 2011–2012 on the early phase of implementation of the Act (see Srivastava & Noronha, 2014a, 2014b, for school- and institutional-level results). To the best of our knowledge, it was among the earliest studies on the implementation of the RTE Act, as it was conducted in the first full year of the implementation in Delhi, which in turn, was among the first to implement certain provisions of the Act.[2] Before we proceed, some notes of clarification follow.

Section 12(1)(c) of the RTE Act applies to private unaided schools, i.e. schools independent of state financing, ownership, and management. They are the focus of this paper. The term 'private schools' is used interchangeably with 'private unaided schools' here. Private aided schools, i.e. privately managed but heavily state-subsidised, have different requirements regarding the provision of free seats. Free seats in these schools are meant to be in proportion to the annual aid or grants received, subject to a minimum of 25% (Section 12[b], Government of India, 2009).

Government provision is also heterogeneous in India, as education is highly decentralised. Education is a 'concurrent subject', meaning there is shared Centre–state responsibility, although the majority of financing and administration are borne by the states. Additionally, schools are run by different levels of government, and some, by different government departments. For the purposes of the discussion here, 'government schools' refers to schools run by state departments of education or local authorities/bodies.[3] Combined, these constitute the largest proportion of schools overall in India, and also the largest share of government provision.

Schooling costs and other barriers

The international literature shows that basic education has not been 'fee-free' in the majority of countries even under free education policies (UNESCO, 2015). Out of 173 countries surveyed in 2006, 135 constitutionally guaranteed free primary education, but 110 usually levied some charges (Hyll-Larsen, 2013). In addition to tuition fees, households bear significant out-of-pocket costs for transportation, books, uniforms, meals, exam and other school fees, and private tuition, etc., even in elementary education. These may not all apply when accessing specific government or private school types, particularly where schools or households are subsidised or are provided some inputs (e.g. in the Indian context, mid-day meal schemes, book/uniform subsidies, scholarships, free private school seats post-RTE).

Nonetheless, there is relative consensus that out-of-pocket costs associated with private school access (particularly, private schools run by independent providers) tend to be higher than in government schools in a number of contexts (Alderman, Orazem, & Paterno, 2001; see Day Ashley et al., 2014, for global review), and in India (Desai, Dubey, Vanneman, & Banerji, 2008; Härmä & Rose, 2012). Out-of-pocket costs negatively affect initial and sustained access. The cost burden has been shown to increase throughout elementary education, and in the transition to and within secondary education in India and elsewhere (Lewin, 2007; Siddhu, 2010). This is related to relatively inequitable sustained access to and within the private sector in India and elsewhere, with negative equity concerns for socially and economically disadvantaged groups (Akyeampong & Rolleston, 2013; Mehrotra & Panchamukhi, 2006; Woodhead. Frost, & James, 2013), even in segments of the sector termed 'low-fee' (Härmä, 2009; Härmä & Rose, 2012).[4]

Comparative global data also show that household out-of-pocket costs account for a large proportion of total education expenditure, supplementing and sometimes outstripping public investment, heightened in countries with low government education expenditure (UNESCO, 2015). UNESCO's 2015 *Education for all global monitoring report* estimates that household expenditure accounted for 31% of the total between 2005 and 2012 in 50 countries with data (UNESCO, 2015, p. 260). The report concludes that the 'share of household contributions is by far the highest in South Asian countries' (UNESCO, 2015, p. 261). In India, the mean public expenditure on education between 2000 and 2012 was only 3.38% of GDP (Srivastava, 2014).[5] This is much below the country's long-standing stated aim of achieving 6% of GDP by 1985, and despite impressive macro-economic growth in the first decade of the 2000s. The 2015 Global Monitoring Report estimates that between 2005 and 2012, total education expenditure in India was just over 6% of GDP, nearly 50% of which came from private household expenditure (UNESCO, 2015, p. 260).

Despite provisions existing in principle since 1950, elementary education has neither been completely free, nor tuition-fee-free in India. At the time of Tilak's (1996a, 1996b) comprehensive analysis on the principles of free elementary education in India, he found that over a third of states did not legislate for free education, despite the national goal in the 1992 National Policy on Education to be met by 1995. Of the states that did, many did not cover a full elementary cycle (eight years), covering primary only (four to five years, depending on the state). A widespread *laissez-faire* attitude to enact and uphold such provisions in government and private sectors (where applicable, as in Delhi) was known to exist (Juneja, 2005; Srivastava & Noronha, 2014a; Tilak, 1996a, 1996b). While all states now have free elementary education rules given the compulsions of the RTE Act, initial studies show bureaucratic delays inhibiting its full implementation and non-compliance by private schools (Mehendale, Mukhopadhyay, & Namala, 2015; Sarangapani, Mehendale, Mukhopadhyay, & Namala, 2014; Srivastava & Noronha, 2014a).

There are additional structural barriers to accessing schooling, such as the complexity of admission processes, physical distance to schools, infrastructure getting to and within schools (e.g. safe road access; girls' toilets; accessible facilities for children with disabilities), etc. Sustained access to and within schooling is further compromised by 'softer' social or hidden normative barriers that may be informally inserted into formal and informal schooling interactions, resulting in exclusion (Kabeer, 2000; Subrahmanian, 2003). Examples include access to more advantageous social networks facilitating entry to higher quality public or private schools; preferential treatment of children from higher socio-economic backgrounds; regressive pedagogic practices and exam systems; and school violence and harassment.

In the Indian context, these barriers or 'push-out factors' (Reddy & Sinha, 2010), have been shown to disproportionately negatively affect children from lower-income households, and from traditionally disadvantaged caste and social groups (Desai et al., 2008; Ogando Portela & Pells, 2015; Ramachandran & Naorem, 2013). The RTE Act has non-discrimination clauses regarding the treatment of EWS and socially disadvantaged groups (Section 8[c] and Section 9[c], Government of India, 2009), and mandates an environment 'free of fear, trauma, and anxiety' for all (Section 29[2][g], Government of India, 2009). It has also instituted a number of provisions to minimise structural barriers to accessing schooling (Sections 13–17, Government of India, 2009), in addition to child-centred pedagogic change (Section 29, Government of India, 2009). Despite this, there have been concerns regarding the viability of the Act and the free seats provision to quell experienced exclusion, particularly regarding (elite) private school access, and where there is a large social distance between the minority accessing freeships and the majority of the clientele. Thus, in addition to the financial impact, this study also attempts to document some aspects of the experienced reality of accessing private schooling and freeships in the early post-RTE context.

Methods

Fieldwork for the full study was conducted between June 2011 and January 2012, and documentary analysis completed in April 2012.[6] We present only the methods for data reported in this paper. The bulk of household-level data were collected in June–September 2011 in a team comprising the authors and research assistants. Data were collected through: a household survey in one resettlement block and adjacent squatter colony in Karampur slum (*n*=290) and semi-structured household interviews (*n*=40) drawn from this larger sample.

Additionally, regulatory analysis conducted at the institutional-level of the larger study was used to analyse actual experiences of accessing schooling, and match household understandings of the RTE Act against official articulations. Data collection instruments were designed by the authors.

As this was an exploratory study, and owing to complications in sampling and capturing households accessing private schools and freeships (see below), survey data were not used to ascertain correlational or causal relationships. Rather, they were used to provide a background frame from which to select households for the more in-depth semi-structured interviews. Household survey data were analysed using descriptive statistics.

The study site

Given the pervasive scepticism on the viability of the Act and the free seats provision in the early implementation phase, Karampur was chosen for a number of particularities. Firstly, it met the basic criteria for site selection: a recognised slum area; a mix of government and local private schools; and familiarity with local NGOs that could facilitate entry. More importantly, it had the added advantage of having relatively more mobilised citizen campaigns than comparable sites, as local NGOs were assisting parents with freeship admission and running RTE information campaigns. We assumed a greater likelihood of capturing freeship households and schools implementing the Act's provisions, crucial in the early implementation phase.

Karampur had a number of 'resettlement colony' blocks. It was well-developed with *pakka* houses and several public facilities. One block was chosen for the sample site because it was adjacent to a squatter (*jhuggi*) colony. Resettlement colony blocks had long rows of back-to-back, mostly two-storied housing on 25 square-yard plots, with 4-foot wide brick-paved lanes. Housing generally had piped water and toilets. In contrast, the squatter colony squeezed a much larger number of houses on 3–9 square-yard plots. These semi-*pakka* or makeshift shacks often only had plastic sheets and odd wooden pieces for roofing, and were served by public taps and a public toilet complex. The narrow, winding pathways had open drains and piles of slushy garbage.

Household survey

The household survey was designed to capture socio-economic status (including basic assets) and education profiles, but specifically, to more systematically generate a household sub-sample with appropriate variation for semi-structured interviews. Names of all schools ever attended and school fees for anyone aged 0–18 were documented. Every household was approached, but since the focus was on schooling access, only those with children aged 6–16 were selected for the survey sample.

The survey was simultaneously conducted in the selected resettlement block and squatter colony to capture a wider spectrum of households (Table 1). However, squatter colony sampling was discontinued after a few days due to negligible private school access. Furthermore, our initial random sample had only four households with freeships. Since this was a prime focus of our study, we included an additional six households with freeships in an adjacent block by snowballing.

A total of 74% of households belonged to traditionally disadvantaged groups (i.e. scheduled caste, scheduled tribe, and other backward classes). Scheduled caste and scheduled tribe households alone constituted 55% of the total. The highest proportion of adults reported having secondary-level education (38.8%), although resettlement colony residents were nearly 2.2 times more likely to have secondary schooling, and adults with no schooling were 2.9 times more likely in the squatter colony. This was followed by 22.8% who reported themselves as illiterate or having no schooling, indicating a wide variation within the sample regarding the education range. Finally, 17.2% had upper primary/lower secondary schooling, and 12.5% primary only.

Overall, the most commonly reported occupation among working adults was 'private service' (50%), referring to a heterogeneous category ranging from domestic maids, drivers, and salesmen, to a very small number of workers in larger companies. Of working adults, a combined 55.6% of squatter colony and 60.7% of resettlement block adults had private or government sector jobs, although all those with prized government jobs (e.g. drivers; peons, etc.) were resettlement colony residents, as were the great majority (91.5%) of self-employed adults (e.g. skilled work like tailors, trades, or micro-enterprise). This was in contrast to a higher proportion of daily wage earners (57.6%), the poorest paid and most erratic form of labour, in the squatter colony.

Semi-structured household interviews

The sub-sample of 40 households was drawn from the survey sample on the basis of maximum variation of school choice to enable understanding on government and private schooling access and experiences. This consisted of four school choice categories (see Table 2).

The semi-structured interview schedule had six parts for all households and a seventh for freeship households. Questions were on: decision-making and school choice processes; perceptions of school quality; schooling costs and fee concessions; experiences of interacting with schools; voice and school responsiveness; understandings of the RTE Act's provisions

Table 1. Total household survey sample.

	Households
Squatter colony	62
Resettlement colony block 1	222
Resettlement colony block 2*	6
Total	290

Note: *Drawn through snowball sampling to include households accessing private schools via freeships.

Table 2. Semi-structured household interview sample.

	Number of households
Category 1: Accessing government schools only	11
Category 2: One or more child in local fee-level 1 private schools*	11
Category 3: One or more child in fee-level 2 private schools**	8
Category 4: Accessing private school(s) through freeship	10
Total	40

Notes: Fee levels were determined by categorising all private schools accessed by survey households in the current year. *Fee-level 1 schools charged Rs. 3600–6000/year at primary level; **Fee-level 2 schools charged Rs. 10,000 or more/year at primary level.

(including attempts at securing freeships); and, for freeship households, experiences of securing the freeship and of inclusion. The interview schedule was piloted in a similar community. Interviews were conducted at participants' homes by two members of the research team in Hindi, lasting approximately 45–60 minutes each. The majority of respondents were mothers, though in several cases both parents responded, and in some cases, elder siblings supplemented parents' responses. Interviews were recorded and documented in detail. Data were analysed and coded in Atlas ti.

Schooling patterns and expenditure

Schooling patterns and perceptions

Survey households accessed a total of 44 government and private schools, indicating a relatively healthy mix of schools available to them (Table 3). The majority of children (57%) attended Delhi Department of Education government secondary schools, almost all of which were integrated schools (Class 1–12). A smaller proportion (14%) accessed local government Municipal Corporation of Delhi (MCD) primary schools. A combined 26% of students accessed private schools on a fee-paying basis, most of these in fee-level 1 schools (see below for specification). Notably, of these, 6% accessed the relatively more expensive fee-level 2 schools. At 2%, students accessing private schools via freeship were indeed, a minority.

We further found private school access to be clustered—89% of all children attending fee-level 1 schools were in four schools, and half of freeship students were in one fee-level 2 school. No household accessed fee-level 1 schools via freeships. School-level data indicated this was because of non-compliance (Srivastava & Noronha, 2014a). Initial results from other studies also show freeship access to be inhibited by non-compliance (Mehendale et al., 2015; Sarangapani et al., 2014).

Similar to existing literature, quality perceptions about government and private schools were mixed (Akyeampong & Rolleston, 2013; Fennell, 2013; Härmä, 2009; Srivastava, 2006). However, regardless of the specific school they accessed, interviewees attributed 'good quality' to government and private schools in neighbourhoods of 'good standard' outside Karampur. This suggests that quality perceptions may be linked with the socio-geographic

Table 3. School participation and reported fees

School type	Annual fees reported by households		Number of children	% Children (rounded)
	Mean	Median		
Central school (*Kendriya Vidyalaya*)(Class 0–12)[+]	3699	3340	8	1
Government senior secondary(Class 1–12; 6–10; 6–12)	259	240	358	57
MCD primary(Class 1–5)	104	150	87	14
Fee-level 1 private(Class 0–5; Class 0–8)	4449	4320	127	20
Fee-level 2 private(Class 0–8; 0–12)	17,127	13,200	38	6
Fee-level 2 private schools (freeship)	0*	0*	12	2
Private aided	2340	2100	3	1

Notes: Most private schools had some pre-school classes (i.e. Class 0). This was sometimes found in government schools.
+Central schools (*kendriya vidyalaya*) are run by the Central Government. They were previously reserved for children of government employees, but are also meant to be instituting a quota under the RTE Act. Cases reported here did not access them via the RTE quota.
*All freeships students accessed fee-level 2 schools. Households reported no tuition fees. However, this is not the same as total out-of-pocket costs. See Figure 2 and Table 4.
Source: Household survey data.

context of the school, an area that is hitherto largely unexplored in the literature on India and the Global South.

Most interviewees felt that local MCD primary schools were the worst compared to other government schools, with the local boys' school at the bottom of the rung.[7] It was visibly prone to violence and insecurity by our own observations. In addition to poor infrastructure and security concerns (particularly in the boys' school), interviewees were negative about teaching and complained about high pupil–teacher ratios, absenteeism, and low teaching time. This could not be independently verified in every case. In the face of this and constrained access to other government or private schools, many parents felt helpless causing anxiety, irritation, and anger.

While similar negative assessments of government schools are prevalent in the literature on India (e.g. De et al. 2011), there is less discussion on positive parental perceptions as was found in some of the data in our study. Not all government schools were reported as dysfunctional. A few boys' and almost all girls' secondary schools were appreciated for their security arrangements and teaching, remarkably, even by households that had transferred from private schools. This was particularly true for integrated government schools that taught English from an early grade, and schools in 'better' localities. Similar to findings here (see Figure 1 below), while the literature notes that the transition from private to government schools is because of increased costs as grade levels increase (see Lewin, 2007; Siddhu, 2010, for review), it does not sufficiently analyse relative quality perceptions/experiences upon transition. In this way, findings in this study may be an important starting-off point for wider-scale analysis.

Fee-level 1 schools had an annual fee of Rs. 3600–6000 at primary (Class 1–5), and were generally within 0.5 km of Karampur. While they had relatively lower fees than fee-level 2 schools, they all charged more than Srivastava's (2006) operationalisation of 'low-fee private' schools as private unaided schools with a monthly tuition fee in elementary education equivalent to a maximum of one day's earnings of a daily wage earner. Household interviewees accessing them felt security was good, and they had strict disciplinary measures (though sometimes harsh) and teaching commitment. While most interviewees felt that children learned more as compared to government schools (not independently verified), learning outcomes were questioned in absolute terms. For example, the quality of English-medium instruction, an often touted benefit of private schools, was criticised by some.

There were other areas of dissension regarding the quality of fee-level 1 schools by those accessing them, and even more so by those accessing the more expensive fee-level 2 private

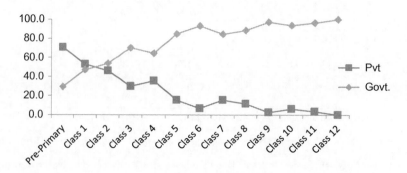

Figure 1. Government and private school access by class level (%). Source: Household survey data.

schools, mirroring the general literature on 'low-fee' schools (Akaguri, 2011; Fennell, 2013; Srivastava, 2006). Some saw little distinction between fee-level 1 and government schools. Interviewees noted high pupil–teacher ratios and limited school infrastructure, and teacher-related concerns such as relative inexperience, frequent turnover, and lack of qualifications. Some interviewees felt that fee-level 1 schools were not 'really' private, but as one fee-level 2 parent put it, 'semi-private' schools, intimating that the term 'private' should be reserved for higher-fee (and thus, in this frame, higher quality) schools.

Similar to other qualitative studies (Fennell, 2013; Srivastava, 2006), social factors seemed to affect perceptions. For example, some interviewees claimed that comparatively lower fees in fee-level 1 schools attracted children from the squatter colony, leading to disruptive school environments and poor hygiene. In fact, our household survey showed negligible private school access by squatter colony residents.

Fee-level 2 schools had an annual fee in primary of Rs. 10,000 or higher, were more heterogeneous, and tended to be outside Karampur in relatively better-off areas. Most would not be considered elite, other than the one accessed by half of freeship students. The more expensive fee-level 2 schools charged approximately Rs. 20,000–30,000/year by conservative estimates, and although highly desirable to parents, were largely unaffordable. The few children in the survey sample that attended them had, with rare exceptions, been admitted via a freeship and did not pay tuition fees, although other costs were incurred. The more frequently accessed among them charged fees closer to the bottom of the range, and contrary to Section 13(1) of the RTE Act, reportedly demanded 'donations' or capitation fees for admission.

Interviewees accessing fee-level 2 schools (full-fee and freeship) reported good infrastructure and facilities, well-guarded premises, and good teaching quality, including English-language instruction (not independently verified in each case). We observed that the elite freeship school had a swimming pool, playroom, games, and computers. The fact that fee-level 2 schools were in middle-class neighbourhoods increased interviewees' satisfaction.

Overall, as class levels increased, so did government school access (Figure 1). Private school access was highest for children in pre-primary (70.8%) and Class 1 (52.9%), but steadily dropped thereafter. The sharpest decline was between Class 4 and 5 (from 35.6% to 15.3%), remaining low upon transition to and within upper primary (Class 6–8), and was negligible by secondary (Class 9–12). Household interviewees indicated that the associated rise in fees and expenses with increasing grade levels was a major reason for this shift, in line with existing literature on the difficulty of sustained private school access (Lewin, 2007; Sidhhu, 2010).

Out-of-pocket household expenditure

Figure 2 presents average annual per child out-of-pocket household expenditure on elementary education for interview households. *All* households, including those accessing government and private schools via freeship, incurred schooling costs. However, there was a large discrepancy in out-of-pocket expenditure between government and private school access, including for children in 'free' seats. As compared to children in government schools, the average annual out-of-pocket expenditure was 6.2 times more for full-fee-paying children in fee-level 1 schools, 8.7 times more for freeship students (all of whom were in fee-level 2 schools), and 18.4 times more for full-fee-paying children in fee-level 2 schools.

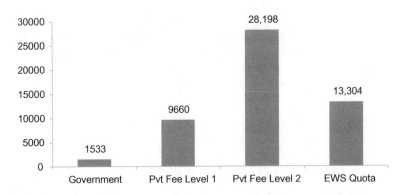

Figure 2. Per child annual average household elementary education expenditure (Rs.) (*n*=39). Source: Semi-structured interview data.

Table 4. Average annual per-child out-of-pocket household expenditure (elementary) as proportion of set income levels

	% Daily wage rate, unskilled labour (Delhi, 2011)*	% Maximum income criterion for freeships (Rs. 100,000)
Government	1.9	1.5
Private fee-level 1	12.5	9.7
Private fee-level 2	36.5	28
Freeship access	17.1	13

Notes: *As reported in Government of NCT of Delhi (2012).
Calculations are derived based on reported out-of-pocket expenditures in Figure 1.

Thus, accessing a 'free' seat was certainly not free (Rs. 13,304). The average cost was more than a full-fee seat in a fee-level 1 private school (Rs. 9660), and well-above the government sector (Rs. 1533), which while not free, was by far the least expensive. Relatively lower out-of-pocket costs in government as compared to private schools has been noted in other literature (Akaguri, 2014; Alderman et al., 2001; Desai et al., 2008; Härmä & Rose, 2012), and for households in this study, remained the case whether accessing private schools on a full-fee-paying or 'free' seat basis.

Table 4 expresses the same average annual per-child out-of-pocket costs as a proportion of the daily wage rate for unskilled labour in Delhi at the time of the fieldwork (Rs. 6422/month), and as a proportion of the maximum income freeship eligibility criterion (Rs. 100,000/year). It is obvious that it would be highly unlikely for anything other than government schools to be affordable or sustainably accessible by these two groups, given the pool of schools in our study. This echoes concerns about the limits of affordability of private schools by poorer segments raised by other studies on India (Härmä & Rose, 2012; Mehrotra & Panchamukhi, 2006), even on the basis of subsidies, given real out-of-pocket costs.

Table 5 presents a breakdown of out-of-pocket expenditure. Although minimal, government school students incurred tuition fee costs, which is against the principles of free education. Six from among the eight full-fee-paying fee-level 2 interview households paid 'donations' for admission. In another case, the Rs. 10,000 capitation fee demanded by the school was waived when that household leveraged existing social networks, and a local politician intervened. Such demands have been noted in the emerging post-RTE literature (Mehendale et al., 2015; Sarangapani et al., 2014).

Table 5. Breakdown of per child average annual expenditure in elementary education (Rs.).

	Tuition fee	Transport	Books	Uniform	Private tuition	Other	Total
Government	72	129	184	230	907	12	1533
Private fee-level 1	4134	875	1564	809	2160	118	9660
Private fee-level 2	18,215	2615	3100	1360	2375	533*	28,198
EWS freeship	0	5182	2491	2373	2454	805	13,304

Notes: Private tuition costs and transport costs have been calculated for 10 months; books and uniform on a one-time basis; fees for 12 months.
*As explained above, there were reported cases of 'donations' (i.e. capitation fees) taken at the time of admission. These are not included here due to inconsistency in reporting.
Source: Semi-structured household interview data.

While freeship students did not pay tuition fees, there were substantial transportation costs since private schools offering freeships were far from Karampur in 'desirable' areas. This had significant implications on taking-up freeships. For example, one household was offered a freeship but declined when the school demanded a lump sum payment of the year's transportation charges upon registration. As freeship students attended relatively more expensive private schools, the type of uniform was also more upmarket and costly. Costs for books were substantial, but lower than for full-fee-paying fee-level 2 private students. According to interviewees, no school exempted freeship students from associated costs. Conversely, households that could afford them expected to pay for these, but were grateful for the tuition fee exemption.

Private tuition costs were substantial for all student groups. While in absolute terms they were lowest for government school students, proportionally, they were the highest, representing 59% of total out-of-pocket expenditure. Among this group, private tuition expenditure was generally for students who had transferred from fee-level 1 private schools. They came from relatively more economically stable households compared to those who had never accessed private schools. Students who had only ever attended government schools were generally unsupported by private tuition. However, they also tended to have parents with little or no schooling, and may have most benefited from supplemental tuition, although cost was a barrier. This suggests a pattern similar to Aslam and Atherton's (2014) study on private tuition in India and Pakistan, where the likelihood of taking private tuition increased with ability to pay.

Barriers to access: household experiences

General admission

While the free seats provision is meant to ease barriers to private school entry for a proportion of children, Sections 13–15 of the RTE Act include other provisions meant to ease initial access. Schools are prohibited from charging capitation fees, or screening parents or children (including testing) (Section 13[1]); should ensure age-appropriate enrolment and cannot refuse admission if documents attesting to age are missing (Section 14); cannot deny admission at any time during the school year (Section 15). In cases of over-subscription for the freeship or otherwise, selection is meant to be random (Section 2[o]).

Households accessing fee-level 1 schools claimed that admission was relatively simple, but affordability was the biggest barrier. Although these schools asked for birth certificates and other documents, unlike in Sarangapani et al.'s (2014) study, parents found them easy to provide and schools were flexible about timing. No one reported testing. Full-fee-paying fee-level 2 households, on the other hand, reported that schools insisted on entry tests, and that admission could be denied. Furthermore, children could be admitted to a class lower than the level that was applied for. The demand for 'donations' was also a barrier. Some parents were hesitant in approaching the more upmarket schools due to their relatively lower socio-economic backgrounds.

No parent reported refusal by local government schools. In fact, even the catchment area was not strictly enforced. However, relative social positioning seemed to affect the ability to access more desirable government schools. For example, several household interviewees reported that it was difficult to access particular government schools prized for teaching quality, safety, or English-medium instruction, characteristics often combined in a single school. Many such schools had a lottery system and a more complicated system of enrolment, with a rush to fill additional forms. The most disadvantaged households with low education levels and poor employment, and who could not get assistance in filling the appropriate forms, were least likely to manage admission.

Freeship admission

Among other procedural issues, the *2011 Delhi Free Seats Order* specified maximum income (Rs. 100,000) and residency requirements (three years) for freeships (Section 2[c]); prohibited testing (Section 5); prohibited teaching freeship students in separate shifts or charging any kind of fee (Section 3); outlined procedures for schools to visibly post free seats and conduct a lottery if over-subscribed (Section 4); and specified required proof of income and residency documents (Section 6) (Government of NCT of Delhi, 2011b).

Despite active NGO campaigning in Karampur and capturing some households that had secured free seats, the overall extent of knowledge about the Act and its provisions was limited, even among the latter. Of the 30 non-freeship interview households, only two had tried to obtain a freeship (but failed). The overwhelming majority were not aware of the provision. Furthermore, perceptions about the Act were coloured by perceptions on the overall climate for education delivery. For example, some interviewees lamented that government education initiatives were often launched but parents were not properly informed; others, that the Department of Education's powers were limited; and some, that corruption would inhibit proper implementation.

Of the households that secured freeships, unsurprisingly, both parents were relatively better schooled than non-freeship households, and the family had a steady (if modest) income and/or personal connections with schools or others 'in the know'. Nonetheless, free-ship households could be divided into two groups—one that secured admission on their own (four households), and the other whose journey was facilitated by an NGO or another parent who understood the process and helped complete forms (six households). All freeship households significantly mobilised their resources (i.e. money, personal contacts and friends/family/acquaintances/employers, NGO help) to ensure success.

The first group were relatively better educated and relatively economically stable. They generally learned of the opportunity through the newspaper, TV, or relatives. Three had private sector jobs and rental income. Two among them were relatively much better-off, one having simultaneously applied to different private schools as a fee-paying client hoping to be successful at any cost. The other household head was the son of a jeweller and had an undergraduate degree. His father simply made a salary certificate saying that his income was well below the limit specified, although this was highly unlikely. The second group had comparatively fewer assets and lower status jobs, although they were above the maximum income threshold. While they may not have been the poorest or most disadvantaged, most freeship households would have been unable to access fee-level 2 schools otherwise.

However, gaining admission was not easy. The process was protracted, tedious, cumbersome, and costly. Applicants went through enormous effort, making the rounds of neighbourhood schools, generally applying for freeships at between three and nine schools, and patiently and persistently following up. Freeship parents claimed that they began the process willing to repeat it the following year if unsuccessful. Once an application was successful, they began strategising for sibling admission.

Private schools were reported as being unhelpful and evasive about dates for submitting forms, the lottery, and announcing successful applicants. There were reported instances of private schools demanding 'extra fees', i.e. bribes, to expedite the process. One interviewee claimed that schools deliberately misplaced applications. Vimal, a successful applicant, recounted experiencing anxiety and tension during the process.[8] He was ultimately successful as a result of contacting a minister through his unique social network:

> … there was a lot of running around. First get the forms, line up, sometimes they say, 'They're available at this time', sometimes at another time. That's how they behave. Then you have to go to submit the forms, line up, give the forms and documents, etc., stamped by two gazetted officers or an MLA [member of legislative assembly]. It seems even MLAs don't have much sway. Maybe ministers, like in our area there's [name of minister deleted] so I got it stamped by him and submitted it. It's somewhat difficult. (Vimal, Father, Freeship Household Interviewee)

Suraj, another father ultimately successful in securing a freeship, explained that some private schools negotiated with parents to avoid accepting full tuition fee waivers, asking them to pay whatever they could:

> I completed a form for [name of school deleted]. My younger son's name got on to the waiting list. Then they called me and said, 'What can you give? Give half the fee amount'. (Suraj, Father, Freeship Household Interviewee)

He ended up accessing another private school for his sons via freeships, and tried to protest when that school demanded a fee of Rs. 3000–4000 per child, but to no avail. This time, he acquiesced. When he asked the school to justify the fee, it insisted:

> '… we have so many expenses, there's this and that'. I said, 'We've been exempted from paying fees by the government'. But they said, 'No, these are the expenses for the teachers, the building'. (Suraj, Father, Freeship Household Interviewee)

Parents reported that the demand of specific documents by private schools was a further complication, and another potential door for them to extort money. Parents had to battle if they were unwilling to bribe, especially for the income certificate, which they reported was the most difficult to obtain. Households were told that the income certificate had a six-month expiry date, and a fresh certificate would be required the following year if they were unsuccessful in securing freeships the first time around. This was contrary to the *2011 Delhi Free Seats Order* which prohibits expelling or barring students who lack this document. It also states that once a student is admitted in a free seat, a self-declaration or affidavit attesting to income is sufficient (Section 6[a], Government of NCT of Delhi, 2011b).

There was general scepticism about the authenticity of the process. Some interviewees felt that those who genuinely met freeship criteria would be kept unaware, or would be too hesitant in approaching schools. This was also mentioned in school-level data by a private school owner and active member of a private school association who claimed to know of a number of 'fake admissions' (Srivastava & Noronha, 2014a, pp. 188–189). One full-fee-paying client in a fee-level 2 private school stressed:

> Those who secure admissions under this quota are so rich that they can probably pay the fees for three children. I know of so many people, I won't name names, who have a monthly income of over 100,000 or 200,000 but their children are going to school under EWS [freeship]. They should change the system and the really needy should get it [...] 90% [who are actually eligible] don't even come forward. They might be hesitant because they are less educated. 99% of those who are benefitting are prosperous ... like people should think these people are paying a van [to bring their children to school], but how? I mean it's all fake, just for show. (Sanjeev, Fee-paying Fee-level 2 Household Interviewee)

Finally, there were mixed feelings among household interviewees about the experience and barriers that children admitted via freeships might face, particularly, in relatively higher-fee and elite schools. On the one hand, those who were aware about the provision were excited by the potential opportunities. On the other, they expressed concern about their relative social background *vis-à-vis* the general peer group. As in the case below, more than one such family had discussions with their children about their experiences:

Payal [mother]:	I also keep asking the children if everything is alright, how do they teach, how are the facilities, everything. To make sure that it's not like anything's being done separately, or that they'll do something separately with the EWS [freeship] children, you know? So the children say that everything is alright, everyone is the same.
Payal's husband [father]:	There is a double shift ... but our children go in the morning shift. This time they're not taking the evening shift, I found out. They're reducing that now. (Payal [Mother] and Payal's husband [Father], Freeship Household Interviewees)

This family accessed the elite fee-level 2 school that half the freeship children in our study attended. Payal's husband was referring to the school's self-described 'slum school project' in which disadvantaged children were taught in a separate shift with separate staff in the evening. This was confirmed by the principal in school-level data for this study (Srivastava & Noronha, 2014a, p. 190), even though operating a separate shift contravenes the Act and the *Delhi Free Seats Order* (Section 3[b], Government of NCT of Delhi, 2011a). While Payal's children were part of the main school, others continued to be taught in the separate evening shift.

Conclusions

As the political centre of the country, pressure to implement and disseminate the provisions of the RTE Act was highest in Delhi in the early days, which continues. Furthermore, we were careful to situate the study in a potentially robust context for success. Karampur was a relatively better resourced slum, served by a healthy mix of government and private schools of varying fee levels, and had the advantage of an NGO active in RTE campaigning and assisting freeship applicants. We believed this would increase the likelihood of capturing a reasonable number of households aware of and successful in securing freeships, and some level of school compliance. We assumed this would help households (particularly, those accessing private schools via freeships) enjoy benefits of free access and fewer barriers. These were serious considerations as it was early in the implementation phase.

While further broad-scale research is required, this study reveals a number of disconcerting findings regarding private school access in the post-RTE context, and similar to the limited emerging literature (Mehendale et al., 2015; Sarangapani et al., 2014). First, access to different school types within and between government and private sectors was segmented. Private school access for very poor households was severely constrained. Government provision remained the main provider for them, and overall for households in the study. This may have been further related to the nearly minimal access to private school freeships for households in the study. Furthermore, successfully securing a 'free' seat also seemed to be linked to a high level of motivation and persistence, better relative social positioning, and advantageous social networks.

Secondly, free education remained an elusive myth for all, including those accessing 'free' private schools seats and government schools. Out-of-pocket expenditure was most severe for full-fee-paying households accessing relatively more expensive private schools among the pool of available schools (although they could not be considered elite schools). Accessing 'free' private school seats was the second costliest option. This may have been because among private schools in the study, only some among the relatively higher-fee schools implemented the provision. As discussed in school-level results elsewhere, non-compliance regarding the free seat and other provisions was a result of institutional mediation, unwillingness, and operational and bureaucratic constraints faced by private schools (Srivastava & Noronha, 2014a). Government access remained the least costly option, by far.

Thirdly, households experienced barriers to access and inclusion despite the RTE Act's numerous provisions, particularly when accessing freeships and relatively more expensive private schools. Access to the relatively lesser expensive private schools (all of which fell above the operationalisation of 'low-fee private schools') was also constrained, perhaps partially because of non-compliance with the free seats provision. Other barriers in contravention of the Act (e.g. testing, documentary proof, separate shifts) were more notable in the relatively more expensive private schools. Households accessing government schools reported the fewest barriers, although access to schools considered relatively better and outside the slum area was difficult because of more complicated application procedures.

Aside from specific application, admission, and cost barriers, households also experienced 'soft barriers' related to their relative social positioning and less access to advantageous social networks/connections. This was particularly the case for households attempting to secure freeships, and access to schools outside the slum area and relatively more expensive private schools. It remains to be seen how children admitted through private school freeships will be included, and socially and academically supported. For example, students attending elite and English-medium private schools via freeships are less likely to have access to supplemental education services, and to experience more social distance as compared to their non-freeship peers, particularly as they progress through the cycle. Thus, soft social barriers experienced as discrimination or 'exclusion' might be the most durable, and they, and the terms on which 'inclusion' is realised (Kabeer, 2000; Subrahmanian, 2003), are perhaps the most necessary to address in order to fulfil the spirit of the RTE Act.

Notes

1.   Karampur is a pseudonym. All names of interviewees are also pseudonyms.
2.   Rules, regulations, and processes were still under revision during the time of the study, and to a certain extent, continue to be so. This paper thus aims to provide somewhat of a baseline or first glance at issues against which further examination may be conducted as the process and implementation unfold.
3.   The 'local authority' is defined in the Act as a 'Municipal Corporation or Municipal Council or Zila Parishad or Nagar Panchayat or Panchayat, by whatever name called, and includes such other authority or body having administrative control over the school empowered by or under any law for the time being in force to function as a local authority in any city, town or village' (Section 2[h], Government of India, 2009).
4.   There is a vociferous debate in existing private school literature on the affordability of the 'low-fee' sector. The authors are intimately aware of the debate and the associated literature, but do not enter into it here in the interest of space. Srivastava (2013) has published elsewhere on the matter.
5.   Calculations using UNESCO Institute for Statistics data as reported in 2014.
6.   The Delhi School Education (Free seats for students belonging to economically weaker sections and disadvantage group) Order, 2011(2011 Delhi Free Seats Order) (Government of NCT of Delhi, 2011b), was issued in January 2011, ahead of the period of the study. It stated the general conditions and procedures for schools to institute the free seats provision.
7.   The local boys' and girls' schools were run in separate shifts in the local MCD school.
8.   All interview excerpts are translated from the original in Hindi. All names are pseudonyms.

Acknowledgments

Research reported in this paper was conducted as part of a larger project funded by the Privatisation in Education Research Initiative (PERI), Open Societies Institute. We would like to acknowledge the following individuals for research assistance with household-level data: Meenakshi Dogra, Neeru Sood, Vedika Khanna, Rakesh Kumar, Ravikant Kumar, Sanjeev Kumar, Sunil Kumar, Vinay Kumar, Surbhi Mahajan, and Deepika Phalswal.

Disclosure statement

No potential conflict of interest was reported by the authors.

Funding

This work was supported by the Open Society Foundations Privatisation of Education Research Initiative.

References

Akaguri, L. (2014). Fee-free public or low-fee private basic education in rural Ghana: How does the cost influence the choice of the poor? *Compare, 44*, 140–161.

Akyeampong, K., & Rolleston, C. (2013). Low-fee private schooling in Ghana: Is growing demand improving equitable and affordable access for the poor? In P. Srivastava (Ed.), *Low-fee private schooling: Aggravating equity or mitigating disadvantage?* (pp. 37–64). Oxford: Symposium Books.

Alderman, H., Orazem, P. F., & Paterno, E. M. (2001). School quality, school cost, and the public/private school choices of low-income households in Pakistan. *Journal of Human Resources, 36*, 304–326.

Aslam, M., & Atherton, P. (2014). Shadow education sector in India and Pakistan. In I. Macpherson, S. Robertson, & G. Walford (Eds.), *Education privatisation and social justice: Case studies form Africa, South Asia and South East Asia* (pp. 137–158). Oxford: Symposium Books.

Day Ashley, L., Mcloughlin, C., Aslam, M., Engel, J., Wales, J., Rawal, S. ... Rose, P. (2014). *The role and impact of private schools in developing countries: A rigorous review of the evidence.* Final report. Education Rigorous Literature Review. UK Department for International Development. Retrieved from https://www.gov.uk/government/uploads/system/uploads/attachment_data/file/307032/Private-schools-2014.pdf

De, A., Khera, R., Samson, M., & Shiva Kumar, A. K. (2011). *Probe revisited: A report on elementary education in India.* New Delhi: Oxford University Press.

Desai, S., Dubey, A., Vanneman, R., & Banerji, R. (2008). *Private schooling in India: A new educational landscape* (Indian Human Development Survey Working Paper Series, No. 11). University of Maryland/National Council of Applied Economic Research. Retrieved from http://www.ihds.umd.edu/IHDS_papers/PrivateSchooling.pdf

Fennell, S. (2013). Low-fee private schools in Pakistan: A blessing or a bane? In P. Srivastava (Ed.), *Low-fee private schooling: Aggravating equity or mitigating disadvantage?* (pp. 65–82). Oxford: Symposium Books.

Government of India. (2009, August 26). *The right of children to free and compulsory education act, 2009.* No. 35 of 2009. New Delhi.

Government of National Capital Territory [NCT] of Delhi. (2011a, November 23). *Delhi right of children to free and compulsory rules, 2011.* No. DE.23(462)/Sch.Br./10/17–33. Delhi: Department of Education, Government of NCT of Delhi.

Government of National Capital Territory [NCT] of Delhi. (2011b, January 7). *Delhi school education (free seats for students belonging to economically weaker sections and disadvantage group) order, 2011.* No. 15 (172)/DE/Act/2010/69. Delhi: Education Department, Government of NCT of Delhi.

Government of National Capital Territory [NCT] of Delhi. (2012). *Current minimum wage* [webpage]. Delhi: Department of Labour, Government of NCT Delhi. Retrieved from http://www.delhi.gov.in/wps/wcm/connect/doit_labour/Labour/Home/Minimum+Wages/

Härmä, J. (2009). Can choice promote Education for All? Evidence from growth in private primary schooling in India. *Compare, 39*, 151–165.

Härmä, J., & Rose, P. (2012). Is low-fee private primary schooling affordable for the poor? Evidence from rural India. In S. L. Robertson, K. Mundy, A. Verger, & F. Menashy (Eds.), *Public private partnerships in education: New actors and modes of governance in a globalizing world* (pp. 243–258). Cheltenham: Edward Elgar.

Hyll-Larsen, P. (2013). Free or fee: Corruption in primary school admissions. In Transparency International (Ed.), *Global corruption report: Education*, Chapter 2.5 (pp. 52–59). Abingdon: Routledge. Retrieved from http://www.transparency.org/whatwedo/publication/global_corruption_report_education

Juneja, N. (2005). Exclusive schools in Delhi: Their land and the law. *Economic and Political Weekly, 33*, 3685–3690.

Kabeer, N. (2000). Social exclusion, poverty and discrimination: Towards an analytical framework. *IDS Bulletin, 31*(4), 83–97.

Lewin, K. M. (2007). The limits to growth of non-government private schooling in sub-Saharan Africa. In P. Srivastava & G. Walford (Eds.), *Private schooling in less economically developed countries: Asian and African perspectives* (pp. 41–65). Oxford: Symposium Books.

Mehendale, A., Mukhopadhyay, R., & Namala, A. (2015). Right to education and inclusion in private unaided schools: An exploratory study in Bengaluru and Delhi. *Economic and Political Weekly, 50*(7), 43–51.

Mehrotra, S., & Panchamukhi, P. (2006). Private provision of elementary education in India: Findings of a survey in eight states. *Compare, 36*, 421–442.

Ogando Portela, M. J., & Pells, K. (2015). *Corporal punishment in schools: Longitudinal evidence from Ethiopia, India, Peru and Viet Nam* (Innocenti Discussion Paper, No. 2015-02). Florence: UNICEF Office of Research. Retrieved from http://www.unicef-irc.org/publications/788

Ramachandran, V., & Naorem, T. (2013). What it means to be a Dalit or tribal child in our schools: A synthesis of a six-state qualitative study. *Economic and Political Weekly, 48*(44), 43–52.

Reddy, A. N., & Sinha, S. (2010). *School dropouts or pushouts? Overcoming barriers for the right to education* (CREATE Pathways to Access Research Monograph, No. 40). Brighton: Centre for International Education, University of Sussex. Retrieved from http://www.create-rpc.org/pdf_documents/PTA40.pdf

Sarangapani, P. M., Mehendale, A., Mukhopadhyay, R., & Namala, A. (2014). *Inclusion of marginalised children in private unaided schools under The Right of Children to Free and Compulsory Education Act, 2009: An exploratory study*. New Delhi. Retrieved from https://www.oxfamindia.org/sites/default/files/wp-inclusion-of-marginalised-children-in-private-unaided-schools-190314-en_0.pdf

Siddhu, G. (2010). *Can families in rural India bear the additional burden of secondary education? Investigating the determinants of transition* (CREATE Pathways to Access Research Monograph, No. 50). Brighton: Centre for International Education, University of Sussex. Retrieved from http://www.create-rpc.org/pdf_documents/PTA50.pdf

Srivastava, P. (2006). Private schooling and mental models about girls' schooling in India. *Compare, 36*, 497–514.

Srivastava, P. (2013). Low-fee private schooling: Issues and evidence. In P. Srivastava (Ed.), *Low-fee private schooling: Aggravating equity or mitigating disadvantage?* (pp. 7–35). Oxford: Symposium Books.

Srivastava, P. (2014). Under-financing education and the rise of the private sector in India. Revue internationale d'éducation de Sèvres [En ligne], Colloque: L'éducation en Asie en 2014: Quels enjeux mondiaux ?, mis en ligne le 11 juin 2014, consulté le 01 septembre 2016. http://ries.revues.org/3863

Srivastava, P., & Noronha, C. (2014a). Early private school responses to India's Right to Education Act: Implications for equity. In I. Macpherson, S. Robertson, & G. Walford (Eds.), *Education privatisation and social justice: Case studies from Africa, South Asia and South East Asia* (pp. 179–198). Oxford: Symposium Books.

Srivastava, P., & Noronha, C. (2014b). Institutional framing of the Right to Education Act: Contestation, controversy, and concessions. *Economic and Political Weekly, 49*(18), 51–58.

Subrahmanian, R. (2003). Introduction: Exploring processes of marginalisation and inclusion in education. *IDS Bulletin, 34*, 1–8.

Tilak, J. B. G. (1996a). How free is 'free' primary education in India? (Part 1). *Economic and Political Weekly, 31*, 275–282.

Tilak, J. B. G. (1996b). How free is 'free' primary education in India? (Part 2). *Economic and Political Weekly, 31*, 355–366.

UNESCO. (2015). *EFA global monitoring report 2015. Education for All 2000–2015: Achievements and challenges*. Paris: UNESCO.

Woodhead, M., Frost, M., & James, Z. (2013). Does growth in private schooling contribute to Education for All? Evidence from a longitudinal, two cohort study in Andhra Pradesh, India. *International Journal of Educational Development, 33*, 65–73.

Extending access to low-cost private schools through vouchers: an alternative interpretation of a two-stage 'School Choice' experiment in India

James Tooley

ABSTRACT

Muralidharan and Sundararaman report a randomised controlled trial of a school voucher experiment in Andhra Pradesh, India. The headline findings are that there are no significant academic differences between voucher winners and losers in Telugu, mathematics, English, and science/social studies, although because the private schools appear to use time more efficiently, they are also able to teach Hindi (the national language). The average per capita cost in private schools is less than a third of that in public schools. So while private schools are more efficient, they are not necessarily leading to higher standards. There are two types of private school in the experiment, English and Telugu medium. Since tests in non-language subjects were conducted in a different language for children in public and English-medium private schools, the results in mathematics and science/social studies are difficult to interpret. There are suggestive comparisons between children in Telugu-medium private and public schools, where children took tests in the same language (and were also not subject to disruption in medium of instruction), which show that students in private schools outperform those in public in all subjects. This suggests that giving children access to private schools through vouchers could be a very important policy reform.

1. Introduction

A recent DFID-commissioned report (Day Ashley et al., 2014) revealed areas of consensus and controversy (see Tooley & Longfield, 2015) around the phenomenon of low-cost private schools serving poor families in developing countries. One area illuminated by the report concerned learning outcomes. The headline finding was that 'Pupils attending private school tend to achieve better learning outcomes than pupils in state [i.e. public[1]] schools' (Day Ashley et al., 2014, p. 15). However, this finding is tempered by the caveat that there aren't many good studies available (they point to only three of 'high quality'); many have the shortcoming of not being able sufficiently to control for background and possible missing variables and selectivity biases. Another set of authors concur:

> There is very little rigorous empirical evidence on the relative effectiveness of private and public schools in low-income countries. Non-experimental studies have used several approaches to address identification challenges and have typically found that private school students have higher test scores, but they have not been able to rule out the concern that these estimates are confounded by selection and omitted variables. (Muralidharan & Sundararaman, 2015, p. 1013)

These authors, in a paper that emerged since the publication of the DFID-commissioned report (so not included as evidence), set out to fill this research lacuna by presenting experimental evidence from a school choice experiment in Andhra Pradesh,[2] India (Muralidharan & Sundararaman, 2015, p. 1013). The study, published in *Quarterly Journal of Economics*, features a randomised controlled trial, with a 'unique two-stage randomization' process, held up as the 'gold standard' of research in this area (see e.g. Mantri & Gupta, 2014). The headline findings of the research show that children using vouchers in private schools attain the same level of academic achievement as those in public schools but at a third of the cost. Furthermore, there are no spillover effects on children in public schools whose parents didn't apply for a voucher or those already in private schools.

These findings have been widely—and disparately—reported as heralding a conclusion to the debate about the relative merits of private and public schooling: For example, Karopady (2014) asserts 'The empirical evidence is increasingly pointing towards private schools not being able to add value as compared to government schools' (p. 51). *The Times of India* suggested:

> The findings of the Andhra Pradesh School Choice research aren't encouraging for voucher systems supporters. Private school kids performed better than government school ones in only the first year; in subsequent years, government ones performed just as well. ... The findings dispel a popular myth that private schools lead to better learning. (Chowdhury, 2015)

Meanwhile, supporters of School Choice rallied to private schools' defence: writing in response to the *Times of India* article, one of the foremost defenders of vouchers comments:

> If I were to write the title for the *Times of India* story, it would be: at three times the cost, government schools are no better than private schools. The *Times of India* headline is: private schools are not adding value. You be the judge! (Shah, 2015)

Note that the research findings are accepted by both critics and supporters of vouchers alike; this paper takes a different approach. While congratulating the authors on their powerful research design, it suggests that there is an important challenge in the research implementation which calls into question the headline results: the challenge is that many voucher-winning students took the tests for non-language subjects in a different language (English) than voucher-losing students in the public schools (Telugu). (They also switched their medium of instruction to English-medium schools, and were therefore subject to disruption in their medium of instruction.) Fortunately, the research paper does give suggestive indications of what a comparison would be like when children in public and private schools *did* take the same tests. This shows a large and statistically significant private school advantage in achievement, as well as the widely accepted cost-effectiveness.

In this paper, I first briefly summarise the methods and findings of the research paper. Second, I point to the key problem with the research implementation which calls these findings into question. Third, I discuss the suggestive results which do allow direct comparisons between children in public and private schools. Fourth, I note other less central issues which may nonetheless be of interest, especially to those trying to design effective comparisons between public and private schools. Finally, I discuss the authors' policy prescriptions and add some reflections of my own.

2. Summary of method and findings

The research examined the impact of the Andhra Pradesh School Choice Project, which conducted a voucher experiment in five districts of rural Andhra Pradesh, south-central India, funded by the Legatum Foundation, the UK's DFID and the World Bank. The experiment featured eight stages:

1.   Villages which were in the same districts as those used in the larger Andhra Pradesh Randomised Evaluation Studies (although in different divisions to avoid any connection with schools in the other studies) *and* in which there was at least one *recognised* private school were selected for the study—there were 180 such villages.
2.   Baseline tests in Telugu and mathematics were given to *all* students in two cohorts: those attending the final year of pre-school and those attending grade 1 of primary school, in both public and private schools in these 180 villages. Tests were conducted in March–April 2008, i.e. at the end of the school year.
3.   Parents of students in public schools in all of these 180 villages were invited to apply for a voucher.
4.   The first part of the two-stage lottery procedure took place: 90 out of the 180 villages were randomly assigned to be 'voucher villages' (Muralidharan & Sundararaman, 2015, p. 1023), while the remaining villages would continue as before.
5.   The second part of the two-stage lottery took place: within the voucher villages, children from public schools were randomly selected to be voucher recipients. Invitations were given to parents of these randomly selected students to apply for a voucher so that they could attend private school. (Thus, importantly, stages 3–5 led to their being 'two lottery-based comparison groups—those who did not get the voucher due to their village not being selected for the program' and 'those who did not get the voucher due to losing the individual level lottery conducted within voucher villages' [Muralidharan & Sundararaman, 2015, p. 1023]).
6.   Recognised private schools in the villages were invited to participate in the voucher programme.
7.   Tests in Telugu, mathematics and English were conducted at the end of two and four years, while tests in science and social studies (called 'EVS' in the paper) and Hindi were given after four years.
8.   Household surveys were conducted once every year in a representative sample of households of the different sets of students, and data were collected from unannounced school visits conducted once a year in all schools in the 180 project villages.

Overall, 23% of government school children in the voucher villages were reassigned to private schools. The baseline tests (conducted when students were at the end of pre-school or at the end of primary grade 1) showed a highly significant difference of 0.65σ in favour of children in private over public schools (Muralidharan & Sundararaman, 2015, p. 1039 and Table II, p. 1027). For children receiving vouchers over the four years of the experiment, however, the conclusion is that differences in favour of private schools are not to do with features of private schools:

> After two and four years of the program, we find no difference between test scores of lottery winners and losers on Telugu (native language), math, English, and science/social studies, suggesting that the large cross-sectional differences in test scores across public and private schools mostly reflect omitted variables. (Muralidharan & Sundararaman, 2015, p. 1012)

However, apparently because they are able to more efficiently allocate time taught on other subjects, private schools in addition teach, inter alia, Hindi, whereas the public schools do not; unsurprisingly lottery-winning voucher students do better at Hindi then than those left in the public schools. Moreover, 'the mean cost per student in the private schools … was less than a third of the cost in public schools' (Muralidharan & Sundararaman, 2015, p. 1012). Hence the final conclusion:

> private schools in this setting deliver slightly better test score gains than their public counterparts (better on Hindi and same in other subjects), and do so at a substantially lower cost per student. (Muralidharan & Sundararaman, 2015, p. 1012)

This is the headline conclusion that as we noted above has been accepted by voucher proponents, as well as critics. We shall explore in the next section why this headline conclusion appears insupportable because some tests used were different for public and private school students.

3. The fundamental problem

Researchers wanting to compare achievements in public and private schools in India have long faced a dilemma: what language should be used for testing children in mathematics and other non-language subjects? (see e.g. Bashir, 1997; Dixon, 2003; Kingdon,1996). The dilemma arises because of differing mediums of instruction in public and private schools. Typically, the medium of instruction in public schools is a regional language, thus Telugu in rural Andhra Pradesh. Private schools on the other hand often purport to be English medium (although the reality is more complex, see below), but others are also (in Andhra Pradesh) Telugu medium. Hence, if a mathematics (or other non-language subject) test is given to children with written instructions in English, this may seem to privilege those from the English-medium private schools, whereas giving instructions in Telugu might appear to be biased against those used to receiving and understanding instructions in English.

Two common solutions have arisen to this dilemma:

1. Ensure that mathematics (and other non-language subject) tests are word-free, e.g. arithmetic operations only and/or wordless cognitive puzzles.
2. Ensure that the instructions given in mathematics (and other non-language subjects) tests are in both languages *on the same paper*, to ensure that students can choose which language to use for instructions on how to address each individual question.

Even in the second case, problems of translation will occur—it's hard for researchers (even those familiar with both languages) to be sure that word questions in mathematics have been identically translated, as it is known that even small changes in words (as well as other features of questions) in mathematics questions can drastically alter student success rates (see e.g. APU, 1988). For this reason, the first solution may be the most preferable even though it does limit the type of mathematical questions that can be asked, although the second is also used.

Nowhere in the paper is it explicitly mentioned, but as the problem is widely known, the assumption must be that the researchers solved this dilemma in one of these two standard ways. Unfortunately, they did not.

Recently, I asked one of the project researchers (acknowledged in Muralidharan and Sundararaman [2015, p. 1011]), to conduct tests to compare the low-cost private schools where I was working, with public schools, in Hyderabad, Andhra Pradesh. His team used different tests in mathematics for public and private schools, with instructions in English for the private schools (which were all, ostensibly at least, English medium) and Telugu for the public. He assured me that this was the method used in the Andhra Pradesh School Choice Project. This was confirmed by one of the authors: while the protocol was for schools and/or pupils to be given a choice of which paper to use, the language used in the mathematics (and other non-language) tests 'tended to follow the medium [of instruction] of the school, with English-medium private school students taking the test in English and Telugu-medium students taking the test in Telugu (the split was roughly 50% each)' (Karthik Muralidharan, personal communication; of the private schools, 50.4% were English medium [Karopady, 2014, p. 49]). Note, importantly, that this is not the same as the second solution to the language dilemma given above. There *both* languages are given on the *same* paper, so that all students still take the same test, but can choose which language to read. In the case in question, students took in effect different tests in mathematics and other non-language subjects.

The aim of creating a Randomised Controlled Trial is as far as possible to ensure that participants in treatment and control groups are treated in *exactly* the same way apart from the unique factor introduced as the intervention—in this case school vouchers. This study it appears has treated the treatment and control groups differently by using two different sorts of tests for mathematics and EVS: one in English, the other in Telugu. Even if it wasn't obvious in what ways this difference in treatment could lead to bias for one or other groups of participants, one would be justified calling into question the results. However, in this case, one can see clearly how the different tests could cause very serious bias.

If it was a comparison between performance in public and private schools in well-heeled urban communities it may be thought that it was less of a problem: the children in English-medium schools are being taught in English, so why shouldn't they be given tests in English? However, in poorer rural (or urban slum) areas of India, the 'English medium' appellation carried by low-cost private schools is typically more of an aspiration, at least in the lower grades, than a reality. As Karopady, from Azim Premji University, who had been closely involved with the project, (acknowledged for his 'constant support' [Muralidharan & Sundararaman, 2015, p. 1011]), put it:

> The medium of instruction is as claimed by the school authorities. In the rural setting, while these schools could have more transactions in English, *they are some distance from being truly English medium.* (Karopady, 2014, footnote 6, p. 52, emphasis added)

This is agreed. I have noted elsewhere, for instance, how it is an 'oft-repeated criticism' of low-cost private schools that they are 'English medium in name only' (Tooley, 2009, p. 179); I also reported that 'Observations in classrooms … suggest that schools describing themselves as English-medium use English only textbooks … with teachers offering a mixture of English and Urdu/Telugu to support their use …' (Tooley, Dixon, & Gomathi, 2007). The low-cost English-medium schools in fact operate as hybrid schools—teaching in the mother tongue in the lower grades, often using English textbooks translated by teachers into the mother tongue, with the aspiration of bringing everyone up to speed in English by higher grades.

Hence even in a simple comparison between public and private schools in rural areas, it would be unfair to give tests with English written instructions to children in private schools (supposedly English medium but in fact teaching in Telugu in the lower grades), as this would penalise them against those being given tests with Telugu instructions. In this particular voucher experiment, the situation appears even more difficult: 'Overall, the students who applied for and accepted the voucher had lower baseline test scores, suggesting that students with lower test scores were more likely to leave the public schools if given the opportunity to do so' (Muralidharan & Sundararaman, 2015, p. 1028). So children switching from Telugu-medium public to English-medium private schools were likely to have been of low achievement levels; for them, trying to figure out mathematics questions in English may have presented huge difficulties.

To illustrate the kind of problem faced by these voucher students when doing tests after being moved to English-language schools, I've translated three of the questions from the mathematics test into Telugu. (I'm assuming not many readers understand Telugu; if they do, they'll need to translate into a language they don't understand.) Readers will have no difficulty with questions like this one:

కింది పరిష్కరించండి

5.57+3 = _____

Although the instruction is in Telugu, it is in effect repeated in the mathematical language too, so as long as we know how to add together two numbers (whilst taking into account place value) we can get this one correct, irrespective of the language of the test (the Telugu says 'Solve the following').

But this next question is entirely different:

ఏ అంకెల సంఖ్య 2345 లో వంద స్థానంలో ఉంది ?

Without knowing Telugu it is simply impossible to answer, however good we are at mathematics. (The question is: Which digit is in the hundred's place in the number 2345?)

Similarly, we will not be able to solve this question, unless we are fluent in Telugu:

వైశాలి ఒక పెన్సిల్ విలువ రూ కొనుగోలు కోరుకుంటున్నారు. 4. ఎనిని 50 పైసల నాణేలు ఆమె పెన్సిల్ కొనుగోలు అవసరం ఉంటుంది ?

(Vaishali wants to buy a pencil worth Rs.4. How many 50 paise coins will she require to buy the pencil?)

The point is that the difficulties we have with these last two questions illustrate precisely the nature of the problem faced by voucher children moved to an English-medium private school. However good they are at mathematics, they will not get these answers correct, except of course through lucky guesses.

Of course, the argument could be framed in the opposite direction—that testing the children in English-medium private schools in Telugu would have been unfair, especially in the later years of the experiment, as by then voucher children's English may have improved because of their greater exposure to the language. However, it must not be assumed that the language children will learn in English lessons is the same language they will need in mathematics, or that there is equal degree of English-language immersion in language and non-language subjects, especially in the grades tested. It is plausible, for example, that mathematics' teachers were less fluent in English than the language subject teachers, and so placed a greater emphasis on teaching in Telugu than language teachers. Moreover, it is well known that the language used in mathematics lessons and tests is often very different from that used in English lessons. There are also problems of unknown or misunderstood vocabulary, with 'different meanings in everyday usage, as with even, odd, and function' (Math Solutions, 2009, p. 5); 'How many are left?' does not signify a directional question at all. A further difficulty is that the same mathematical concept can be conveyed using many different words—e.g. 'add', 'and', 'plus', 'sum', 'combine'. There are confusing mathematical and non-mathematical homonyms, such as 'sum/some' and 'whole/hole'. And mathematics questions often come 'embedded in language that makes the problem unclear or difficult to comprehend' (p. 5). Overall, those learning English as a second (or greater) language 'typically experience difficulty understanding and therefore solving word problems, and this difficulty increases in later grades of elementary school as the word problems become more linguistically and conceptually complex' (p. 6), out of synch with the language taught in the corresponding grade English lessons.

The key points are, first, the only fair way of assessing the students in different language-medium schools would be to follow one of the two methods outlined above, using word-free tests, or using tests with both languages translated side-by-side. As this was not done, secondly, we *simply do not know* what the impact of having used these different tests will be on student performance. This therefore leads to the following re-phrasing of the headline findings of the Andhra Pradesh School Choice Project, given that the results are for both English- *and* Telugu-medium private schools combined, compared to Telugu-medium only public schools:

- In Telugu, the regional language, there is *no significant difference* between achievement of those in public schools and those receiving vouchers to attend private schools. However, private schools spend significantly less time on Telugu so they are *much more efficient* than public schools.
- In mathematics and EVS, we *do not know* what advantage or otherwise the private or public schools have. As children took different tests, *there is no basis for comparison*.
- In English, the international language, children with vouchers in private schools *perform slightly better* than those in public schools.
- In Hindi, the national language, children with vouchers in private schools *perform better* than those in public schools. (This is not surprising, however, given that public schools do not teach Hindi.)

That is, in the five subjects tested in year 4, voucher children in private schools perform (at least slightly) better in two (international and national languages) and the same in one (regional language); in the other two non-language subjects, we cannot tell what the difference is.

In fact, the finding in English may also not be robust, because of further difficulties with the English test. The English tests (as well as the other subjects) 'were carefully designed to assess the common curriculum in government and private schools so as to ensure that there was genuine comparability' (Karopady, 2014, p. 49). But this presents an immediate difficulty for English as opposed to other subjects: English is taught in private schools from Class I whereas in public schools only from Class III (p. 50). The *same* tests administered in public and private schools would then bring in problems of potential bias: if the tests covered what the private school children had covered, then they would be unfair to the public school children. If they measure what public schools have covered by Class III, then they would be too easy for the private school children, leading to a ceiling effect on what they were able to demonstrate. It turns out that there may well have been such a ceiling effect. The researchers, aware of the low level of achievement of all students, designed the tests to include items from the tested grade and several lower grades too (personal communication, Karthik Muralidharan). This means that the English results are likely to underestimate the true private school effect.

It is obviously disappointing that we can't say anything about mathematics (or science and social studies). However, as roughly half the students in private schools (those in Telugu-medium private schools), *did* take the same mathematics and science/social studies tests as those in public schools, can't we look at the results for these children to get a fairer comparison between public and private? Helpfully the researchers did explicitly compare these groups, with revealing results.

4. Suggestive results comparing like with like

The researchers did disaggregate results for the Telugu- and English-medium private schools, and found rather interesting results. It is important to stress that the discussion in this section, following the caveats in Muralidharan and Sundararaman (2015, pp. 1047–1055), is *suggestive* only, ('some suggestive patterns emerge in the results' [p. 1054]), for two major reasons: first, the standard errors, when following a 'conservative IV [instrumental variable] strategy' are 'too large for meaningful inference' (p. 1054); moreover, even 'with a precise IV estimate', the researchers note that the medium of instruction of the school 'is correlated with other school characteristics' (p. 1054). However, reinforcing the above discussion that the different tests used may have distorted the results, they note that in general English-medium schools 'have *superior* indicators of school quality—including facilities; teacher experience, qualifications, and salary; and annual fees charged per child' (p. 1054). It is counter-intuitive to expect student outcomes in these better equipped schools to be lower than in schools with fewer advantages.

The results disaggregating children in English-medium and Telugu-medium private schools are as follows:

> At the end of four years of the voucher program, we find that the causal impact of attending an English-medium private school varies sharply by subject, with students doing worse (than staying in the public school) in Telugu, math and EVS but much better in English and Hindi. The mean impact across subjects is positive (0.22σ) but not significant. (Muralidharan & Sundararaman, 2015, p. 1051)

We must reinforce again the point raised above that the mathematics and EVS scores here are called into question. Because the children took different tests in the English-medium private and Telugu-medium public schools, we simply do not know about the relative achievement of children in public and private in mathematics and EVS.

However,

> On the other hand, the estimated impact of attending a Telugu-medium private school is positive for every subject, and the mean impact across subjects is positive (0.53σ) and significant. (Muralidharan & Sundararaman, 2015, p. 1051)

Table 1. Comparing like with like. Telugu-medium private schools and public schools: impact on test scores in standard deviations of attending private school with a voucher compared to public school.

	Telugu	Math	English	EVS	Hindi	Combined all subjects	Combined math/EVS
Year 2	−0.033	0.062	0.408	n/a	n/a	0.143	
	−	+	+			+	
Year 4	0.259	0.255	0.043	0.746**	1.384***	0.532***	0.496*
	+	+	+	+	+	+	+

***Significant at the 0.01 level; **significant at the 0.05 level; *significant at the 0.1 level.

Because in the Telugu-medium private schools all tests were the same as those in the public schools, and there was no confounding variable introduced of medium of instruction, it is fair (although only suggestive, for the reasons given above) to compare children in Telugu-medium private schools with those in public schools. Table 1 (simplifying the researchers' Table X [Muralidharan & Sundararaman, 2015, p. 1052]), shows the results of comparing like with like.

The results can be summarised as follows:

- In year 2, estimated score differences between private and public schools are positive in favour of those having vouchers for all subjects apart from Telugu.
- By year 4, estimated score differences are positive for every subject, and the mean impact when subjects are combined is large and positive (0.53 standard deviations) and statistically significant. Importantly, this is not simply the effect of Hindi distorting the results: combining mathematics and EVS also gives a large (0.50 standard deviations), positive, and statistically significant difference, albeit at the 10% level (Muralidharan & Sundararaman, 2015, p. 1052, Table X).

Children with vouchers in the private schools outperformed those in the public schools *in all subjects after four years of the voucher programme*; the combined result shows a large, statistically significant difference in favour of private schools. This is a hugely positive, albeit suggestive, finding for the voucher debate.

The authors see the significance of these findings as follows: 'students who switched from attending a public school to a Telugu-medium private school did better than those attending an English-medium one (especially on non-language subjects)'. This suggests for the researchers that 'private schools may have been even more effective when students did not experience the disruption of changing their medium of instruction' (Muralidharan & Sundararaman, 2015, p. 1015).

Ceteris paribus, this might be a useful explanation to explore in terms of 'education psy-chology literature, which suggests that first-generation learners may be better off being taught in their native language, which can be reinforced at home' (Muralidharan & Sundararaman, 2015, p. 1055). But other things were not equal; as already discussed, children in English-medium private schools were given different tests to those in the Telugu-medium schools, so we simply do not know what their relative performance actually was. As indicated above, there may not be a major difference between the language of instruction for younger children in the (supposedly) English-medium private schools and the Telugu-medium private and public schools, so testing them in different languages is likely to be unfair. All are likely to be taught, at least predominantly, in their mother tongue, perhaps in one case using

English-language textbooks. Hence, because of the research implementation using different tests, we are not able to confirm whether or not the school language of instruction actually impacts on student performance given these results.

5. Miscellany of minor issues

Some other issues may be worth highlighting, in lesser detail (given space constraints), each of which illustrates the difficulties that need to be overcome in order to produce 'gold standard' research in this area.

5.1. Pupil attrition

One of the major difficulties that arose in this research—and which perhaps could not reasonably have been anticipated—is pupil attrition. The researchers write: 'We attempted to administer the written tests to the full set of students' (Muralidharan & Sundararaman, 2015, p. 1029), but initially failed to do so because of high levels of student attrition (of around 40%), most of which was caused by 'students who had migrated and could not be found, as opposed to students still attending schools but not present for testing' (footnote 18, p. 1029). Given this, the researchers then had to mount an 'intense effort … to track down all the students who had applied for the voucher'. Once done, they had to conduct an additional round of testing in each village outside school hours. The same process—this time not unexpectedly—was required in year 4 of the scheme (footnote 18, p. 1029).

5.2. Class size

In the research, 'a large fraction (23%) of public school students moved out to private schools' (Muralidharan & Sundararaman, 2015, p. 1045). *Prima facie*, then, one would assume as a result class sizes had *decreased* in public schools and *increased* in private schools, which could have led to bias against private schools and certainly would have violated the principles of Randomised Controlled Trials, of keeping as much as possible the same for both control and treatment groups. However, the authors 'verify that being in treatment villages does not change the average of several key school characteristics between treatment and control villages over the course of the study (results available on request)' (footnote 19, p. 1030). Two reasons are given for the lack of private school class size *increase*: first, private schools 'used the additional resources provide by the voucher payments to … keep enrolments constant' (footnote 19, p. 1030). Anecdotally, I've rarely heard of a private proprietor who didn't want to get more income, so it seems odd that any would turn pupils away. Second, the private schools hired 'enough staff so that average characteristics (such as class size) did not change on average'. This also doesn't gel with my experience, as typically low-cost private schools in villages do not operate at full capacity. So if a school gets more children (on vouchers) then they would fill up spaces rather than employ extra teachers to create new classes (especially as it is stipulated that no class had more than 25% of its enrolment as voucher kids).

5.3. KG or not?

Did the public school children attend kindergarten or not? There appears to be a contradiction in the paper here. On the one hand, the authors write:

> a major limitation in the cross-sectional comparisons is that private school students typically have two years of pre-school education (nursery and kindergarten) *compared to public school students (who typically start in the first grade)*. Thus, comparisons of test score levels at a given primary school grade confound the effectiveness of private schools and the total years of schooling. (Muralidharan & Sundararaman, 2015, footnote 9, p. 1018, emphasis added)

In passing we can note that it doesn't seem an impossible task to control for this variable (ask the children and/or the families how many years of schooling they have had, including pre-schooling). But more importantly, on the other hand we are also told that for children in both private *and* public school samples, 'The cohorts covered were students attending kindergarten and grade 1 in the previous school year (2007–08)' (footnote 13, p. 1021). In other words all children tested, both public and private, were in school, either anganwadi (public pre-school) or private kindergarten. This is confirmed in other reports of the same research: 'A baseline test … was administered during March–April 2008 to children in anganwadi or KG' (Karopady, 2014, p. 49). Indeed, the experiment 'was *intended* for students who were studying in anganwadis or in KG in the academic year 2007–08 and who had intended to study in government schools' (p. 49, emphasis added). Hence, whether it is true or not, as the authors claim, that in general children in public schools don't attend pre-school, for the chosen sample this was not true—they were actually selected whilst in a public or private pre-school.

6. Conclusion: discussion and implications

While the recent DFID-commissioned 'rigorous literature review' (Day Ashley et al., 2014) reported that children in private outperform those in public schools, this conclusion is based on findings from a relatively small number of studies, none of which has been experimentally-based. One recently published study aimed to fill this lacuna. Muralidharan and Sundararaman (2015) conducted an experiment to ascertain the impact of 'School Choice' in Andhra Pradesh, India. They used the 'gold standard' research method of Randomised Controlled Trials (RCTs), with an innovative two-stage randomisation procedure. The headline results reportedly showed that children given vouchers to attend private schools did not in general outperform those left in public schools. However, private schools delivered the same results as public schools at a third of the cost, so reforms to allow vouchers in private schools will be more cost effective than public schools.

However, it turns out that the same tests were not used for children in public and private schools, violating a key principle of Randomised Controlled Trials, that the different groups should be treated in exactly the same way. This means that the headline results are called into question: roughly half of the private schools ('English medium') used non-language tests with English instructions, whereas the public schools and the remaining private schools ('Telugu medium') were given tests with instructions in Telugu. This means that like was not compared with like, and so we are unable to say what the differences are between public and private in non-language subjects.

Fortunately, the researchers were able to disaggregate the results in English-medium and Telugu-medium private schools, although these results are subject to important caveats so are suggestive only. Comparing the results for children in Telugu-medium private schools with those in public schools, where exactly the same tests had been given, children given vouchers to attend private schools achieved better in *all* subjects (Telugu, mathematics, English, science/social studies and Hindi) than those left in public schools. In other words, these findings are suggestive that voucher children in private schools significantly outperform those in public schools, for a fraction of the cost.

The issue of cost needs to be addressed. The private schools in the sample had an average annual cost (which presumably is more or less equivalent to the average annual fee) of around Rs.1849 per child, or Rs.185 per month over 10 months (about USD 4 per month using historical exchange rates) (Muralidharan & Sundararaman, 2015, Table III, p. 1031). This was significantly lower than the average annual cost of public schools (at Rs.8390 per child). Certainly, on average, schools in the sample are low-cost (see Tooley and Longfield [2016] for a discussion of 'low-cost').

One of the ways in which such schools are able to keep costs low is by paying teachers lower wages than in government schools (Muralidharan & Sundararaman, 2015, p. 1032), which some view as exploitative (Day Ashley et al., 2014, pp. 21–22). Indeed, in India this comparative advantage of low-cost private schools *prima facie* appeared to be outlawed under the 'Right of Children to Free and Compulsory Education Act' (2009), usually known as the Right to Education Act (RTE). Under RTE, regulations for private schools have been created which are focused on input measures, including teacher qualifications and salaries. As it stands, this would seem to make the operation of many low-cost private schools illegal, and thousands of unregistered schools have been closed as a result (see e.g. Francis, 2014). However, the *prima facie* emphasised above is important. Under the Indian constitution, although states are obliged to implement the Act, they are permitted flexibility in interpreting and modifying the regulations, provided that the basic provisions are not violated. At least two states, Gujarat and Rajasthan, have significantly modified the regulations, allowing in some cases schools to be judged in large part on their student outcomes rather than on inputs (see Gujarat Government, 2012, Appendix 1). In these states, and if this approach to the regulations became more widely accepted, then it would appear that low-cost private schools could continue as before in the way they pay teachers, provided of course that they achieve high enough student outcomes.

Muralidharan and Sundararaman (2015) note some policy prescriptions of their research findings:

> Our results on private school productivity suggest that it may be possible to substantially increase human capital formation in developing countries like India by making more use of private provision in the delivery of education. (p. 1058)

However, they note important caveats to this, including:

> there may be a trade-off between a libertarian approach to school choice that believes that parents will make optimal schooling choices for their children and a paternalistic one that believes that parents (especially poor and uneducated ones) may make misguided evaluations of school quality based on visible factors that may not contribute to more effective learning. (pp. 1061–1062).

They continue:

> While we find that private schools are much more productive than public schools from the perspective of a social planner, it is not obvious that they represent a better value for the marginal

parent *who is paying for private schools* over a free public school. Since test scores did not improve in math and Telugu, the marginal parent would have to place a high value on Hindi scores to justify paying for the typical private school in our sample. Although we cannot rule out this possibility (or that parents valued other non-academic aspects of private schools), it is also possible that *parents were not able to easily determine the effectiveness of schools at improving learning outcomes* …. (p. 1062, emphasis added)

Two points can be made about this caveat. First, the suggestion of this paper is that we do not know what the results for test scores in mathematics were, given that different tests were used in English- and Telugu-medium schools, so it is not clear if parents are really so poor at judging school effectiveness. However, there are suggestive results, comparing only Telugu-medium schools, which point to improved performance in all subjects when the same tests are used; this could well be the outcome of an experiment in private schools in general which overcame the problem of using different tests.

Second, this caveat also raises a possible conflation of two different meanings of school choice. In the research paper, the 'School Choice' of the title means choice through top-down reform, where children are given vouchers to leave public to go to private schools, and it is this major policy debate which is of concern to the authors. However, this is not the only kind of school choice—the other is where parents choose to go to private schools and pay out of their own funds. Elsewhere I have dubbed these two approaches 'School Choice' (the capitals signifying a top-down approach, where typically governments fund parents through vouchers etc., to attend private school) and 'school choice' (small letters indicating the spontaneous order of parents choosing private schools and paying themselves) (Tooley, 2014).

It is worth making this distinction because in this paper it appears the implications of findings from the first kind of School Choice through top-down reform are illegitimately being transferred across to the second kind of spontaneous choices of parents. The authors suggest that their research findings raise questions about whether the 'marginal parent' is justified *paying fees* to send their child to private school. But parents paying fees for schools was not the object of this research, which was instead based on parents receiving vouchers, a completely different approach. Results of an experiment on vouchers (School Choice) won't necessarily apply to parents paying fees (school choice).

In fact, some results are given in passing for this spontaneous kind of 'school choice'. For instance the authors report that there are 'large cross-sectional differences in math and Telugu test scores (of 0.65σ)' (Muralidharan & Sundararaman, 2015, p. 1039) on the baseline tests in favour of private schools, when students had been in either Grade 1 or pre-school for a full year. But, they argue, as their overall findings show no academic benefit to *voucher* children being in private schools, this suggests that these large differences in favour of private schools 'are mostly driven by omitted variables and not by differential effectiveness of public and private schools' (p. 1039). Given the doubts raised about their headline research findings, it may be that these 'omitted variables' are not as important as had been thought.

This kind of conflation can be seen in popular commentaries on the research (there is no suggestion that the current researchers agree with these commentaries). One author notes that 'contrary to popular perception, private schools are not adding value, as compared to government schools … after adjusting for socio-economic factors' (Karopady, 2014, p. 51), and asks: 'If private schools are not adding any value, why then do parents still prefer them?' (p. 52). The *Times of India* points to parents' misguided choices of private schools which 'ironically, have little to do with outcomes' (Chowdhury, 2015).

Again, these are conflating the two types of school choice. The results referred to are about children using vouchers, not about children whose parents have paid for private school. Indeed, Karopady himself concurs that, after adjusting for socio-economic factors, the children in private schools by their parents' volition (i.e. those paying school fees) perform 'significantly better than their government school counterparts in all four subjects' (Karopady, 2014, p. 51). However, just as for Muralidharan and Sundararaman (2015), for Karopady the results from the voucher experiment bring into question this superior private school performance: 'The findings seem to indicate that the reasons for better performance of … children … who would have gone to private school in any case … may need to be looked for outside the school' (Karopady, 2014, p. 52). Again, perhaps not to the extent envisaged.

The recent research from Muralidharan and Sundararaman (2015) adds significantly to the research literature on the impact of low-cost private schools. Although the research implementation was hampered by using different tests in non-language subjects for children in different school types, within the research paper there are findings which suggest that when families are offered vouchers to allow them to access private schools, significantly higher academic achievement compared to those children left in public schools is achieved, at only a fraction of the per capita cost of public education. This suggests that allowing children to access private schools using vouchers could be an important policy reform improving educational opportunities and outcomes for the poor.

Notes

1. We follow international convention, as did Muralidharan and Sundararaman (2015), rather than the conventions used in Britain and India, and describe government schools as 'public', to be contrasted with private schools.
2. The study was conducted before the bifurcation of this state—which now consists of two states, Telangana and one still called Andhra Pradesh.

Disclosure statement

No potential conflict of interest was reported by the author.

References

Assessment of Performance Unit (APU). (1988). *Mathematical development; A review of monitoring in mathematics. 1978–1982, Parts 1 and 2.* Slough: NFER.
Bashir, S. (1997). The cost effectiveness of public and private schools: Knowledge gaps, new research methodologies and an application in India. In C. Colclough (Ed.), *Marketizing education and health in developing countries: Miracle of mirage?* (pp. 124–164). Oxford: Clarendon Press.
Chowdhury, S. R. (2015, February 27). Private schools are not adding value: Study. *Times of India.*

Day Ashley, L., Mcloughlin, C., Aslam, M., Engel, J., Wales, J., Rawal, S. ... Rose, P. (2014). *The role and impact of private schools in developing countries: A rigorous review of the evidence.* London: Department for International Development.

Dixon, P. (2003). *The regulation of private schools for low-income families in Andhra Pradesh, India: An Austrian economic approach* (Unpublished PhD thesis). Newcastle University, UK.

Francis, A. (2014, March 6). Why India's landmark education law is shutting down schools. *BBC News.* Retrieved from http://www.bbc.com/news/world-asia-india-26333713

Gujarat Government. (2012, February 18). *The Gujarat Government Gazette Extraordinary, LIII*(54). Retrieved from http://gujarat-education.gov.in/education/Portal/News/159_1_MODEL%20 RULES%2029.2.12.PDF

Karopady, D. D. (2014, December 20). Does school choice help rural children from disadvantaged sections: Evidence from longitudinal research in Andhra Pradesh. *Economic and Political Weekly, XLIX*(51), 46–52.

Kingdon, G. (1996). The quality and efficiency of private and public education: A case study in urban India. *Oxford Bulletin of Economics and Statistics, 58,* 57–81.

Mantri, R., & Gupta, H. (2014, January 6). Azim Premji, please listen to Steve Jobs and Bill Gates: Not about technology, but about your educational philanthropy. *Livemint.* Retrieved from http://www.livemint.com/Opinion/301G41LuZJGgs8qLE3clxN/Azim-Premji-please-listen-to-Steve-Jobs-and-Bill-Gates.html

Math Solutions. (2009). Teaching math to English language learners. In *Supporting English language learners in math class, Grades K–2.* Math Solutions.

Muralidharan, K., & Sundararaman, V. (2015). The aggregate effect of school choice: Evidence from a two-stage experiment in India. *Quarterly Journal of Economics, 130,* 1011–1066.

Shah, P. (2015, February 27). Retrieved from http://spontaneousorder.in/private-schools-are-not-adding-value-you-be-the-judge/

Tooley, J. (2009). *The beautiful tree: A personal journey into how the world's poorest people are educating themselves.* New Delhi: Penguin.

Tooley, J. (2014). The role of government in education revisited: The theory and practice of vouchers, with pointers to another solution for American education. *Social Philosophy and Policy, 31,* 204–228.

Tooley, J., Dixon, P., & Gomathi, S. V. (2007). Private schools and the millennium development goal of universal primary education: A census and comparative survey in Hyderabad, India. *Oxford Review of Education, 33,* 539–560.

Tooley, J., & Longfield, D. (2015). *The role and impact of private schools in developing countries: A response to the DFID-Commissioned 'Rigorous literature review'.* London: Pearson.

Tooley, J., & Longfield, D. (2016). Affordability of private schools: Exploration of a conundrum and towards a definition of 'low-cost'. *Oxford Review of Education, 42,* 444–459.

Non-state actors, and the advance of frontier higher education markets in the global south

Susan L. Robertson ⓘ and Janja Komljenovic

ABSTRACT

This paper examines the growth of global non-state and multilateral actors in the 'global south' and the creation of frontier markets in the higher education sector. These developments are part of market-making changes in higher education as the sector is opened to new actors, logics, and innovative services, aimed at 'the global south'. Yet making a higher education market that brings in new investors, providers, and consumers from within and across the global north and south is a complex process that requires imagining and materialising through new social devices, norms, and institutions so that the higher education sector works like a capitalist market based on competition, credit, commodification, and creativity. The paper examines these processes through three entry points: recruiters of international students; for-profit providers of HE; and financial agents providing new forms of credit. We argue that these developments both play off, and reinforce, older and newer asymmetries of power between individuals, social groups, and nations, within and between the global north and south, creating an even greater learning divide.

Introduction

This paper examines the growth of global non-state and multilateral actors in the higher education sector and the creation of frontier markets in the global south (Marber, 2014). These developments are part of 'market-making' changes in higher education as the sector is opened to new actors, logics, and innovative education services aimed at 'the global south' (Connell, 2007a, 2007b; Santos, 2014).

Yet making a higher education market that also brings in new investors, providers, and consumers from within and across the global north and south is a complex process (see Komljenovic & Robertson, 2015; Robertson & Komljenovic, 2016). As Beckert (2013) shows, it requires imagining and materialising through the creation and deployment of new social devices, norms, and institutions, so that the higher education sector increasingly works like a capitalist market based upon competition, credit, commodification, and creativity.

We begin by elaborating our use of the concepts, 'global north' and 'global south'. We then bring these concepts into conversation with wider political, economic, and technological conditions for the ongoing expansion of capitalist market-making processes in geographically-located higher education sectors. We then introduce three case studies to explore these processes, and the corresponding non-state actors who work in, on, and through, the global north and south: (i) lubricating the wheels of student mobility via 'recruiters' and 'brokers'; (ii) lubricating the wheels of new 'providers' in the sector who put into place very different higher education practices targeted at a different student demographic; and (iii) lubricating the wheels of student access via new modalities of credit, involving new relationships between education investors and debtors.

We conclude by arguing that there are also considerable frictions confronting these projects, as not only must market-making contend with existing imaginaries and practices regarding the public good nature of higher education and how it should be invested in, but when rogue traders, failed markets, increased indebtedness, and wealth inequalities are made visible, these act as a contrast to, and also shed light upon, these very different projects and their social relations for the north and the south.

The 'global south'—a social, spatial, and relational concept

The idea of the global south has several distinct, though related, meanings and it is important to distinguish them so as to avoid flattening class and other relations in any one territorial space.

The more commonly shared meaning of the 'global south' refers to a large number of territorially-located countries in Africa, Central and South America, and Asia, who face major economic and other development challenges. Reference to the global south here is nevertheless a relational concept, in that the level of development that is being referred is contrasted with other parts of the world—Europe and North America in particular—who in turn constitute the 'global north'. Around 160 of a total of 195 independently recognised states are broadly included in the global south; the other 35 countries make up the global north—often also referred to as the OECD, or rich countries, club[1] (Woodward, 2009).

A second meaning of the concept 'global south' is also social and relational, but in this case we use it to refer to those communities/populations whose circumstances (economic, cultural, political, technological), when compared to the rest of the population in that territory, are highly precarious and marginal. In this case, the global south can also mean individuals and communities in developed countries. Examples include groups living on or under the poverty line,[2] asylum seekers who have limited access to social welfare, or ethnic and other groups who find themselves marginalised from the mainstream in what are otherwise wealthy countries.[3] Alternatively we might see a global north in the geographic global south; for example, the gated communities and exclusive education aimed at local and international political and economic elites in countries such as Nigeria, South Africa or Brazil.

In this paper we will show that it is not only the emerging middle class and elites in the geographic global south who are the targets of the new for-profit providers and recruiters and recruiting universities from the north, or universities located in those cities and countries—for example the University of Johannesburg in South Africa, who exercise a degree of hegemony across the region. The horizon has expanded to include poorer and marginalised populations in the geographic north with the offer of specially developed online programmes, and credit via new financial products to fund their studies. Similarly, new for-profit providers in the United States have focused a great deal of attention in their marketing strategies on aspirational minority groups in the US who have historically not participated in higher education (Deming, Goldin, & Katz, 2011).

Higher education and the global south

It follows from our argument so far we are not only examining the role of non-state actors in exploiting frontier markets in low-income countries. Rather we are also focusing attention on those populations in the south and the north who have historically *not* accessed higher education, and who have become the object of attention by the higher education recruiters and brokers, investors, and for-profit providers. In doing so we are not suggesting that the inclusion of otherwise excluded groups from higher education is a bad thing. Far from it. Rather, we are pointing to the tendency in frontier market-making to exploit the aspirations of the marginalised populations by offering them often inferior higher education experiences at significantly higher costs and levels of indebtedness.

The broad contours of the higher education sector in the global south, both historically and recently, have been shaped by the dominance of a hegemonic global north (aka 'the west', 'developed west', etc.), with its civilisational project—modernity—and its privileging of western science as the engine of progress and principle form of reasoning (Araya & Marber, 2013; Santos, 2004). And though many countries in the south had their own institutions of higher learning for the political and cultural elite well before the creation of the medieval and modern European universities—from Pakistan to China, India, Egypt, and Vietnam— these were eventually to be eclipsed by the globalising of a particular set of localisms from within the West around a particular set of ideas[4] defining a university, with its distinctive forms of knowledge production, and relations to the wider world. In most cases, expanding empires and their colonial projects into Africa, Latin America, Oceania, and Asia drove these movements and transformations. They also bought with them western disciplinary-based knowledges, and created new dependencies through alignments with universities in the global north. This included educating the university's faculty in the north, funded as part of a university's international mission, or by national and regional aid programmes (for example, the Colombo Plan, established in 1950 to provide development support to the Asia Pacific Region, including scholarships for further studies).

However, many universities in the global south were highly dependent on state funding, and it was this relationship to the state which would become problematic for institutional survival by the early 1990s (Robertson, 2009; Salmi, Hopper, & Malee Bassett, 2009; Samoff & Carrol, 2003). Many of the low-income countries in the global south found themselves in the vortex of structural adjustment programmes and the limits that were placed on state investment in higher education; a condition placed on them by the World Bank and the conditionalities it imposed (Robertson et al., 2007).

By the early 1990s, the twin effect of neoliberal structural adjustment policies, on the one hand, and little or limited state investment, on the other, generated a crisis in the sector with a preferred set of solutions regarding its resolution: embracing the private sector as a provider; leveraging new sources of funds through loans and other fiscal arrangements; cross border higher education trade; funded studies abroad and other initiatives; and capacity building partnerships with the global north (Lancrin, 2005). The wide embrace of 'knowledge economy' policies in many countries—with knowledge now regarded as a crucial pillar of human development worldwide (World Bank, 2002,

p. ix)—the turn to trade in services—including in higher education—for the global north, the growing dominance of English as a global lingua franca, together with pressures to acquire symbolic capital in the form of an education in a 'western' institution to power social mobility, all injected new momentum into the already existing uneven relationship between and within the global north and global south. Yet we do not want to suggest that this newer way of thinking about the economy and society, the legitimacy of a neoliberal market society, and the role of higher education in it, could be or was manufactured overnight. Rather these projects have demanded considerable work—ideologically, materially, and institutionally—in the face of competing and existing projects—as we show below.

From old to new HE imaginaries

Social imaginaries organise collective understanding and meaning-making; social imaginaries also descriptively normalise things as they are and normatively frame them as they should be (Taylor, 2002). Imaginaries cater for emergence, existence, and the legitimation of multiple ideologies and they also condition common sense. Once sedimented into the DNA of any society through its institutions and cultural frames, they make it difficult to imagine possibilities beyond them as they curtail questions that are asked at a societal level and the possible answers that are considered viable (Stein & de Andreotti, 2015).

Beckert (2013) argues that shaping imaginaries, and thus the decisions of individual actors, is a particularly important task in capitalist dynamics, as capitalism as an economic system depends upon being able to anticipate that the future will be like the present, though by definition the future *is* the future and can only be anticipated, and not known. Beckert (1996, 2013) draws attention to the ways in which political regulators and their speech acts in the field of the economy aim to shape the decisions, expectations, and actions of actors, and the social and political structures underlying and reproducing those expectations. This demands a great deal of ideological and institutional work, and particularly so in seeking to bring a sector like higher education into the economic field as a commodity. He identifies four Cs of capitalism—commodification, credit, creativity, and competition—which lubricate the wheels of capitalism and which need to orient expectations to ensure ongoing accumulation (Beckert, 2013).

Imaginings work at multiple levels—from the macro- to the meso- and micro-levels (Komljenovic & Robertson, 2015). The idea of a knowledge-based economy (Jessop, Fairclough, & Wodak, 2008; Jessop & Sum, 2014) emerged as a distinct imaginary advanced at the macro-structural level by the OECD and those member countries (the USA, UK, Australia, New Zealand, and Canada) who have sought to position themselves as services economies in contrast to their former status as primarily producers of goods. Since the late 1980s, higher education has also been constructed as part of a globally-competitive services sector represented in global trade figures (Hughes, Porter, Jones, & Sheen, 2013). This has meant viewing higher education, not as a public good or public service, but as a commodity that can be bought and sold in the marketplace, with sophisticated market intelligence, marketing strategies and systems of credit to oil the wheels of its ongoing expansion. Locking in higher education as an economic good to be managed by the market, and not challenged by politics, is the objective of ongoing global and regional trade negotiations (Robertson & Komljenovic, 2015).

A raft of technologies has also been creatively developed and promoted over the past 30 years aimed at promoting competition, commodification, and credit through institutionalising this political project, through social devices and norms that shape, and ensure, its ongoing social reproduction. This includes technologies like university rankings (Hazelkorn, 2009); global competitiveness indexes dependent on proxies like publications in international (English language/US scientific) journals that align knowledge production with global competition (Schwab & Sala-i-Martín, 2014); benchmarks and indicators such as the OECD's *Education at a Glance* (OECD, 2015); and the EU's indicators (DG EAC, 2014) which normalise ideas like competition, efficiency, consumerism, individualism, privatisation, innovation, talent, knowledge, student loans, and debt. Such competition is for a bigger possible share of international students, a higher place in university rankings, higher student enrolment rates, a higher share of public and private investment in education, and so on.

The knowledge economy imaginary also normalises competition in regional, national, and institutional infrastructures, in turn shaping actors' expectations about theirs and others' futures. This can be evidenced in institutional, national, and supranational policies, programmes, and practices, where the direction of travel is 'a race to the top' as a globally-competitive knowledge economy (Australian Government, 2015; HM Government, 2013b). Higher education is reframed as an object of national or regional competitiveness governance, where competitiveness and commodification favour market forces over other criteria of judgement (Jessop & Sum, 2014; Sum & Jessop, 2013).

Market-making also requires those who are the object of such discourses to 'buy into', and thus 'buy', these ways of looking at the world. Here Howarth (2009) draws attention to psycho-social processes, like fantasy. Similarly Beckert (2013) points to the ways in which desiring and imagining a better life become the rationale for indebtedness, with the expectation (fictional as one cannot know what the future will actually hold) this will be a good investment for the future. Concepts like fantasy and desire enable us to explore how personal/individual, institutional, national, and regional wishes and desires are mobilised through marketing and recruitment campaigns which speak to aspirations to 'do well', to 'be western', to acquire the status of 'a good English speaker', and so on, which in turn reproduce and strengthen 'global north' and 'global south' relations now shaped through market imaginaries and relations.

Lubricating the wheels of market-making in the global south

So far we have argued that the global south is a target for many new non-state actors to expand markets. In this section we explore key processes at work through three new kinds of actors in the HE sector: (i) recruiters/brokers for international student recruitment; (ii) new for-profit providers; and (iii) new forms of credit available from new kinds of investors. And whilst they do not exhaust the new actors and processes in the sector, they reveal a great deal about how the global south is 'spoken to' and enrolled in capitalist market relations. The data for this section come from selected policies, interviews conducted over 2014, and from secondary data and analyses.

Lubricating the wheels 1: creating a pipeline—recruiters/brokers

In this first case we focus particularly on the rise of international student mobility and the role of recruiters as specialised agencies who now interact with universities and other HE providers. An international student recruitment agent is:'... an individual, company, or organization that provides educational advice, support, and placement to students in a local market who are interested in studying abroad'(De Luca, 2008, p. 36). In the past, agents mainly sent people abroad to undertake language training courses. What we report here is a relatively new phenomenon in the higher education sector (since the late 1980s starting in Australia and the UK). Agents began to sense students were looking for opportunities to study at a university in a foreign country as a result of factors such as limited home capacity, the desire for social mobility, and learning English as competitive advantage in the labour market. Much of the industry literature frames this in terms of the growth of a middle class in these countries, with aspirations for education and the resources to spend (OECD, 2014). This dynamic has created opportunities for recruiting agents to expand their business to include HE studies more generally.

Despite this emerging phenomenon, few studies focus attention on the role of recruitment agents. As a result, we know little about how many of the four and a half million internationally mobile students (OECD, 2015) use agents, and whether or not agents are influential in students' decision-making. This matters in that many institutions spend increasing amounts of money on international student recruiters.

The British Council, in a report in 2011, found that '... 48% of interviewed East Asian students had contacts with an agent, compared to 41% in Africa, 39% in South Asia, 30% in Latin America, and 23% in Europe'(ACA, 2011). Pimpa (2003) report that recruitment agents and peers are the most influential factors for Thai students in Australia, and that agents exercise a stronger influence than peers. The Observatory on Borderless Higher Education (2014) found that 56% of international students in Malaysia are recruited by agents, 56% of international students in Australia, 47% in New Zealand, 41% in Canada, 38% in the UK, 20% in the Netherlands, and 11% in the USA. Agents have thus become increasingly more important and powerful players in international student mobility flows over time (Thomson, Hulme, Hulme, & Doughty, 2014).

Recruiters have also expanded their orbit of interests and influence—from one largely based on the colonial relations of language to now a newer, though no less colonial and imperialistic economic project. Nevertheless, the practice of using agents is controversial in most 'receiving' countries (see Chopra, 2015; Raimo, 2014), in that what is implied is that commercial interests and 'hard sell' trump academic standards at universities and enable immigration scams. This is indicative of the struggles and frictions present when a market is being constructed in a sector where previously the language of price/consumerism/competitive markets has been an alien idea.

A given market becomes stable when the product gains legitimacy with customers (Fligstein, 2001). In the case of transforming public sectors into capitalist market relations, this means securing legitimacy within the public realm. Cultural acceptance of using recruitment agents depends on 'instituting' this market in specific locations, to use Polanyi's (1944) terminology. Where there is growing thickening or 'institutedness' of higher education institutions—in particular the UK, USA, Canada, Australia, and New Zealand—we can see recruiting agents also being more freely used.

In the UK, agents are an explicit part of government strategies (HM Government, 2013a, 2013b). The British Council, a public agency which has historically promoted and provided English-language courses, now manages an agents' database, provides training for agents, and issues 'good practice' guidance for agents and universities (British Council, 2015; Raimo, Humfrey, & Huang, 2014). Thomson et al. (2014) report that in the last decade, the British Council has reduced its direct presence in African markets and instead expanded its partnership with agents who have a presence in, and thus also operate, locally.

Large exporters of education services (measured in terms of international student mobility), like Australia and New Zealand, have national approval systems for agents (ICEF Monitor, 2014). Agents are also part of national strategies for increasing numbers of international students (Australian Government, 2015). Education New Zealand (ENZ)—a governmental structure—provides training for agents, manages a database of trained and reliable agents, manages all promotional material and resources for these agents, and provides general support for the higher education institutions and agents they are working with (Custer, 2014; Education New Zealand, 2015).

In 2012, education officials from the UK, Australia, Ireland, and New Zealand adopted a Code of Ethics for international recruitment agents in what is now known as the 'London Statement' (British Council, 2012; British Council & Australian Government: Australian Education International, 2012). Each country was to implement the principles by 2013. This statement was prepared in a forum called a

> Roundtable Discussion on the Integrity in International Education—a Forum at which Australia, the UK, Canada, Ireland, New Zealand and the US meet to share knowledge and experience and identify common areas of practice and concern, as well as scope for collaboration. (Australian Embassy Thailand, 2012)

These global north countries share a common language, history, and culture. They are also deeply engaged in advancing neoliberalism as a political project, and a market society as an outcome. It is therefore not odd that they are cooperating in an attempt to keep their country at the top regarding competition for a share of the global student market, a place in the global rankings (of which one measure is the international nature of the student population), a share of talent, and a healthy economic return in GDP terms.

The practice of using recruitment agents within and between the global south and north in turn restructures their social and power relations in the higher education sector. It means those universities who use agents have effectively out-sourced a large proportion of their institutional representation in fairs and other venues of the student application and selection processes, application support, and ongoing consultation services. Universities instead pay fees to agents, usually ranging between 10 and 17.5% of first year's tuition fee (ICEF Monitor, 2014). In the UK, a Times Higher investigation found that among 158 higher education institutions in the UK, the average agent fee was £1,767, though this was dependent on the region, market, and institution (Havergal, 2015). This means universities effectively 'buy' students through agent's services. The question we ask here is: how, and in what ways, do these practices transform the relationship between the university and a student? When this relationship is mediated through a consumer exchange relation, does it change perceptions of the use value of education? And, how does the student view themselves in relation to their learning, to academics, and their enrolling institution?

Our research reveals that the practice of using recruitment agents has allowed for innovation and experimentation in the education sector, including possibilities for a new and diverse range of products and services that can be bought and sold, enabling new suppliers to come into the sector. And it is here when recruiters now act as 'edu-brokers' by setting up market encounters between sets of actors and charging a fee for this service. As edu-brokers they forge new economic encounters, and thus change the nature of the social relations between education institutions and recruitment agents (these are private companies, the leading being: Alphe from the UK, BMI from Brazil, FPP EduMedia from Brazil, ICEF from Germany, and Weba from Switzerland). These encounters are organised in the form of workshops with much of the agenda aimed at 'speed dating' types of meetings. Education institutions pay fees to attend these events (between £1,050 and £3,700 depending on the company, type of workshop, and location) whilst agents do not. In this respect institutions are paying for the 'promise' they will be able to meet reliable recruitment agents (Mazzarol, 1998).

As Beckert (2013, p. 332) reminds us, 'trustworthiness' is critically important in making markets so as to generate confidence regarding the promise of a return into the future. For this fee, institutions receive access to material to prepare themselves for the workshop, such as access to the meeting schedule, agents and their details, a table at the workshop where agents move every half an hour, and participation in receptions and parties. These workshops aim to reduce risks and accelerate trust in agents by higher education institutions. They are also predictable and safe spaces. Recruiting companies differ amongst themselves as to types of workshops offered, locations of workshops, and degrees of rigor regarding quality check of agents.

Some companies have recently begun to transfer the practice of workshops from institution-to-agent to flow back in the other direction; from institution-to-institution. In doing so, they have created a new service at a price, producing an increasingly more mature and dynamic market. The locations of workshops follow market trends in student flows and recruitment agents. These workshops are organised so that either western institutions can travel to countries of student origin in the global south, or where agents from the global south can travel to the most popular study destination countries (typically the north).

In this sense the brokers' market does not need to be materialised locally, or territorially embedded (Hess, 2004). But it does need to be fixed, or stabilised, in places in order for it to be reproduced in what Jessop (2006) describes as a 'spatio-temporal fix'. These workshops are efforts at *fixing* social relations at the same time as being *flexible* and *fluid*. In this way, brokers create multiple points of fixity, whilst also being responsive by moving to new places, depending upon imagined future markets. In doing so, brokers reinforce the asymmetries between the global north and the global south, whilst providing opportunities for 'new players' on each side to enter.

Lubricating the wheels 2: new logics, markets, and products—'for-profit providers'

In this second 'lubricating' of higher education market-making, we focus on the expansion of for-profit providers. Global and national education corporations include Laureate Education, Kaplan, Bridgewater, INTO, Apollo Group, DeVry University, and Kroton amongst others. We are particularly interested in the conditions that have enabled their presence as competitors, how they position themselves in the sector and in relation to what kind of student base, the ways the 'for-profit' logic is managed to secure trust, and how they legitimate their presence to ensure, and stabilise, their longer-term futures as sellers of higher education services. We also explore how and in what ways for-profit actors ameliorate or exacerbate global north–south relations and their attendant social inequalities given that in many cases they legitimate their presence by arguing they bring higher education to a neglected population.

We find Deming et al.'s (2011, pp. 3–4) definition of the for-profit provider helpful:

> The for-profit postsecondary school sector, at its simplest level, is a group of institutions that give post-high school degrees or credentials and for which some of the legal 'non-distributional requirements' that potentially constrain non-profit schools do not bind. For example, for profit institutions can enter the equity markets and there are few constraints on the amounts that they can pay their top managers.

Private and public universities who are not-for-profit might make a surplus, but as their legal status is as a charitable body, any excess must be reinvested in the development of the institution rather than valorised as profits. However, many of the owners and managers of for-profit universities based in the US and beyond take out high levels of CEO compensation, with some CEOs earning the super-salaries (Chronicle of Higher Education, 2010) which Piketty (2014) identifies as part of the 1% of the top 10%. Not only do the owners and managers of the global education corporations take out a highly lucrative salary, but in public liability companies the manager works for the shareholders and not the students or academics teaching in the institution.

For-profit private institutions have (until recently) been the fastest growing part of the US higher education sector—increasing from 0.2% in the 1970s to 9.1% of total enrolment in degree awarding higher education institutions in 2009 (Deming et al., 2011). Their rise in the USA, as in countries like Brazil and the UK, has been enabled by: growing pressure on adult learners to acquire credentials; the rising cost of tuition, online provision as a result of technological developments; and more porous boundaries around nation-state enabling global expansion.

For-profits are highly diverse in their range of programmes and sizes (Hentschke, Lechuga, & Tierney, 2010; Morey, 2004). They also have the highest fraction of non-traditional students obtaining the greatest proportion of their total revenue from federal student aid (loans and grants) programme. In 2009 they enrolled 1.85 million US students—many in shorter certificate rather than degree programmes (Deming et al., 2011).

For-profit firms are not just active in the USA, though they are particularly prominent there. Recently there has been a major growth in activity in Brazil as part of the overall expansion of HE enrolments (though it is still less than 20% of the 18–24 aged cohort—with government plans to increase the level of participation to 33%). Ten of the largest for-profits now educate about two million post-secondary students and account for over a third of Brazil's students. Recently the largest Brazilian for-profit provider bought Anhanduera, the second largest, with a stock market value of more than $8 billion and a clientele of one million (Tierney & Iloh, 2014).

Many of the for-profits also tend to serve a particular student population; one that we earlier identified as the 'global south' in the 'global north'. If we look at US-based data, we can see that the for-profits serve older students, women, African Americans, Hispanics, and those who are single parents, with much lower family incomes (Deming et al., 2011, p. 7) and likely to be living under the poverty line. Many of these students are entitled to receive federal financial aid in the form of loans and grants (and in some cases, large national chains like Kaplan University and the University of Phoenix receive more than 80% of their revenues from federal sources) which they must pay back immediately when studies are completed. It needs to be pointed out, however, that at least in the USA, for-profit courses are more expensive than many state universities, and students also need to take out additional loans in the form of credit to pay for the cost of tuition (see below). In the UK, on the other hand, for-profit universities, such as Pearson College, charge close to 50% less than the average student annual undergraduate fee of £9,000 (Hughes et al., 2013, p. 65).

In Brazil the global north (meaning the local social elites) attend the best universities which are both public and free, whilst poorer students have historically attended not-for-profit private higher education providers (Gomes, Robertson, & Dale, 2013; Horch, 2014). The existence of this older private sector servicing the poor has made it easier for the for-profits to enter and survive. That a 'left-wing' government also supports the expansion of for-profit higher education providers to meet its own political objectives, of expanding access to HE service a knowledge economy, in turn shapes acceptance.

Across the countries that we looked at where for-profits are active, the business model for the sector is based on taking a successful programme and using new web technologies to offer standardised curriculum, often in an online environment, with a very small back-office staff, to a very large number of students located across the chain, paying part-time instructors (Deming et al., 2011; Morey, 2004). Like all corporations, they benefit from economies of scale and scope, as well as the use of flexible employment practices. As a chain they have centralised sales and advertising—and deploy very large budgets to do so (around 24% of revenue). They have dedicated marketing people acting as recruiters with monthly targets (Robertson & Komljenovic, 2016).

Many for-profit higher education providers are highly innovative in how they have established themselves in the sector, expanding their 'customer' base and accessing sources of credit (often state-backed loan books) to ensure viability and profitability. One example is Laureate Education, whose footprint in the global south tops that of any American higher education institution; 80% of its revenues come from outside of the USA (Redden & Fain, 2012) and around 60% of its operations are in developing countries such as Brazil, South Africa, and Turkey. In its operations in the USA, students are able to access federal loans to fund some of the cost of their studies. In 2015 it enrolled a million students spread across 28 countries and 88 institutions around the globe (Fain, 2014a, 2014b; Laureate Education, 2015) employing 70,000 employees, faculty, and staff (Laureate Education, 2015). Students study in low-cost programmes, such as education, health sciences, business education, engineering, and hospitality management.

Tracing through the history of Laureate Education helps illustrate one model of expansion: the use of private equity investors; buying up highly indebted or ailing institutions; operating in those parts of the world where the regulatory environment is more conducive to their operations; a strong marketing department; most recently, a tranche of investment funds from the World Bank's private investment arm, the International Finance Corporation (Laureate Education, 2013); and legitimacy through courting the rich and the famous to appear at its conferences and be on its governing board. These elements combine to make a particular kind of competitive global higher education provider reshaping the HE sector as a result of enabling new buyers (students) of higher education services.

Like most for-profits, Laureate invests a great deal in marketing; its budget is around $200 million, using telemarketers who have scripts and recruitment targets (Çalışkan & Callon, 2010), with those turning in good sales performances given bonuses (Kimes & Smith, 2014).

This means cost savings elsewhere; in comparison to a more conventional university, Laureate has most of its academic teaching staff on part-time contracts, and contracts which do not involve and value other cost-adding activities, such as research.

One of the biggest issues facing for-profit providers most particularly in the USA is the lower level of performance of the students, and a high rate of loan defaults, causing the government to try and regulate the sector. At the same time, critics point out that this is not a 'normal' population, and that their minority and disadvantaged profile has a significant bearing on student outcomes (Deming et al., 2011). Others point to the 'hard sell' tactics of the recruiters whose own pay is based on demanding performance targets. The angle on selling is to tap into the desires of marginalised populations—to be someone, and their aspirations for the future of their family. This commodification of aspirations is a form of exploitation. More importantly, in understanding capitalist markets and higher education, this kind of practice generates a lack of trust and the real possibility the investors will not get their money back into the future as the populations targeted will never earn the level of income that enables them to service the debt. This creates an unstable market with wary investors and buyers, as expectations about a future return do not materialise.

Lubricating the wheels 3: expanding HE as a commodity—financial actors

In this third case, we look at the rise of financial actors in the non-state sector. Their role is particularly in ensuring the supply of credit so as to enable the creation of capitalist markets. Credit is an indispensable element in enabling capitalism's economic growth (Beckert, 2013, p. 330). This axiom led Joseph Schumpeter (1954) to observe that, at its most basic, capitalism was a system of indebtedness. 'Capitalism is that form of private property economy in which innovations are carried out by means of borrowed money, which in general … implies credit creation' (Schumpeter, 1939, p. 223). Indeed the 'capitalist engine' cannot be understood '… without reference to its credit operations and a distinctive monetary system involving the creation of money by banks through the selling of debt' (Schumpeter, 1954, pp. 318–320).

Why is credit, or the selling of debt, so important? It is because the accumulation of capital and growth of the economy depends on a higher level of demand than that which the owners of capital can create through their own payments.

Credit needs to be explained based on the (speculative) expectations of future profits (investment credit) and the desire for a higher living standard in the present (consumer credit). Through credit, an investor obtains purchasing power in the present against a promise—the promise to repay the loan at a specified point in time, together with an additional sum called interest (Beckert, 2013, p. 331).

Profit-maximising actors, such as those we referred to in the previous two 'lubricatings'—the recruiters and brokers, and the new for-profit providers—all use credit to the extent that their investments generate higher profits than the cost of interest. From the point of view of the creditors, for example Banco Santander which sells students in higher education 'loans' to cover their fees and other costs, this provides them with a new market from which to gain additional wealth, and to avoid the depreciation of money over time through inflation.

As Beckert (2013, p. 331) points out, what makes credit and money so interesting from a sociological point of view is that though there is an expectation that the debtor (e.g. the student, a university, other edu-business actors, the state) will live up to their promise to repay the loan, this cannot be rationally calculated because the future cannot be known or foreseen. Here creditors must act as if they can *anticipate* the future. And as we will see in the examples we will explore regarding new financial products in the sector, a range of 'risk' checks are built into the assessment of whether or not to lend money, at what rate of interest, with what kind of repayment scheme, over what time period, and so on.

In many countries around the globe, higher education places have been either fully or partly subsidised by the state though this is changing as the sector itself becomes a mass rather than an elite system (OECD, 2014). And whilst the state might lend money to service its public debts, here we are interested in exploring efforts by interested actors and political institutions, such as Lumni, Upstart, and Parthenon-EY, and the World Bank's private lending arm the International Finance Corporation, to put into place, and normalise, opportunities for investors to enter into the higher education sector offering new and innovative credit arrangements to students and institutions in the higher education sector.

Since the early 2000s, the International Finance Corporation (IFC) has been promoting higher education as a frontier and emerging market, where it argues the private sector could, and should, play a larger role (Mundy & Menashy, 2012). Over the period 2000–2007 the IFC provided $237 million in financing to 37 private education projects in 20 global south countries. Some of these loans were tagged for helping students from poorer households to access higher education places. But they were also used to encourage local entrepreneurs and transnational firms to develop private fee-paying education. Here the availability of credit then enables students to pay private fees. In 2008, for example, the IFC set up a loans scheme in Jordan with the Omnix International and Cairo Amman Bank to enable 3,000 students to take out loans to cover the cost of their tuition (Robertson, 2009, p. 127). We noted above that the IFC also made a significant investment in Laureate Education in 2014, as itself an investor and not just a political regulator in shaping expectations and actions regarding market-making practices.

In 2015 the IFC published the report *Learning from global best practice and financial innovations*, with Parthenon-EY (IFC, 2015). Parthenon-EY also produced a further report in 2015—*Driving grades, driving growth: how private capital in education is increasing access, inspiring innovation and improving outcomes.* EY here is Ernst and Young, one of the top four global consulting firms. Parthenon was created in 1991 as the Parthenon Group with a focus on the education sector. In 2014, the Parthenon Group merged with Ernst and Young to form Parthenon-EY. This partnership is presented as a strategic one; it aims to combine Parthenon's extensive strategy capabilities across the Global 1000, private equity, and education markets, with Ernst and Young's global reach. What is important to note here is that this is a strategic investment by both parties to promote a new kind of imaginary; that investors can generate income through selling credit in the higher education sector, whilst students can seek credit to enable them to access higher education places, and an ensuing career.

Three issues are to be noted here. The first is that there is considerable work being done in these IFC-backed reports in 'normalising' the presence of private capital and new financial products in the HE sector. For example, in their introduction, the authors' state:

> Whilst the report is supportive of private investment in education, it is also acutely aware of the risks involved when 'private capital engages with public goods'. Among acknowledged risks is the danger that profits take precedence over societal impact and that private investment will exacerbate inequality. (Assomull, Abdo, & Pelley, 2015, p. 3)

This is a major issue of legitimacy—or trust and confidence—and one that will continue to challenge those actors actively promoting the making of higher education markets in that it makes it also vulnerable to political intervention and thus regulation of a kind that might be detrimental to rent seeking and profit-making. Flagging awareness is an attempt to proactively manage the strength of an alternative imaginary that continues to shape the overall form and scope of higher education in many countries. Similarly, Laureate Education, until recently an entirely private equity-backed company,[5] has rebranded itself a 'public interest corporation'. Here we might read this 'rebranding' as a response to the lack of trust that surrounds for-profits in the higher education sector and thus commitment to education as a public good versus a profitable good.

The second is the claim that, despite the reservations noted above, the presence of private capital in higher education will be a 'game changer' (Assomull et al., 2015, p. 5). They argue that it is only private capital that can generate the level of innovation and expansion that will meet the needs and aspirations of the middle classes in the global south, with their aspirations for high quality education and a willingness to invest in education. There is little evidence to support this, and indeed much evidence—as we can see from our previous section on the for-profit providers—that this is not the case. But this is not the major point. The main purpose here is to generate sufficient trustworthiness and confidence about the role of the private sector in creating innovative financial products that will in turn generate better learning, greater equity, and so on as the return on the investment.

The third is the substantive content of the reports; the range of highly creative and inno-vative start-ups and products they are now promoting to service newly emerging higher education markets and market actors—most prominently low-income students. These prod-ucts include Social Impact Bonds, Development Impact Bonds, Asset-Backed Securities, Crowd Funding, Peer-to-Peer Loans, Human Capital Financing, amongst other products. We will elaborate briefly on two of these to highlight the emerging competition amongst inves-tors, the ways in which these products are legitimated to generate trustworthiness and confidence, as well as how the nature of the credit relation between student and investor challenges and changes what it means to be a learner (i.e. human capital bonded into the future).

Social Impact Bonds (pay for success bonds) were pioneered in the UK, Australia, India, and the USA. The service provider enters into a contract with the public sector to administer projects that have a social outcome (inclusion of hard to reach populations in a foundation year leading to studies in a university). If the social impact has been met, the relevant gov-ernment body pays the investors, along with a proportion of the realised savings (e.g. unem-ployment benefits).

Human Capital Financing, or Income Sharing Agreements, mostly use web presence to bring an investor into a contractual relationship with a debtor/student. In this case, the investor lends the money to cover the costs of higher education with a view to taking a share of the debtor's employment income over a fixed period into the future. Online intermediaries, like Lumni and Upstart, map the risk of the investment to the investor using statistical models that assess plans, country of residence, academic performance, and the job market. These risks are then used to determine repayment requirements and loan amounts. Lumni has been a pioneer in this field, and has financed nearly 7,000 students in Chile, Colombia, Mexico, Peru, and the United States since its launch in 2001.

The risk to the investor is what happens if the student does not pass, or does not secure well-paid future employment. For the moment we know very little about these products, and how they do and don't work (and for whom). What the 'risk calculation' tools suggest, however, is a class bias in that it is seeking to determine who is likely to do well at university and the proxy for this is family background and the reputation of the university. Like with credit more generally, those with poorer credit records (or from asset poor homes) are likely to be charged higher rates of interest to manage the 'risk'. These kinds of products also point to the normalisation of indebtedness as part of the making and expansion of higher education markets, on the one hand, and the ways in which expectations around repaying might need to be generated also through global institutions in the face of more global working populations, on the other.

Conclusion

This paper set out to make a contribution to work on education markets, this time focusing attention on the growth of global non-state and multilateral actors in the higher education sector and the creation of 'frontier markets' in 'the global south'. Our purpose was to shed light on processes involved in market-making, and to make visible newer actors in the sector whose activities and interests often go un-noticed. Our interest in the global south is a response to this special issue, and an opportunity to highlight the importance of developing a relational, spatial, and social approach to higher education markets within and between the north and the south. It also draws attention to projects and processes that are exploitative of aspirations, given the structural changes in the global economy which Brown, Lauder, and Ashton (2011, p. 148) describe as the 'broken promise' of the relationship between education, jobs, and income.

Our cases reveal that the global south is simultaneously viewed as a space and potential population for the north, using its comparative advantage to sell higher education as a commodity through innovative and creative approaches to recruitment, new modalities of provision (especially part-time/online), and financial arrangements. We also show that it is important to view neither the north nor the south as ontologically flat in terms of power and social relations. The aspirations of learners we broadly referred to as the 'global south in the north' are now targeted as requiring ongoing development, or 'servicing', in terms of 'higher education'. The aspiring north in the south are also the object of highly creative approaches in the competition between institutions for stabilising the international student mobility pipeline, with agents developing and selling a range of products. Beckert's (2013) work has been particularly helpful to us in showing the fragility of higher education market-making in that they require ongoing work to ensure confidence and trust, whilst being faced with questions about whether or not higher education sector should be a commodity, that the poor should be the target of such a high level of indebtedness, that the north should be able to recruit from the global south, and so on.

There are also considerable frictions confronting these projects, as not only must market-making contend with existing imaginaries and practices regarding the 'public good' nature of higher education and how it should be invested in, but when 'rogue traders', 'failed markets', increased indebtedness, and wealth inequalities are made visible this acts as a contrast to, and sheds light upon, these very different projects and their social relations for the north and the south.

Notes

1. The total GDP of the OECD countries is US$49.3 trillion (see OECD [2015] *Gross domestic product [GDP] [indicator]*. Retrieved from: 10.1787/dc2f7aec-en, last accessed 19 December 2015). The total GDP for the world is US$78.28 trillion (see https://www.cia.gov/library/publications/the-world-factbook/geos/xx.html, last accessed 19 December 2015). This means that 160 countries share 37% and 34 countries share 63% of the world's GDP.
2. For example, despite being one of the wealthiest countries in the world, the US Census Bureau in 2014 reported that in the United States, 14.5% of all Americans lived below the poverty line; 33% of all households headed by a single mother live below the poverty line, whilst 42% of all households headed by a single black mother live below the poverty line (see http://www.census.gov/prod/techdoc/cps/cpsmar13.pdf, last accessed 19 December 2015).
3. 'Today, OECD member countries account for 63 percent of world GDP, three-quarters of world trade, 95 percent of world official development assistance, over half of the world's energy consumption, and 18 percent of the world's population' (see http://usoecd.usmission.gov/mission/overview.html, last accessed 19 December 2015).
4. Newman's 'The idea of a university' in 1873, along with the von Humboldt's view that knowledge should be created by research, were to have a profound effect on the nature and shape of the modern university, and this version has been the one that has been globalised.
5. In October 2015 it made an Initial Public Offer to shareholders.

Disclosure statement

No potential conflict of interest was reported by the authors.

ORCiD

Susan L. Robertson ⓘ http://orcid.org/0000-0002-6757-8718

References

ACA. (2011). Why students use agents—demand and supply. Retrieved from http://www.aca-secretariat.be/index.php?id=29&tx_smfacanewsletter_pi1[nl_uid]=82&tx_smfacanewsletter_pi1[uid]=2703&tx_smfacanewsletter_pi1[backPid]=272&cHash=121017b964072268c279f78e7b8731df

Araya, D. & Marber, P. (Eds.). (2013). *Higher education in the global age: Policy, practice and promise in emerging societies*. New York, NY: Routledge.

Assomull, A., Abdo, M., & Pelley, R. (2015). *Driving grades, driving growth: How private capital in education is increasing access, inspiring innovation and improving outcomes*. Retrieved from http://www.wise-qatar.org/sites/default/files/asset/document/parthenon_wise_research_report.pdf

Australian Embassy Thailand. (2012). Statement of principles for the ethical recruitment of international students. Retrieved from http://thailand.embassy.gov.au/bkok/AEI_London_Statement.html

Australian Government. (2015). Draft national strategy for international education (for consultation) April 2015. Retrieved from https://internationaleducation.gov.au/International-network/Australia/InternationalStrategy/Documents/DraftNationalStrategyforInternationalEducation.pdf

Beckert, J. (1996). What is sociological about economic sociology? Uncertainty and the embeddedness of economic action. *Theory and Society, 25*, 803–840.

Beckert, J. (2013). Capitalism as a system of expectations: Toward a sociological microfoundation of political economy. *Politics & Society, 41*, 323–350.

British Council. (2012). Landmark 'International code of ethics' for education agents. Retrieved from http://www.britishcouncil.org/organisation/press/landmark-international-code-ethics-education-agents

British Council. (2015). *Education agents*. Retrieved from http://www.britishcouncil.org/education/education-agents

British Council & Australian Government: Australian Education International. (2012). Landmark 'International code of ethics' for education agents. Retrieved from http://thailand.embassy.gov.au/files/bkok/AEI_LondonStatement.pdf

Brown, P., Lauder, H., & Ashton, P. (2011). *The global auction: The broken promises of education, jobs and income*. Oxford: Oxford University Press.

Çalışkan, K. & Callon, M. (2010). Economization, part 2: A research programme for the study of markets. *Economy and Society, 39*, 1–32.

Chopra, N. (2015). *Universities, agents and international students: Contribution and the controversy.* Retrieved from http://blog.thepienews.com/2015/05/lets-get-this-straight-shall-we/

Chronicle of Higher Education. (2010). *CEO compensation on publicly traded higher-education*. Retrieved from http://chronicle.com/article/Graphic-CEO-Compensation-at/66017/

Connell, R. (2007a). *Southern theory*. Cambridge: Polity.

Connell, R. (2007b). The northern theory of globalisation. *Sociological Theory, 25*, 368–385.

Custer, S. (2014). Education NZs new agent training programme. PIE News. Retrieved from http://thepienews.com/news/education-new-zealand-launches-agent-programme/

De Luca, M. (2008). 'Agent'—a dirty word? *IIE Networker, 36*–38.

Deming, D. J., Goldin, C., & Katz, L. F. (2011). *The for-profit secondary school sector: Nimble critters or agile predators?*. Cambridge, MA: National Bureau of Economic Research.

DG EAC. (2014). *Education and training monitor 2014*. European Commission: Directorate General of Education and Culture. Retrieved from http://ec.europa.eu/education/library/publications/monitor14_en.pdf

Education New Zealand. (2015). Agent familiarisation programme. Retrieved from http://enz.govt.nz/how-we-work/business-development/regionbal-agent-funding-programme

Fain, P. (2014a, May 20). Laureate looks forward. *Inside Higher Ed*. Retrieved from https://www.insidehighered.com/news/2014/05/20/ceo-global-profit-its-expansion-accreditation-and-profit-debate

Fain, P. (2014b, June 2). Moody's downgrades Laureate's credit outlook. *Inside Higher Ed*. Retrieved from https://www.insidehighered.com/quicktakes/2014/06/02/moodys-downgrades-laureates-credit-outlook

Fligstein, N. (2001). *The architecture of markets: An economic sociology of twenty-first-century capitalist societies*. New Jersey: Princeton University Press.

Gomes, A., Robertson, S. L., & Dale, R. (2013). Globalising and regionalising higher education in Latin America. In D. Araya & P. Marber (Eds.), *Higher education in a global age.* (pp. 160–183) New York, NY: Routledge.

Havergal, C. (2015). *Agents paid an average of £1,767 per non-EU recruit*. Retrieved from https://www.timeshighereducation.co.uk/news/agents-paid-an-average-of-1767-per-non-eu-recruit/2018613.article

Hazelkorn, E. (2009). Rankings and the battle for world-class excellence: Institutional strategies and policy choices. *Higher Education Management and Policy, 21*(1), 1–22.

Hentschke, G., Lechuga, V., & Tierney, W. (2010). *For profit colleges and universities*. Stirling, VA: Stylus.

Hess, M. (2004). 'Spatial' relationships? Towards a reconceptualization of embeddedness. *Progress in Human Geography, 28*, 165–186.

HM Government. (2013a). *International education—Global growth and prosperity: An accompanying analytical narrative. Industrial strategy: Government and industry in partnership*. Retrieved from https://www.gov.uk/government/uploads/system/uploads/attachment_data/file/340601/bis-13-1082-international-education-accompanying-analytical-narrative-revised.pdf

HM Government. (2013b). *International education: Global growth and prosperity. Industrial strategy: Government and industry in partnership*. Retrieved from https://www.gov.uk/government/uploads/system/uploads/attachment_data/file/340600/bis-13-1081-international-education-global-growth-and-prosperity-revised.pdf

Horch, D. (2014). *As demand for education rises in Brazil, for-profit colleges fill the gap*. Retrieved from http://dealbook.nytimes.com/2014/06/19/as-demand-for-education-rises-in-brazil-for-profit-colleges-fill-the-gap/?_r=0

Howarth, D. (2009). Power, discourse, and policy: Articulating a hegemony approach to critical policy studies. *Critical Policy Studies, 3*, 309–335.

Hughes, T., Porter, A., Jones, S., & Sheen, J. (2013). *Privately funded providers of higher education in the UK*. London: Department for Business, Innovation and Skills.

ICEF Monitor. (2014). *The agent question: New data has the answer*. Retrieved from http://monitor.icef.com/2014/09/the-agent-question-new-data-has-the-answer/

IFC (2015). *Learning from global best practice and financial innovations*. Washington, DC: World Bank Group.

Jessop, B. (2006). Spatial fixes, temporal fixes, and spatio-temporal fixes. In N. Castree & D. Gregory (Eds.), *David Harvey: A critical reader* (pp. 142–166). Oxford: Blackwell.

Jessop, B., Fairclough, N., & Wodak, R. (Eds.). (2008). *Education and the knowledge-based economy in Europe*. Rotterdam: Sense.

Jessop, B., & Sum, N.-L. (2014, February 24). *A cultural political economy approach to competitiveness, the knowledge-based economy, and higher education*. Lecture at the University of Bristol.

Kimes, M., & Smith, M. (2014, January 16). Laureate, a for-profit education firm, finds international success (with a Clinton's help). *Washington Post*. Retrieved from http://www.washingtonpost.com/business/laureate-a-for-profit-education-firm-finds-international-success-with-a-clintons-help/2014/01/16/13f8adde-7ca6-11e3-9556-4a4bf7bcbd84_story.html

Komljenovic, J., & Robertson, S. L. (2015). The dynamics of 'market-making' in higher education. Article under review at the *Journal of Education Policy*. Retrieved from https://susanleerobertson.files.wordpress.com/2009/10/the-dynamics-of-market-making-in-higher-education.pdf

Lancrin, S. (2005). *Building capacity through cross-border tertiary education*. London: OBHE.

Laureate Education. (2013). *IFC, a member of the World Bank Group, makes largest ever education investment—$150 million equity stake in Laureate Education, Inc*. Retrieved from http://www.laureate.net/NewsRoom/PressReleases/2013/01/IFC-Member-of-the-World-Bank-Group-Makes-Largest-Ever-Education-Investment

Laureate Education. (2015). *About*. Retrieved from http://www.laureate.net/AboutLaureate

Marber, P. (2014). Higher education and emerging markets: Opportunity, anxiety, and unintended consequences amid globalisation. In D. Araya & P. Marber (Eds.), *Higher education in a global age* (pp. 11–44). London & New York: Routledge.

Mazzarol, T. (1998). Critical success factors for international education marketing. *International Journal of Educational Management, 12*, 163–175.

Morey, A. I. (2004). Globalization and the emergence of for-profit higher education. *Higher Education, 48*, 131–150.

Mundy, K., & Menashy, F. (2012). The role of the International Finance Corporation in the promotion of public private partnerships for educational development. In *Public private partnerships in education: New actors and modes of governance in a globalizing world* (pp. 81–103). Cheltenham: Edward Elgar.

OECD (2014). *Education at a glance 2014: OECD indicators*. Paris: OECD Publishing. Retrieved from. doi:10.1787/eag-2014-en.

OECD (2015). *Education at a glance 2015: OECD indicators*. Paris: OECD Publishing.

Piketty, T. (2014). *Capital in the twenty-first century*. Boston, MA: Harvard University Press.

Pimpa, N. (2003). The influence of peers and student recruitment agencies on Thai students' choices of international education. *Journal of Studies in International Education, 7*, 178–192.

Polanyi, K. (1944). *The great transformation*. Beacon Hill, Boston: Beacon Press.

Raimo, V. (2014). Universities rely on agents to recruit international students—they shouldn't try and hide it. Retrieved from https://theconversation.com/universities-rely-on-agents-to-recruit-international-students-they-shouldnt-try-and-hide-it-35067

Raimo, V., Humfrey, C., & Huang, I. Y. (2014). Managing international student recruitment agents: Approaches, benefits and challenges.

Redden, E., & Fain, P. (2012, October 10). Going global. *Inside Higher Ed*. Retrieved from https://www.insidehighered.com/news/2013/10/10/laureates-growing-global-network-institutions

Robertson, S. L. (2009). Market multilateralism, the World Bank Group, and the asymmetries of globalizing higher education: Toward a critical political economy analysis. In R. Malee Bassett & A. Maldonado-Maldonado (Eds.), *International organizations and higher education policy: Thinking globally, acting locally?* (pp. 113–131). New York & London: Routledge.

Robertson, S. L., & Komljenovic, J. (2015). *Forum shifting and shape making: New spaces for trade in services negotiations and the changing shape of higher education*. Presentation at ECPR 2015, Montreal, Canada.

Robertson, S. L., & Komljenovic, J. (2016). Unbundling the university and making higher education markets. In A. Verger, C. Lubienski, & G. Steiner-Kamsi (Eds.), *World yearbook in education* (Global edu) (pp. 211–227). London: Routledge. Retrieved from https://susanleerobertson.files.wordpress.com/2009/10/robertson-and-komljenovic-2016-unbundling-higher-educationfinal.pdf

Robertson, S. L., Novelli, M., Dale, R., Tikly, L., Dachi, H., & Alphonce, N. (2007). *Globalisation, education and development: Ideas, actors and dynamics. Researching the issues* (Vol. 68). London: Department for International Development.

Salmi, J., Hopper, R., & Malee Bassett, R. (2009). Transforming higher education in developing countries: The role of the World Bank. In R. Malee Bassett & A. Maldonado-Maldonado (Eds.), *International organizations and higher education policy* (pp. 99–112). London & New York: Routledge.

Samoff, J., & Carrol, B. (2003). From manpower planning to the knowledge era: World Bank policies on higher education in Africa. *UNESCO forum on higher education, research and knowledge*. Stanford, CA: Stanford University. Retrieved from http://afaq.kfupm.edu.sa/features/Carrol.pdf

Santos, B. de S. (2004). *The world social forum: A user's manual*. University of Wisconsin.

Santos, B. de S. (2014). *Epistemologies of the south: Justice against epistemicide*. London & New York: Routledge.

Schumpeter, J. (1939). *Business cycles: A theoretical, historical and statistical analysis of the capitalist process* (2nd ed.). New York, NY: McGraw Hill.

Schumpeter, J. (1954). *History of economic analysis*. Oxford: Oxford University Press.

Schwab, K., & Sala-i-Martín, X. (2014). *The global competitiveness report 2014–2015*. Geneva: World Economic Forum. Retrieved from http://www.weforum.org/pdf/Global_Competitiveness_Reports/Reports/factsheet_gcr03.pdf

Stein, S., & de Andreotti, V. O. (2015). Cash, competition, or charity: International students and the global imaginary. *Higher Education*. Retrieved from http://link.springer.com/10.1007/s10734-015-9949-8

Sum, N.-L. & Jessop, B. (2013). *Towards a cultural political economy*. Cheltenham & Northampton: Edward Elgar Publishing Limited.

Taylor, C. (2002). Modern social imaginaries. *Public Culture, 14*, 91–124.

The Observatory on Borderless Higher Education. (2014). The agent question: Insights from students, universities and agents.

Thomson, A., Hulme, R., Hulme, M., & Doughty, G. (2014). Perceptions of value: Assessing the agent/commission model of UK higher education recruitment in Africa. *Africa Review, 6*, 105–120.

Tierney, W. G., & Iloh, C. (2014). *A marriage of convenience: For-profit higher education in Brazil*. Retrieved from http://evolllution.com/opinions/marriage-conveniencefor-profit-higher-education-brazil/

Woodward, R. (2009). *The organization for economic cooperation and development*. London & New York: Routledge.

World Bank. (2002). *Constructing knowledge societies: New challenges for tertiary education. Higher education in Europe* (Vol. 28). Washington, DC: The World Bank. Retrieved from http://www.tandfonline.com/doi/abs/10.1080/0379772032000110125

Towards a human rights framework to advance the debate on the role of private actors in education

Sylvain Aubry and Delphine Dorsi

ABSTRACT
Part of the debate on the impact of privatisation in and of education lies in determining against which standards of evidence should the phenomenon be assessed. The questions 'what impacts of privatisation in education are we measuring?' and its corollary 'what education system do we wish to have?' are crucial to determining the response. Hence, some of the disagreements surrounding the analysis of empirical evidence on privatisation in education come from differences in the normative framework chosen. Some may, for instance, give a higher weight to equality and equity concerns, while others will consider choice as a structural principle. These disagreements have fundamental implications as to how research is done, interpreted, and used by policy makers, in particular in the Global South where the issues are especially acute. How can we reflect on these key disagreements? This article contends that human rights law, and in particular international human rights standards, as a universally agreed legal normative framework, must be considered and should be a cardinal reference to reflect on privatisation in education, and can provide a useful tool to provide a third way to reflect on this polarised debate. This stems in part from the fact that all countries in the world are party to one or more international treaties protecting the right to education and are thus legally bound to enforce it. However, the human rights framework contains inner tensions, that give it richness, but also require analysis to be able to use it. On one hand, it guarantees the right to mandatory and free quality education for all without discrimination, requiring that education systems 'do not lead to extreme disparities of educational opportunity for some groups in society at the expense of others', while on the other hand, it provides for the liberty of parents to choose or establish a private school—which may be a source of inequality. This paper gives a preliminary assessment of this tension by providing an overview of what we know of the normative human rights framework, as a first step towards a broader project aiming at developing comprehensive guidelines unpacking the normative framework on the right to education relevant to privatisation. It is hoped that this preliminary assessment can help to reflect on some of the fundamental debates with regards to the effect of privatisation of education in the Global South.

1. Introduction

The role of private actors in education and the related questions with regards to the merit or not of privatisation in and of education is without a doubt a contentious issue. Some of the contention stems from the debates around the empirical data on the impact of private actors in education. Evidence is still scant, incomplete, and subject to interpretation, in particular in the Global South. For example, studies such as the United Kingdom Department for International Development (DFID)'s *Education Rigorous Literature Review*, a rigorous review of evidence on the role and impact of private schools on the education of school-aged children in developing countries (Day Ashley et al., 2014), still lead to controversies, such as on the reading of evidence (Tooley & Longfield, 2015).

Part of the contention around privatisation in and of education is also a normative one. Any empirical research consists in collecting data to assess the reality against certain norms, generally put as hypotheses or research questions. Yet, some of the criticisms of Tooley and Longfield (2015) to DFID's review is on 'the framing of several of the assumptions' which underpin the hypotheses of the paper. What we could call the 'normative privatisation debate' is thus to determine the standards against which evidence should be assessed, what researchers generally call the 'research questions' or 'hypotheses' to test.

These questions are crucial, both for researchers and policy makers, because depending on the concepts used, research about privatisation in the same area may be designed totally differently, and/or the same data may be interpreted in different ways. The challenge is then to find a common set of underlying concepts about what a good education system is, which can be widely agreed upon and used as a basis for empirical and policy discussions. This challenge is particularly relevant and crucial for countries in the Global South, where the involvement of private actors in education provision raises most acute questions and is most studied, while States are seeking policy options to respond to the privatisation trend that is rapidly affecting their education systems.

This article will explore how human rights law, and in particular international human rights standards, can provide a normative framework to assess the role of private actors in education. All countries in the world are party to one or more international treaties protecting the right to education and many have enshrined this right into their domestic legislation. The human rights framework related to education is thus a nearly universally legally binding framework. This paper contends that this near universal framework can help to address the normative privatisation debate, which should in turn help to guide the design and interpretation of empirical research as well as policy debates.

As will be discussed below, the human rights framework is however itself open to different nuances in its interpretation, and much research remains to be done to provide clarity for its use. This paper thus only gives a preliminary analysis of what we know, for the moment, on its applicability to the issue of private actors in education. The paper focuses on primary education, which is the level where the debates are the fiercest, and the legal framework is the clearest. It is a first piece as part of a broader and longer-term project aiming at developing guiding principles unpacking the normative framework related to the right to education relevant to the role of private actors in education.

2. Using human rights law as a normative framework to assess private actors in education

Human rights are, partly, moral and political concepts (Freeman, 2002; Macklem, 2015). In short, human rights are morally and philosophically justified, by the necessity to protect the inherent dignity of human beings. This is the root of their legitimacy. However, as any philosophical and political concepts, such as 'social justice' (Macpherson, Robertson, & Walford, 2014, p. 17), they are open to controversies (Freeman, 2002, p. 42).

Yet human rights differ from other theories by the fact that they have been positivised and enshrined in national and international law, that legally binds States. All States in the world ratified at least one treaty protecting the right to education; in particular the International Covenant on Economic, Social and Cultural Rights (ICESCR) (1966), which has been ratified by 164 States, and the Convention on the Rights of the Child (ConRC) (1989), which has been ratified by 196 States. State parties to such conventions are bound to respect the right to education, and the vast majority of them are bound by several norms, at the international, but also at the regional and national levels.

For these reasons, this paper draws only from human rights *law*, rather than the philosophical or political broader understanding of human rights. It mostly focuses on international standards, as being the broadest expression of agreement on certain norms, but without excluding reference to domestic standards, which signal a level of legal enshrinement and consensus, though more geographically limited. This does not mean in any way that non-legal approaches are of less value. It also does not mean that this process excludes moral and political reflections, which are integrally connected to the legal dimension (Macklem, 2015), in particular as human rights are also 'interpreted by a political process' (Freeman, 2002, p. 10).

3. The tension between the freedom and social-equality dimensions of the right to education

Most international human rights conventions frame the right to education in similar terms. The International Covenant on Economic, Social and Cultural Rights, as one of the main human rights texts protecting the right to education, provides a good starting point to analyse the application of this right in relation to the role of private actors in education. Key parts of its Article 13 read as follows:

(1) The States Parties to the present Covenant recognize the right of everyone to education. They agree that education shall be directed to the full development of the human personality and the sense of its dignity, and shall strengthen the respect for human rights and fundamental freedoms. They further agree that education shall enable all persons to participate effectively in a free society, promote understanding, tolerance and friendship among all nations and all racial, ethnic or religious groups, and further the activities of the United Nations for the maintenance of peace. (…)

(2) The States Parties to the present Covenant recognize that, with a view to achieving the full realization of this right:

(a) Primary education shall be compulsory and available free to all;

(b) Secondary education in its different forms, including technical and vocational secondary education, shall be made generally available and accessible to all by every appropriate means, and in particular by the progressive introduction of free education;

(...)

(3) The States Parties to the present Covenant undertake to have respect for the liberty of parents and, when applicable, legal guardians to choose for their children schools, other than those established by the public authorities, which conform to such minimum educational standards as may be laid down or approved by the State and to ensure the religious and moral education of their children in conformity with their own convictions.

(4) No part of this article shall be construed so as to interfere with the liberty of individuals and bodies to establish and direct educational institutions, subject always to the observance of the principles set forth in paragraph I of this article and to the requirement that the education given in such institutions shall conform to such minimum standards as may be laid down by the State.

Article 13 of the ICESCR contains broadly two main dimensions, which are in tension. On one hand, paragraphs 13-1 and 13-2 mostly outline what Sandra Fredman (2015) calls education as a social right and an equality right. It describes the entitlements rights holders have (e.g. free and compulsory primary education, education directed to the full development of the human personality and the sense of its dignity), and corresponding positive obligations States have to fulfil this entitlement (e.g. developing a system of schools). This dimension is further defined in the cross-cutting rights of the ICESCR, in particular the right to non-discrimination and equality (articles 2.2 and 3 of the ICESCR), which form an integral part of the entitlements related to the right to education.[1] On the other hand, the two other paragraphs, 13-3 and 13-4, provide for a different dimension, related to parents' educational liberty—which may be called the liberty dimension. It outlines what should be parents' liberty to choose for their children non-State schools, in connexion with their liberty to ensure the religious and moral education of their children, which is itself complemented by the liberty of individuals and organisations to establish and manage educational institutions. This liberty is guaranteed in all treaties protecting the right to education.

The human right framework therefore recognises the need to provide education as an entitlement that ought to be guaranteed by the State, but it also acknowledges the need to leave space for private education, partly in order to resist the risk of the manipulation of the education system by an authoritarian State, learning from the experience of Nazi abuses (Grau, 2015), which heavily influenced the drafting of human rights texts.

As can be imagined, these two dimensions can be in tension, and it is this tension which is the root cause of the conflicting debates in privatisation in and of education. For instance, the EFA Global Monitoring Report (2015, p. 216) reported that 'in Chile, New Zealand, Sweden and the United States, substantial freedom to choose schools often leads to increased inequality'—such inequality being protected under the social-equality right dimension of the right to education.

In interpreting this tension, it is important to note that the UN Committee on Economic, Social and Cultural Rights (CESCR), which is the body of experts chosen by States to interpret and monitor the implementation of the ICESCR, including the right to education, underlined, regarding the steps that have to be taken to realise economic, social and cultural rights, that the Covenant 'neither requires nor precludes any particular form of government or economic system being used as the vehicle for the steps in question, provided only that it is democratic and that all human rights are thereby respected'.[2] This means that the ICESCR

> is neutral and its principles cannot accurately be described as being predicated exclusively upon the need for, or the desirability of a socialist or a capitalist system, or a mixed, centrally planned, or *laisser-faire* economy, or upon any other particular approach.[3]

Two preliminary remarks on the tension between the social-equality rights and liberty dimensions can be made. Firstly, article 13-4 itself contains some limitations to the liberty to establish private schools. It stipulates that this liberty is

> subject *always* to the observance of the principles set forth in paragraph 1 of this article and to the requirement that the education given in such institutions shall conform to such minimum standards as may be laid down by the State. (Emphasis added)

This shows very directly that this liberty can be limited by the State. This implies, as a minimum, a strong regulation role for the State, which corresponds to its obligation to *protect* the rights from third party abuses. It also demonstrates that whatever the prevalence of private and public actors in an education system, the role of the State is central, at least for regulatory purposes.

Secondly, although Fredman (2015) calls the second dimension related to liberty described above as 'a freedom right', the term 'right' is an overstatement, at least when looking at articles 13-3 and 13-4 of the ICESCR (and its clones in other human rights texts). Indeed, as seen above, human rights texts do not use the term 'right' to provide for individuals' liberty to choose and establish schools. Instead, treaties carefully require that States have a duty to undertake to 'have respect *for the liberty of* …' (emphasis added), rather than respect for the *rights* of parents to choose. Significantly, this particular wording was explicitly discussed during the drafting of the ICESCR (whose wording and approach in this respect has been copied as such in subsequent texts), and States made a clear and deliberate choice to reject the term 'right' to qualify parents' possibility to choose, and to consider it merely as a 'liberty' (Coomans, 1995, p. 15; Saul, Kinley, & Mowbray, 2014, p. 1151).[4] At the supra-national level, only two regional human rights systems, the European and the Inter-American ones, use a different wording, by providing for a *right* of parents to ensure education in conformity with their own religious and philosophical convictions.[5] However, this remains an exception, and even in those systems, the scope of the right has been found by courts to be limited to ensuring education in conformity with the parents' education,[6] and has been interpreted as excluding State obligation to fund private education. There is thus no internationally recognised *right* to choose or establish non-State schools.

This is an essential point that requires further research. One difference that is clear is that it involves different levels of State obligations. For example, courts have found that States do not have an obligation to fund private schools.[7] Another *likely* difference is that when the social-equality right conflicts with the liberty dimension, as in the cases of privatisation quoted above by the EFA Global Monitoring Report team, the social-equality right dimension has greater legal weight and/or scope. This would mean that the liberty of choosing or establishing a school cannot be done at the expense of the social-equality right dimension, for instance at the expense of the realisation of the right to free education or the right to non-discrimination and equality. By contrast, the liberty to choose or create schools may be limited (though without being nullified) to ensure the realisation of the right to education.

Thus, contrary to common perception, it cannot be said, at least legally, that parents' choice of schools or the creation of private schools is an absolute and unlimited liberty, or right.

4. Methodology: towards defining a common human rights framework

Applying the human rights framework to the role of private actors therefore requires an analysis of its internal tension. It also involves unpacking its relatively abstract wording, which does not give clear guidance on the respective role of public and private actors. To do so, we have, with a number of partners, been conducting since 2013 theoretical research on the human rights framework, and concretely testing its legal application, with a focus on primary education in the Global South.

In terms of theoretical research, the UN Special Rapporteur on the right to education, Mr Kishore Singh, has recently published three reports (UN Special Rapporteur on the right to education, 2014, 2015a, 2015b) dealing with privatisation of education. Additional theoretical research has been carried out by non-governmental organisations. The Right to Education Project has conducted a review of some of the case-law relevant to the issue.[8] It has also analysed national laws relevant to private actors in education (Right to Education Project, 2016). In the meantime, the Global Initiative for Economic, Social and Cultural Rights (GI-ESCR), along with national partners, have collected and analysed national level data in several countries on the role and impact of private actors in education. They applied the human rights framework to these country data, and published several reports.[9] At the time of writing, research had been conducted in 11 countries (Brazil, Chile, Ghana, Haiti, Kenya, Morocco, Pakistan, the Philippines, Uganda, Nepal, and the United Kingdom with regards to its development aid). RTE and GI-ESCR have also reviewed the existing (but meagre) legal literature, and analysed other sources of interpretation of the law, such as General Comments, which are interpretative documents written by bodies of experts, and resolutions from the Human Rights Council.

With regards to legal testing, the research in these countries has also provided the basis for systematic testing of the scope of the right to education in the context of privatisation of and in education in various countries. For each country, the organisations involved have presented this research to regional or United Nations human rights mechanisms which were reviewing the implementation of relevant human rights conventions that protect the right to education. These mechanisms are bodies of experts set up by States to provide guidance on the interpretation and implementation of human rights treaties—with one different body for each human rights treaty. As part of their monitoring function, they periodically review the implementation and progress of the Conventions they monitor by the States parties and each review offers an occasion for civil society to present its analysis. Based on the information presented to them, these mechanisms ask questions and make recommendations to States, which help to provide clarity on the scope of the right to education.

On the basis of this research and testing, we have come up with a *draft* human rights analysis framework, which unpacks the basic legal criteria outlining the conditions under which private operators can act, essentially for primary formal education. This framework will be presented in the next part. It is critical to highlight that both the theoretical research and legal testing are still underway, and we expect that it will take one or two more years before being completed. The framework presented here is thus a *preliminary* reflection, that is likely to evolve as our understanding progresses.

A final methodological point to note is that the only actor that the human rights framework addresses is the State. For any situation, the objective is to know whether States (including all public entities, such as decentralised public authorities) have done what they should to meet their obligations and improve human rights fulfilment. The focus is not on any private actor, whether private schools, investors or parents, and any concern should ultimately be connected to the responsibility of a State.

5. A human rights analysis framework

Based on the preliminary analysis presented in Section 3, the general human rights position can be summarised as follows: while private schools should, generally, be legally allowed to exist, and parents should be allowed to put their children in those schools, the liberty dimension of the right to education is limited by legal criteria or conditions, which stem from the rights and principles guaranteed in other parts of the law, and in particular the social-equality dimension of the right to education. That leaves States the possibility to have different arrangements of public and private actors in education that are compatible with the human rights framework. The aim of our work is to find out what are those legal criteria or conditions under which private actors can operate in order to assess which of these arrangements between public and private actors are acceptable under human rights law.

The following draft framework outlines five 'dimensions' which are five criteria that the operation of private schools should not infringe. These criteria are inter-connected, may partly overlap, and they represent a sort of *red line*: if the existence or growth of private actors in education affects negatively *any* of those criteria, it is not acceptable, and likely, a violation of human rights law. Conversely, when *all* of these criteria are met, the role of private actors in education is acceptable under the human rights normative framework. Importantly, these criteria apply to States in the management of their domestic education system, but also equally to donor States, which should respect those criteria when funding education systems—including private schools—in other countries.[10]

Therefore, while private providers of education are permitted, States must ensure that the involvement of private actors in the provision of education does not affect the five following criteria.

5.1. Non-discrimination, inequality, and segregation

The exercise of educational liberties should not lead to any form of discrimination or segregation, or create or increase inequality. This is perhaps the most crucial principle, both because increased inequality is one of the most criticised negative effects of privatisation in education, and because of the strength of the legal protection for the right to non-discrimination and equality.

Equality and non-discrimination are immediate and cross-cutting obligations in the ICESCR, the Convention on the Rights of the Child (ConRC),[11] and most human rights texts.

The States Parties' obligations with respect to non-discrimination are immediate (as opposed to being subject to progressive realisation) and require States to pay particular attention to vulnerable or marginalised groups. States are required to protect the right to education of everyone from both direct and indirect discrimination, and to not only eliminate discriminatory laws and policies but also to adopt special measures and affirmative action when needed.[12]

In addressing the balance between the freedom dimension and the other aspects of the right to education, the CESCR stated that

> Given the principles of non-discrimination, equal opportunity and effective participation in society for all, the State has an obligation to ensure that the liberty set out in article 13 (4) does not lead to extreme disparities of educational opportunity for some groups in society.[13]

Similarly, following a General Day of Discussion on private actors and the Convention on the Rights of the Child (ConRC), the UN Committee on the Rights of the Child (CRC), which is the body of experts tasked to interpret and monitor the implementation by States of the ConRC, adopted the following recommendation relating to the principle of non-discrimination (Article 2 of the ConRC):

> Likewise, the general principle of non-discrimination as enshrined in article 2, [of the Convention] … assume[s] particular importance in the context of the current debate, with the State party equally being obliged to create standards consistent and in conformity with the Convention. For instance, privatization measures may have a particular impact on the right to health (art. 24), and the right to education (arts. 28 and 29), and States parties have the obligation to ensure that privatization does not threaten accessibility to services on the basis of criteria prohibited, especially under the principle of non-discrimination.[14]

This issue has also been directly addressed by UN human rights bodies in their concluding observations, which are observations and recommendations they make to States following the periodic review of the implementation of human rights treaties by these States. For instance, in 2014, in the case of Morocco, the CRC expressed concern that

> Private education is developing very quickly, especially at primary level without the necessary supervision regarding the conditions of enrolment and the quality of education provided, which has led to the reinforcement of inequalities in the enjoyment of the right to education.[15]

Fees charged in private schools can in themselves be problematic if they create discrimination, as in the case of Brazil, where the CRC indicated it was concerned about 'the high fees in private schools which exacerbate existing structural discrimination in access to education and reinforce educational inequalities'.[16] UN human rights bodies have also made some similar analysis for secondary education.[17]

In a crucial move, UN human rights committees have recently explicitly linked discrimination to socio-economic segregation, and considered the latter as being contrary to human rights law. With regards to Chile, the CRC expressed its concern about 'the high level of segregation in the school system' and recommended that the State 'promptly take measures to decrease segregation and to promote an egalitarian and inclusive educational system, prohibiting all schools, independently of the source of funding, public or private, to select students on arbitrary criteria or socio-economic background'.[18] The CESCR later confirmed this assessment of Chile.[19] Socio-economic segregation is here considered as a breach of human rights because of its effects on discrimination, but it remains to be seen whether it can be considered as a standalone principle and equally applicable on other grounds. For instance, it is not sure whether segregation would also be prohibited if it has no discriminatory effect, as could be imagined with 'affirmative action' programmes[20] that would organise classes by academic level with the intent of helping the weakest if a positive effect can be shown—although the challenge may be to holistically demonstrate such a positive effect.

5.2. The right to compulsory free quality education and the role of public education

Free education for all has been recognised as an essential element of the right to education[21] and the only way to reach the most marginalised groups (Bhalotra, Harttgen, & Klasen, 2014). Human rights treaties make very clear that everyone has a right to free compulsory education at primary level and that free education should be progressively introduced at the secondary and higher levels. Human rights treaty bodies have repeatedly and consistently considered that fees should be eliminated as soon as possible, and that their introduction was contrary to the right to education, often also noting their discriminatory impact.[22]

The right to education includes a right to an education which is available, acceptable, and adaptable.[23] These are three of the four components of the right to education outlined by the CESCR (the fourth one being 'accessible') which includes a notion of what is more commonly understood as 'quality'. Quality is a complex concept to define, measure, and assess, which is captured in a more nuanced way by these three terms, but it is an integral and important part of the right to education.

Since education is costly, the only way to make it truly free for all (excluding the unlikely case of a system that is fully funded by philanthropic actors, which would in any case raise other issues, which we will not address here) is necessarily to have some sort of public involvement in education, for the public authorities to either directly provide it for free, or to fully fund the costs of private schools. Options where private fee-charging schools become, or threaten to become, the only options available for some people, are therefore clearly in violation of human rights law.

The general principle is then that private fee-charging educational institutions may exist, but in addition to or as an alternative to free schools. This is also the understanding of the UN Special Rapporteur on the right to education, who emphasised that: 'governments should ensure that private providers only supplement public education, the provision of which is the Government's responsibility, rather than supplant it', adding: 'it is important to ensure that States do not disinvest in public education by relying on private providers' (UN Special Rapporteur on the right to education, 2014, para. 96).

It is not clear, however, whether the UN Special Rapporteur refers to all private providers, or specifically those charging fees. The right to free education is very clear; what is less clear is the provider: does it have to be the State itself providing free education, or can it be a private provider? This raises the possibility of an education system fully run by private schools, but with all the fees and expenses paid for by the State, in a form of public–private partnership (PPP). Would such a system be compatible with the human rights framework? Or, said differently: is there a right to *public* education? This is one of the most difficult questions in interpreting the human rights framework. Part of the response lies in the effect that such an arrangement would have on the other areas of the analytical framework, such as non-discrimination or segregation. This was a major issue in the context of the funding of private schools through vouchers in Chile (GI-ESCR & Sciences Po Law School Clinic, 2014), as were the implications over the control of the content of education, and civil and political rights such as the rights related to participation in public affairs.[24] A number of indications tend to suggest nevertheless that, generally, the principle is that public schools should be the norm.

Firstly, as discussed, the ICESCR (article 13.3) recognises the liberty of parents to choose for their children schools 'other than those established by the public authorities'. Equally, article 2 (c) of the UNESCO Convention against Discrimination in Education (1960) allows the establishment or maintenance of private educational institutions '*if* the object of the institutions is not to secure the exclusion of any group *but* to provide educational facilities *in addition to those provided by the public authorities* ...' (emphasis added). This wording assumes that there is a system of public schools available, which private educational institutions provide an alternative to.

Secondly, the jurisprudence and treaty body practice also supports the idea that human rights require a certain amount of public schools to exist. The CESCR underlined that 'article 13 [of the ICESCR] regards States as having principal responsibility for the *direct provision* of education in most circumstances', and 'an enhanced obligation to fulfil (provide) regarding the right to education', in particular at the primary level.[25] This principle was recalled in recent concluding observations on Uganda.[26] In several cases, the CRC recommended to place stronger emphasis on public education, so as to 'prevent any risk of discrimination' in Lebanon,[27] or rebalance the budget in Colombia.[28] In a recent case about Kenya, the CRC recommended the State 'to prioritize free primary quality education at public school over private schools'.[29]

Thirdly, emerging treaty body practice and jurisprudence suggests that while public funding of private schools can exist, it cannot, generally, be the unique or dominant solution for a whole country. In a striking statement, the CRC recently recommended that Brazil

> phase-out the transfer of public funds to the private education sector and review its policies with regard to fiscal and tax incentives for enrolment in private education institutions in order to ensure access to free quality education at all levels (...) by strictly prioritizing the public education sector in the distribution of public funds,

and 'stop the purchase of standardized teaching and school management systems by municipalities from private companies'.[30] In the case of Chile, which is the most emblematic case of large-scale PPPs, the CRC recommended that the State 'accelerate the allocation of increased targeted resources to education, in particular in free public schools'.[31]

If it is accepted that public schools should be the primary form of education delivery, two questions remain, however: what proportion of non-public schools are acceptable, and is there a limit? And what is the exact scope of the notion of *public schools*: do private schools organised under certain forms of PPPs where they're closely integrated in the State system, such as in the Netherlands or in Belgium, qualify as public or private schools?

5.3. The necessity to guarantee a humanistic mission of education

Article 13.1 of the ICESCR states that education is 'directed to the full development of the human personality and the sense of its dignity, and shall strengthen the respect for human rights and fundamental freedoms'. Article 29 of the Convention on the Rights of the Child furthers this provision and lists a number of aims education must be directed at:

(a) The development of the child's personality, talents, and mental and physical abilities to their fullest potential;

(b) The development of respect for human rights and fundamental freedoms, and for the principles enshrined in the Charter of the United Nations;

(c) The development of respect for the child's parents, his or her own cultural identity, language and values, for the national values of the country in which the child is living, the country from which he or she may originate, and for civilisations different from his or her own;

(d) The preparation of the child for responsible life in a free society, in the spirit of under-standing, peace, tolerance, equality of sexes, and friendship among all peoples, ethnic, national, and religious groups and persons of indigenous origin;

(e) The development of respect for the natural environment.

The CRC further elaborated that

Efforts to promote the enjoyment of other rights must not be undermined, and should be rein-forced, by the values imparted in the educational process. This includes not only the content of the curriculum but also the educational processes, the pedagogical methods and the envi-ronment within which education takes place, whether it be the home, school, or elsewhere.[32]

The committee also insisted on the fundamental principle of the best interest of the child which should be at the heart of all education systems and processes. It underlined that

The overall objective of education is to maximize the child's ability and opportunity to participate fully and responsibly in a free society. It should be emphasized that the type of teaching that is focused primarily on accumulation of knowledge, prompting competition and leading to an excessive burden of work on children, may seriously hamper the harmonious development of the child to the fullest potential of his or her abilities and talents. [...] Schools should foster a humane atmosphere and allow children to develop according to their evolving capacities.[33]

The UN Special Rapporteur on the right to education (2014, para. 54) perhaps best cap-tured this dimension by referring to the 'humanistic mission of education', which is based on these principles. He indicated (2014, para. 117) that

Education benefits both the individual and society and must be preserved as public good so that the social interest is protected against the commercial interests in privatized education. Public authorities should not allow private providers to vitiate the humanistic objectives of education.

What a 'humanistic mission' exactly entails still needs further research but does include:

(1) 'preserving the social interest in education' (UN Special Rapporteur on the right to education, 2014, para. 54), and to 'giv[e] primacy to common human values and the public character of education, as is done in France and Greece, among other countries' (UN Special Rapporteur on the right to education, 2015a, para. 82);

(2) to preserve 'cultural diversity' (UN Special Rapporteur on the right to education, 2015a);

(3) to 'not allow the pursuit of material values to the detriment of a humanist mission of education' (UN Special Rapporteur on the right to education, 2015a, para. 124); and

(4) to not allow 'the propagation by private schools of a value system solely conducive to the market economy' (UN Special Rapporteur on the right to education, 2015a).

It is also closely connected to a 'holistic approach to education' (UN Special Rapporteur on the right to education, 2015a, para. 82), which was developed in the Delors report (UNESCO, 1996, pp. 20–21): 'learning to know, learning to do, learning to live together and learning to be', and further expanded in a UNESCO report (2015) 'Rethinking education: Towards a global common good?'. Connexions have additionally been made to the concept of 'education as a public good' (UN Special Rapporteur on the right to education, 2014, para. 54), but 'public good' is originally an economic term whose applicability to education is still fiercely debated (Devarajan, 2014), and which needs further discussion.

Growth of private actors that would undermine these dimensions would thus be contrary to the human rights framework. But perhaps most controversial and problematic is whether commercial, for-profit, private actors in education are compatible with this principle. The UN Special Rapporteur on the right to education (2015a, para. 81) tends to indicate that it is not, as 'the commercialization of education necessarily involves the pursuit of material values to the detriment of the humanist mission of education'.

The treaty body practice gives limited although meaningful indications on this dimension. Addressing whether standardised tests are compatible with this principle, the CRC considered with respect to the highly marketised education system in Chile that 'education being strictly evaluated according to instrumental and cognitive standards and indicators, excluding values and attitudes such as equality of rights between men and women, development of empathy, respecting commitments, participation in democratic life and respect for the environment' would be problematic under the Convention.[34] More strikingly, it also indicated, with respect to Brazil, that it should regulate private providers' education to ensure 'that they are not engaged in for-profit education', referring to the UN Special Rapporteur's reports.[35] It recently reiterated this statement with respect to Haiti.[36] The CESCR considered that Chile should take the necessary measures to 'ensure the effective implementation of the Inclusive Education Act, which [...] stipulates that educational establishments receiving State support must be non-profit-making'.[37] Importantly also, confirming this trend from a different perspective by highlighting the obligations of donor States, the CRC was recently concerned about the United Kingdom's funding 'of low-fee, private and informal schools run by for-profit business enterprises' in developing countries, and it recommended that it 'refrain[n] from funding for-profit private schools'.[38] These statements indicate that certain types of private schools can be banned for the effect they have on the aims of education, and that for-profit schools are, at least in some cases, and in particular when they receive public funds, non-compatible with the realisation of the right to education.

5.4. Private educational institutions should conform to minimum educational standards

As stipulated in the treaties, private educational institutions should conform to minimum educational standards established by States.[39] These minimum standards may relate to issues such as admission, curricula and the recognition of certificates and must be consistent with the educational objectives set out by international law.[40] States must adopt specific measures that take account of the involvement of the private sector in education delivery to ensure the right to education is not compromised.[41]

In this regard, the Committee on the Rights of the Child emphasised that 'enabling the private sector to provide services, run institutions and so on does not in any way lessen the State's obligation to ensure for all children within its jurisdiction the full recognition and realization of all rights in the Convention'.[42] States are therefore required to monitor and regulate private schools. This obligation was particularly highlighted by the UN Special Rapporteur on the Right to Education (2015a) in a report dedicated to this issue, which recommends that States adopt a regulatory framework for private providers setting out their responsibilities and accountability requirements. He advised in particular that States regulate school fees charged by private providers and strengthen the humanistic mission of education through laws and policies.

The Committee on the Rights of the Child has recommended to several States to regulate and monitor private educational institutions,[43] either for ensuring the respect for the principle of non-discrimination and promoting inclusion and respect for diversity (Chile)[44] or for ensuring the quality of education (Kenya,[45] Zimbabwe[46]). Crucially, having laws and standards is not enough; they need to be adequately implemented. UN treaty bodies recommendations also include a request not only to regulate but to monitor private schools.[47] More specifically, UN Committees have for instance also called on Uganda to use 'oversight mechanisms',[48] or Ghana to regulate and monitor 'through the Private School Desk within the Ghana Education Service'.[49] The UN Special Rapporteur on the Right to Education (2015a, para. 101) also calls States to establish monitoring mechanisms, including to oversee the operations of public–private partnerships (UN Special Rapporteur on the Right to Education, 2015b, para. 134). This point has further been confirmed through case-law. For instance, the Supreme Court of India held that, central, State, and local governments have an obligation to ensure that all schools, both public and private, have adequate infrastructure.[50] Finally, a June 2015 resolution from the Human Rights Council adopted by consensus urges all States to 'monito[r] private education providers and hol[d] accountable those whose practices have a negative impact on the enjoyment of the right to education'.[51] It also underlines another key aspect related to this principle, urging States to 'strengthe[n] access to appropriate remedies and reparation for victims of violations of the right to education'.[52]

5.5. Principles of transparency and participation

If different systems, while different levels of involvement of and support to private actors may be compatible with the human rights framework, decisions about the arrangement of public and private actors within education systems must be subject to public scrutiny and respect for the human rights principles of transparency and participation. In this regard, decisions and developments in relation to the education system, including the involvement of private education, must be done in consultation with, and with the participation of, various groups of society, including the poorest. This obligation has been highlighted in particular by the Committee on the Rights of the Child which recommends that

> States Parties, when considering contracting out services to a non-state provider—either for-profit or non-profit, or international or local—undertake a comprehensive and transparent assessment of the political, financial and economic implications and the possible limitation on the rights of beneficiaries in general, and children in particular.[53]

The CRC also emphasised 'the role of national-level monitoring which seeks to ensure that children, parents and teachers can have an input in decisions relevant to education'.[54] For instance, in several concluding observations, UN treaty bodies raise concerns about the lack of transparency in the management of education resources.[55]

6. Conclusion

This framework partly stems out of empirical research on the extent to which the existence or growth of private school provision in the 11 countries studied is in line with the human rights obligations of those States, which were mostly in the Global South, and were all States where there were issues. Consequently, the framework only focuses on providing a tool to assess what situations are *not* compatible with the human rights framework. Much needed is a more comprehensive articulation of all the applicable principles of what *can* and cannot be done.

In this regard, the next step is to define human rights Guiding Principles on the role of private actors in education. The Guiding Principles will draw from the analysis presented here to develop a list of norms of how States should address private education provision. Work has already started, and aims to be completed by early 2018. It will require wide consultation to address some key questions that have come up through the work on the current five-dimensions framework, such as:

- How to take into account the progressive nature of the right to free quality education?
- How does the human rights framework apply to other forms of private involvement in education, related to endogenous privatisation *in* education, such as performance related pay?
- Under what conditions are different forms of education PPPs compatible with the human rights framework?
- What if any difference does the financial motive of the school, for-profit or not, make in human rights terms?
- In what ways are commercial, for-profit schools compatible, or not, with the right to education?
- How do the principles listed here apply to other sub-sector or forms of education, such as higher education, or non-formal education?

When the Guiding Principles are finalised, they will help, in turn, to refine the assessment framework presented in this paper, which is focused on assessing realities on the ground. As a result, some of the dimensions mentioned above will likely be reframed, perhaps merged, and others may be added. However, we believe that what is presented here is a legally solid starting point.

Notes

1. See also CESCR, General Comment 20.
2. CESCR, General Comment 3, para. 8.
3. *Ibid.*
4. UNGA, Draft International Covenant on Human Rights: Report of the Third Committee (Rapporteur Mr Carlow Manuel Pox [PERU]), A/3764 (5 December 1957), paras. 46–47.
5. See First Protocol to the European Convention for the Protection of Human Rights and Fundamental Freedoms (1952), retrieved from http://www.echr.coe.int/Documents/Convention_ENG.pdf, article 2; American Convention on Human Rights (1969), retrieved from http://www.oas.org/dil/treaties_B-32_American_Convention_on_Human_Rights.htm, article 12; Additional Protocol to the American Convention on Human Rights in the Area of Economic, Social and Cultural Rights (1988), retrieved from http://www.oas.org/juridico/english/treaties/a-52.html, article 13.
6. E.g. European Court of Human Rights (No. 1) (1967), Series A, No. 5 (1979–1980) 1 EHRR 241; (No. 2) (1968), Series A, No. 6 (1979–1980) 1 EHRR 252.
7. E.g. European Court of Human Rights, (No. 1) (1967), Series A, No. 5 (1979–1980) 1 EHRR 241; (No. 2) (1968), Series A, No. 6 (1979–1980) 1 EHRR 252.
8. Right to Education Project, Case-Law on Privatisation available on the privatisation page, retrieved from http://www.right-to-education.org/issue-page/privatisation-education.

9. See http://bit.ly/privatisationproject.
10. See generally the Maastricht Principles on Extraterritorial Obligations of States in the Area of Economic, Social and Cultural Rights (2011), retrieved from http://www.etoconsortium.org/nc/en/main-navigation/library/maastricht-principles/?tx_drblob_pi1%5BdownloadUid%5D=23; and the concern raised with regards to schools 'funded by foreign development aids' in CRC, Concluding Observations, CRC/C/KEN/CO/3-5, para. 56 (2 February 2016).
11. Article 2 ConCR; article 2(1) ICESCR.
12. CESCR, General Comment 20.
13. CESCR, General Comment 13, para. 30.
14. Committee on the Rights of the Child, Report on the Thirty-First session, CRC/C/121, 11 December 2002, para. 4.
15. CRC, Concluding Observations, CRC/C/MAR/CO/3-4, paras. 60–61 (19 September 2014). See also CRC, Concluding Observations: Chile, CRC/C/CHL/CO/4-5, paras. 67–68 (15 October 2015).
16. CRC, Concluding Observations: Brazil, CRC/C/OPAC/BRA/CO/1, paras. 75–76 (28 October 2015); CRC, Concluding Observations: Lebanon, CRC/C/15/Add.169 (2002), para. 12; CESCR, Concluding Observations: Uganda, E/C.12/UGA/CO/1, para. 36 (24 June 2015).
17. CRC, Concluding Observations: Zimbabwe, CRC/C/15/Add.55, para. 19 (7 March 2016).
18. CRC, Concluding Observations, CRC/C/CHL/CO/4-5, paras. 67–68 (15 October 2015).
19. CESCR, Concluding Observations, E/C.12/CHL/CO/4, para. 30 (19 June 2015). See also CESCR, Concluding Observations, E/C.12/MAR/CO/4, paras. 47–48 (22 October 2015).
20. Which can be legitimate under human rights law: CESCR, General Comment 20 (2 July 2009) E/C.12/GC/20, para. 9.
21. CESCR, General Comment 13, para. 51.
22. E.g. Myanmar CRC/C/15/Add.237, para. 62; Republic of the Congo CRC/C/COG/ CO/1, para. 68; Nicaragua CRC/C/15/ Add.265, para. 57.
23. CESCR, General Comment 13.
24. See e.g. article 25 of the International Covenant for Civil and Political Rights.
25. CESCR, General Comment 13, para. 48 (emphasis added).
26. CESCR, Concluding Observations: Uganda, E/C.12/UGA/CO/1 (24 June 2015), para. 36.
27. CRC, Concluding Observations: Lebanon, CRC/C/15/Add.169 (2002), para. 33; Lebanon, CRC/C/15/Add.169, paras. 48 and 49.
28. CRC, Concluding Observations: Colombia, CRC/C/COL/CO/3 (8 June 2006), para. 76.
29. CRC, Concluding Observations: Kenya, CRC/C/KEN/CO/-5, paragraph 57 (2 February 2016).c
30. CRC, Concluding Observations: Brazil, CRC/C/OPAC/BRA/CO/1 (28 October 2015), para. 76.
31. CRC, Concluding Observations: Chile, CRC/C/CHL/CO/4-5 (15 October 2015), para. 68.
32. CRC, General Comment 1: Aims of Education, para. 8.
33. CRC, General Comment 1: Aims of Education, para. 12.
34. CRC, Concluding Observations: Chile, CRC/C/CHL/CO/4-5, paras. 69–70 (15 October 2015).
35. CRC, Concluding Observations: Brazil, CRC/C/OPAC/BRA/CO/1, paras. 75–76 (28 October 2015).
36. CRC, Concluding Observations: Haiti, CRC/C/HTI/CO/2-3, para. 59 (29 January 2016).
37. CESCR, Concluding Observations: Chile, E/C.12/CHL/CO/4, para. 30 (19 June 2015).
38. CRC, Concluding Observations: United Kingdom, CRC/C/GBR/CO/5, paras. 16–17 (3 June 2016).
39. ICESCR, Articles 13.3 and 13.4; CRC, Article 29.2.
40. Committee on Economic, Social and Cultural Rights, General Comment 13, para. 29.
41. Committee on the Rights of the Child, General Comment 16, para. 34, retrieved from http://ow.ly/RDZdF.
42. CRC, General Comment 5, para. 44.
43. E.g. CESCR, Concluding Observations: Uganda, E/C/UGA/Q/, para. 36 (24 June 2015).
44. CRC, Concluding Observations: Chile, CRC/C/CHL/CO/4-5, para. 68 (15 October 2015).
45. CRC, Concluding Observations: Kenya, CRC/C/KEN/CO/-5, para. 57 (2 February 2016).
46. CRC, Concluding Observations: Zimbabwe, CRC/C/ZWE/CO/2, para. 69 (29 January 2016).
47. E.g. CRC, Concluding Observations: Haiti, CRC/C/HTI/CO/2-3, paras. 58–59 (29 January 2016).
48. CESCR, Concluding Observations: Uganda, E/C.12/UGA/CO/1, para. 36 (24 June 2015).
49. CRC, Concluding Observations: Ghana, CRC/C/GHA/CO/3-5, para. 58 (9 June 2015).

50. Supreme Court of India, Environmental & Consumer Protection Foundation v Delhi Administration & Others [2012] INSC 584.
51. Human Rights Council, Resolution: The right to education, A/HRC/29/L.14/Rev.1, para. 2.
52. *Ibid.*
53. Committee on the Rights of the Child, *The Private Sector as Service Provider and its Role in Implementing Child Rights,* para. 11, retrieved from http://bit.ly/1KtWXKz.
54. Committee on the Rights of the Child, General Comment 1: The Aims of Education, para. 22, retrieved from http://bit.ly/1EDKAcB.
55. CRC, Concluding Observations: Morocco, CRC/C/MAR/CO/3-4, paras. 60–61 (19 September 2014); CRC, Concluding Observations: Ghana, CRC/C/GHA/CO/3-5, paras. 57–58 (9 June 2015).

Disclosure statement

No potential conflict of interest was reported by the authors.

References

Bhalotra, S., Harttgen, K., & Klasen, S. (2014). Background paper prepared for the Education for All Global Monitoring Report 2013/4: The impact of school fees on educational attainment and the intergenerational transmission of education. Document 2014/ED/EFA/MRT/PI/22: UNESCO. Retrieved from: http://bit.ly/1JQAQeU

Coomans, F. (1995). Clarifying the core elements of the right to education. In F. Coomans et al. (Eds), *The right to complain about economic, social and cultural rights*. SIM Special No. 18 (pp. 11–26). Utrecht: Netherlands Institute for Human Rights.

Day Ashley, L., Mcloughlin, C., Aslam, M., Engel, J., Wales, J., Rawal, S. ... Rose, P. (2014). *The role and impact of private schools in developing countries: A rigorous review of the evidence*. Final report. Education Rigorous Literature Review. Department for International Development

Devarajan, S. (2014, July 18). Education as if economics mattered. In: *Future development: Economics to end poverty*. Retrieved from: http://blogs.worldbank.org/futuredevelopment/education-if-economics-mattered

EFA Global Monitoring Report Team. (2015). *Education for all 2000–2015: Achievements and challenges* (2nd ed.). Paris: UNESCO. Retrieved from: http://unesdoc.unesco.org/images/0023/002322/232205e.pdf

Fredman, S. (2015, January 27). Talk delivered by Sandy Fredman at Pembroke College, Oxford. Retrieved from: https://oxforduniversity.hosted.panopto.com/Panopto/Pages/Viewer.aspx?id=a6216084-901a-4d3b-8398-003689e2a33a

Freeman, M. (2002). *Human rights: An interdisplinary approach*. Cambridge: Polity Press.

GI-ESCR & Sciences Po Law School Clinic. (2014). Alternative report Presented to the United Nations Pre-sessional Working Group of the Committee on the Rights of the Child at its 70th Session for its consideration of the List of Issues for Chile. GI-ESCR. Retrieved from http://bit.ly/1xelYDh

Grau, I. (2015, December 15). Sobre cómo se llegó a 'Los padres tendrán derecho preferente a escoger el tipo de educación que habrá de darse a sus hijos'. *OIDEL*. Retrieved from: https://oidel.wordpress.com/2015/12/15/sobre-como-se-llego-a-los-padres-tendran-derecho-preferente-a-escoger-el-tipo-de-educacion-que-habra-de-darse-a-sus-hijos/#_ftnref1

Macklem, Pa. (2015, December 10). What are human rights? In: *OUPblog*. Retrieved from http://blog.oup.com/2015/12/what-are-human-rights-moral-political-legal-theory/

Macpherson, I., Robertson, S., & Walford, G. (Eds.). (2014). *Education, privatisation and social justice: Case studies from Africa, South Asia and South East Asia*. Oxford: Symposium Books.

Right to Education Project. (2016). *National legislation on private provision of education*. Retrieved from http://bit.ly/22zY8NB

Saul, B., Kinley, D., & Mowbray, J. (2014). *The international covenant on economic, social and cultural rights: Commentary, cases, and materials*. Oxford: Oxford University Press.

Tooley, J., & Longfield, D. (2015). The role and impact of private schools in developing countries: A response to the DFID-commissioned 'Rigorous Literature Review'. Pearson. Retrieved from: https://research.pearson.com/content/plc/prkc/uk/open-ideas/en/articles/role-and-impact-of-private-schools/_jcr_content/par/articledownloadcompo/file.res/150330_Tooley_Longfield.pdf

UN Special Rapporteur on the right to education (Kishore Singh). (2014). *Privatization and the right to education*. A/69/402. Retrieved from: http://ap.ohchr.org/documents/dpage_e.aspx?si=A/69/402

UN Special Rapporteur on the right to education (Kishore Singh). (2015a). *Protecting education against commercialization*. A/HRC/29/30. Retrieved from: http://ap.ohchr.org/documents/dpage_e.aspx?si=A/HRC/29/30

UN Special Rapporteur on the right to education (Kishore Singh). (2015b). *Public private partnerships and the right to education*. A/70/342. Retrieved from: http://www.un.org/en/ga/search/view_doc.asp?symbol=A/70/342

UNESCO. (1960). UNESCO Convention against Discrimination in Education. Retrieved from http://portal.unesco.org/en/ev.php-URL_ID=12949&URL_DO=DO_TOPIC&URL_SECTION=201.html

UNESCO. (1996). *Learning: The treasure within—Report to UNESCO of the International Commission on Education for the Twenty-First Century*. Paris: UNESCO Publishing. Retrieved from http://unesdoc.unesco.org/images/0010/001095/109590eo.pdf

UNESCO. (2015). *Rethinking education: Towards a global common good*. Paris: UNESCO. Retrieved from: http://www.unesco.org/new/fileadmin/MULTIMEDIA/FIELD/Cairo/images/RethinkingEducation.pdf

Index

Note: Page numbers in *italics* refer to figures
      Page numbers in **bold** refer to tables